THE
Olive
Season

THE
Olive
Season

Amour, a New Life
and Olives Too

Carol Drinkwater

An *Abacus* Book

First published in Great Britain in 2003
by Little, Brown
This edition published in 2003 by Abacus
Reprinted 2003 (twice)

A CIP catalogue record for this book is
available from the British Library.

ISBN 0 349 11549 4

Typeset by M Rules
Printed and bound in Great Britain by
Clays Ltd, St Ives plc

Abacus
An imprint of
Time Warner Books UK
Brettenham House
Lancaster Place
London WC2E 7EN

www.TimeWarnerBooks.co.uk

www.TheOliveFarm.net

www.caroldrinkwater.com

Contents

A cknowledgements

My very special thanks go, as always, to my loyal agent, Sophie Hicks, and to the team at Ed Victor, whom I regard as champagne-quaffing buddies and without whom my professional life would grind to a halt: Maggie Phillips, Hitesh Shah and Grainne Fox.

While out promoting the first volume of this story, *The Olive Farm*, I met some of the people whose job it is to sell books. I understood then what a vital role booksellers play in the publishing process, so my thanks to them, too, for supporting me, welcoming me into their stores and promoting my work.

Almost without fail, when working on a film or television drama, I get a really uplifting kick from the team spirit it engenders. Now, for the first time since I have been pottering about in the publishing world, I know it elsewhere: at my publishing house, Time Warner Books. The group of people who have worked on *The Olive Farm* and *The Olive Season* are too numerous to name. They include the sales guys I have travelled about with, signing books and grabbing sandwiches; the marketing people; the design team who have given me such stunning jackets; fabulous publicists and, of course, the editorial team. I mention one out of such a splendid force because he has become an inspiration to me, my editor and friend Alan Samson.

For Michel,
I was born in love with you.

And for my mother. Our friendship has been a
long time in the budding. But now that I have
understood what she was fighting for, I want
her to know how much I love her.

The Ancients sang their way all over the world.
They sang the rivers and ranges, salt-pans and sand
dunes. They hunted, ate, made love, danced, killed:
wherever their tracks led they left a trail of music.
They wrapped the whole world in a web of song;
and, at last, when the Earth was sung, they felt tired.

Bruce Chatwin, *The Songlines*

This is a true story. A fragment of my own and, because it is my own, I have taken certain liberties: bent time, changed names, rejigged the script here and there. 'To protect the innocent,' as they say in the movies. As well as a few of the guilty lurking within these pages.

CD

Getting Spliced, Polynesian-Style

The car draws to a halt in the leafy lane that not so many years ago was barely a mule track. In front of us is a set of tall, Matisse-blue gates. Ours.

'*C'est bon*, we'll walk the rest of the way,' Michel informs our driver.

Our man at the wheel is puzzled, and so am I.

Michel smiles, and insists. '*Vraiment*, there's no need to take us further.'

In the boot of this Mercedes taxi is an extremely heavy suitcase, an aluminium briefcase containing Michel's video-camera equipment, two laptops and one hand-painted didgeridoo measuring close to four foot in length, as well as sundry pieces of rather battered hand luggage. It is evident to anyone that carrying all this will be no easy exercise. It is also obvious that beyond the locked gates there is a drive which snakes up a steep hillside, and we are both exhausted and jet-lagged. We have been travelling for more than twenty-four hours. Yes, the prospect of carting our luggage by hand and tramping the hill on foot feels like more than I am able to face, but now I see what Michel has seen.

Our three dogs, led by Lucky, the Alsatian, are bounding down the drive. Lucky, who had been abandoned, and who I found curled up like a moth-eaten mat at the foot of our property, bone-thin and nervy. We decided to adopt her, and here she is now, airborne at the gates, barking and growling at the innocent driver.

He stares fearfully at her. '*Ah, vous avez raison, monsieur.*'

Our bags are swiftly unloaded, the fare is settled and, once the car has safely rounded the corner, Michel unlocks the iron gates. They creak like a mummy's tomb as I pull them open and three sets of canine paws land firmly on my stomach, tails wagging.

We are home.

I scan the terraces, planted with row upon row of ancient olive trees. It is April, late spring. Here in the hills behind the Côte d'Azur, the olive groves are delicately blossomed with their tiny, white-forked flowers. Beyond them, perched halfway up the slope of the hill, our *belle époque* villa comes into view. Abounding in balustrade terraces, nestling among cedars and palms, facing out at a south-westerly angle, overlooking the bay of Cannes towards the sun-kissed Mediterranean, there it is, Appassionata, awaiting us.

'Mmm, it's good to be back,' I murmur.

'Would you like me to carry you?' asks Michel.

'Carry me? I know I'm tired, but I'm not that exhausted!'

'Over the threshold, *chérie*,' he adds with a grin and a wink.

Ah, yes. I had momentarily forgotten. We are returning to our olive farm as man and wife. We tied the knot a week ago at the whackiest of wedding ceremonies. Our nuptials took place on the tiny tropical atoll of Aitutaki, one of the Cook Islands in the South Pacific.

'You know, I never thought I'd go through with it,' I giggle.

'What's that?'

'Getting married.'

'Well, there you go.'

I smile, reminding myself of how it all came about.

The first time Michel proposed to me was in Australia on our very first date. We were sitting side by side at a table in an open-air restaurant in Elizabeth Bay; shy strangers awaiting two plates of Sydney Bay prawns.

'I think we have a problem,' Michel said to me.

I looked across at him in surprise.

'I've fallen in love with you,' he muttered softly. 'Will you marry me?'

I confess that I was completely blown away and reacted as any amazed woman might, which was to gulp down a huge mouthful of my Brown Brothers Chardonnay and shrug off the proposal with a confused laugh. The fact is, I didn't take this handsome, blue-eyed man seriously. In any case, I was a career girl, a thirty-something actress, independent, ambitious, in demand and not the type to settle down. Or so I was perpetually reminding myself in those days. Terrified of commitment, scared of losing or being hurt was probably closer to the truth. And although within months of that first dinner in Australia we had scrambled together the rather substantial cash deposit to secure this gloriously dilapidated property, I hedged my bets as far as marriage was concerned. Until one morning, the following autumn, Michel flew in to London from Paris, arrived at my flat, went down on one knee, small, square jewellery box in

one hand and the other holding mine, and said: 'We have
known each other a year now. A year to the day, exactly. We
have our olive farm. Soon all the papers will be signed and
it will officially belong to us. I think we are very happy.
Both my daughters adore you, Carol, *chérie*, and I, *je t'aime
avec tout mon coeur*. So will you, please, accept to be my
wife now?'

My heart was beating like a clapperboard. I love Michel
passionately, but was I capable of taking that final step?

Out popped my answer. 'Only if the King of Tonga mar-
ries us.'

What did I know of the King of Tonga? No more than
anyone else: that he was famous for his massive girth, was
the ruling monarch of a small archipelago of Pacific islands
and that he was Polynesian. It was a flippant response
intended only to buy me more time and keep that final itsy
bit of commitment at bay. But even then, after so many
months of living with Michel, I was underestimating the
measure of his love for me and the tenacity of a film producer's spirit – or this one's, certainly – for they can usually
be counted upon to provide whatever mise en scène has been
requested.

A few weeks later I was back in Sydney and at work. I was
filming a series based on a book written by me and produced by Michel. A fax arrived at the hotel from the
kingdom of Tonga, addressed to me. Buried in the make-
believe world of the role I had created for myself, I had
completely forgotten my careless riposte of weeks earlier
and so the fax bemused me at first. It was handwritten by the
King's personal secretary. Standing in the hotel lobby, I read
on. The communication sought photocopies of my and my
parents' birth certificates and my current passport, details of
criminal record, if any, religious adherences, etc. I flipped to
the next page, heart palpitating, beginning to anticipate what

was coming. Continuing, His Highness's secretary explained that the King insisted all betrothed visiting his island be scrupulously investigated before any 'joining in holy matrimony blessed by His Royal Highness could be approved'.

I dashed upstairs to my seaview suite, telephoned Paris, woke Michel and immediately began to interrogate him. 'Is this a practical joke?' I cried. 'Is it? I mean, what's it all about?'

I could almost hear the smile in his voice as he confirmed that, as I had entreated, we were to be married in the royal kingdom by none other than King Taufa'ahau Tupou IV, the King of Tonga. To say that I was stunned when I replaced the receiver would be an understatement. Still, after a minor panic attack, my enthusiasm for the idea began to grow. A South Sea-island wedding, warm, spumy waves lapping our naked toes as they sank into golden sands, a portly Polynesian potentate waving a scarlet hibiscus or two over our heads, muttering blessings in an incomprehensible tongue . . . Mmm, I thought, if I've got to go, then this is the way to go.

Having furnished the necessary mountain of paperwork, I then learned that the wedding ceremony would be a very different function to the one I had been dreaming of. The King was a devout Methodist. There would be no beach celebrations, no champagne. Prayers, countless hymns and a protracted service would be the order of the day, and no alcohol. I have nothing against such weddings for those who select them but it was not what I had envisaged for us, and so I rang Michel again. This time to explain, rather sheepishly, that I didn't fancy the wedding he was organising.

'Couldn't we just forget it?' I muttered, all too aware of the trouble he must have gone to to bring the arrangements thus far.

He accepted my reservations without complaint. All plans

were halted, and not much more was said on the subject of marriage until three years later, which is to say a little more than a month ago.

We were back in Sydney, the city where we met four years earlier, having dinner with a fellow television producer and longstanding friend of Michel's, Roger. During the course of the meal he asked, in the rather blunt manner Australians sometimes favour: 'I thought you folks were getting spliced. What happened? Decided yer don't like one another? I warned yer she'd be too much for yer, mate!'

I blushed as Michel recounted my objections to the almost forgotten Tongan escapade. Roger guffawed and laughed. 'Bloody lucky escape, I'd say, mate. That old bugger's a religious nut. And they're all still cannibals at heart. You must have heard the story about his mother, the old Queen, when she travelled on the *QE2*?' And before we could reply, Roger proceeded to recount the well-known anecdote about Queen Salote who, when handed the dinner menu at the captain's table, perused it briefly before passing it back to the waiter, saying, 'There's nothing there I fancy. Please bring the passenger list.'

'Listen, why don't you go to Rarotonga? The — Hotel will put on a good do for yer, and no questions asked. Won't even check if y'er already married! Get yerselves spliced, Polynesian style.'

Rarotonga, I learned then, is the capital of the fifteen Cook Islands, which remain, loosely speaking, a protectorate of New Zealand. As it turned out, Michel and Roger had filmed the pilot for a television series on one of the southern islands, Aitutaki, which they claimed was 'absolutely gorgeous'.

'I'll send a fax to the manager. He knows me. They'll do it for yer almost on the spot and it'll only cost yer thirty dollars. Lot cheaper than the divorce'll be.' He grinned at me with a wink. 'Two days on the island is all you'll need. Buy the certificate on yer way in; they'll stamp and date it for two days later and Bob's yer uncle. Sit on the beach and tank up on a few tinnies while they get all the festivities rolling. I'd come along, be worst man for yer, but I can't leave, mate, I'm in pre-production.'

And so we arrive in Rarotonga, where blustering rain greets us, armed with a copy of the telex sent to the hotel by best mate Roger as well as his rather splendid, if a touch cumbersome wedding gift to us: a hand-painted, hand-carved didgeridoo which stands chest-height off the ground and which neither of us can raise a sound out of.

The rain rattles like gunshots against the corrugated roof as we enter the customs shed.

'Film producer?' enquires the customs officer.

Michel nods.

'Are you carrying any unsuitable film material or pornographic magazines with you?' Michel assures him that we are not while I, waiting alongside them, silently marvel at the proportions of this man. I am reminded that when I visited Fiji for the first time I never ceased to be amazed by the size of everyone's feet. Great paddles, they were, in sturdy brown leather sandals, creaking and slapping against the dry, dusty earth. The locals here are Maoris, Polynesians, not Melanesians, as the Fijians are. Still, this officer's feet, his whole physique, are simply stupendous. Michel is over six feet tall but in order to look this man in the eye he is obliged to crane his neck. My husband-to-be explains that the purpose of our visit is to get married. The man smiles jovially and we are, as Roger promised, furnished with a piece of paper – our wedding certificate – dated (but not yet signed by a church minister) for two days hence.

A taxi takes us through the sloshing, muddied capital of

Avarua and delivers us to our beachside hotel, where the
native staff greet us in a friendly, if ponderous way. We
introduce ourselves to a pretty desk clerk at reception and
she plods off in search of Jim, the manager. He is a complete contrast: a harassed New Zealander who bursts from
his office as though on the run and greets us anxiously.
'Welcome,' he mutters distractedly, not looking us in the
eye, while pumping our hands. 'Yes,' he says, he has been
expecting us and, yes, he received the telex and he has
come up with an idea. He will arrange for one of his staff
to row us and the minister out to a speck of an islet about
forty yards offshore, where the service will take place, and
then row us back for a champagne breakfast in the dining
room.

'Sounds good,' we smile uncertainly.

We are standing at the entrance to the lobby, hemmed in
by streaming rain. I glance towards this balding manager –
what hair remains is powdered with dandruff; his eyes are
bloodshot, bleary-looking with heavy, puffy bags semi-
circling them; his nicotine-stained fingers are trembling and
it occurs to me that he might have a drink problem – and
then I peer out to sea, squinting at where he is pointing, but
I see nothing. The sheet of rain coming in off the steel-grey
ocean has obscured the islet in question.

'Don't worry, it will be clear and dry by Saturday. There
might even be a nice breeze, if the weather forecast is to be
believed.' But his nasal whine suggests that nothing in life
can be counted on. 'The monsoon season finished a month
ago. This shouldn't be happening,' he adds, desperately
attempting to conceal concern.

I smile again and stare back towards the dining room. It
is remarkably dark. In fact, everywhere in the hotel is dark.
The place has a neglected, lost-in-the-middle-of-oblivion
feel to it. In all the hotels on all the Pacific islands I have

ever visited I have always been thrilled by the beauty of the brilliantly coloured, erotically shaped flowers displayed in vases at reception, the robust succulents growing in the surrounding gardens. Here there are none. None at all. I don't like it here, I am thinking. We have been flying for five hours, so it is probably my mood and the depressing weather. Tomorrow, after a good night's sleep and a bit of tropical sunshine, I will be bursting with excitement at the approach of our wedding day. I must buck up. Still, standing in this godforsaken lobby, I find it hard to believe not only Rarotonga's claims to have one of the densest tourist trades in the South Pacific but that it is a much sought-after and applauded holiday destination.

Our room is up two flights of darkly varnished wooden stairs. It is a simple space, not dissimilar to a room in a downmarket motel. Simple and damp. It smells musty, of mothballs and well-trodden carpet. The furnishings are worn. There is one chair covered in a threadbare fabric, limp burned-orange curtains, our double bed, with its sickly-white counterpane and sunken centre, a built-in wardrobe and one wooden shelf at knee-height which now holds our suitcase, Michel's camera equipment and our didgeridoo. Adjacent to this is our en-suite, cupboard-sized bathroom with its slanting tiled floor and a shower nozzle in the ceiling a couple of feet to the left of the electric lightbulb, which is screened by a white plastic, tulip-shaped shade with a crack up one side of it.

The view from our only window looks out over the car park towards the interior of the island where, in this filthy weather, the volcanic mountains tower, black and threatening.

Perhaps my desire for these days, this occasion, to be perfect is unrealistic. But however naïve and sentimental I may be, by any standards this is not promising. I feel choked with emotion but unable to communicate any of it. I am thirty-eight years old and have never been married before. Fear of commitment, a violent childhood and an over-acute sense of romanticism have kept me single. I wanted this to be *special*. I have travelled a fair amount in my adult life and ended up alone in some dead-end dives, yet I have almost always managed to retain a modicum of humour or at least my sense of adventure by assuring myself that at some point in an unforeseen future the situation will make good copy. But this is different. Or so some inner voice keeps repeating.

Is this Roger's idea of a bloody good practical joke, cobber?

I decide to put on a brave face and unlock our suitcase ready to begin the unpacking. Michel is on the telephone alongside the bed – an ancient cream appliance with no dial which looks as though it has been thrown out and found its way to a bric-à-brac stall. He is trying to contact reception. Finally, he gives up and decides to walk back downstairs.

'I'm going to see if they have another room,' he mutters impatiently as he closes the door. I cross to the window and gaze out at the rain. It is falling like a barrage of knitting needles. I cross to the bed and lie down, sinking into the pillow, which smells awful and is humid against my clammy cheeks. A tear falls, and I feel miserable.

The storm persists throughout Friday. Its density prevents us from going out in the rowing boat to visit the islet where the wedding is to take place. Jim, desperate to keep his cool, now suggests a contingency plan which is that, should the rain not let up, we will be married at the point of a roofed pontoon that juts a few metres out to sea from the hotel beach. We see little alternative but to accept, and so the plans are rearranged.

Miraculously, fortunately, somewhere around eleven on Saturday morning, the weather clears, blown away by a tradewind approaching from the south-east, from the direction of the Tropic of Capricorn and Easter Island. The sodden, palm-covered pontoon is now swaying back and forth in the surging swash like the tail of a gigantic prehistoric reptile.

Still damp from my shower, I stare at it from our room on the first floor – we moved yesterday – while water from my shampooed hair drips on to my shoulders and runs in rivulets down my naked body. I have no idea where Michel is; I have hardly seen him these last two days except during our meals together in the cheerless dining room. It has been too wet to consider wandering in to town. I dress myself in a bathing costume and sarong and decide to dry my hair in the wind on the beach. Anything to get out of this bloody room.

A glimmer of sun breaks through the banks of fast-moving clouds. My hair is whipping against my face, streaking my eyes, as I perch on a boulder and look out across the South Pacific to a horizon barely delineable. I am thinking about life back at our olive farm, and our future plans for it, wishing I was there, when, suddenly, carried on the wind, I hear my name and turn to see Michel running towards me, waving wildly. I leap to my feet.

'What's up?' I cry.

'Get dressed, we're leaving!' he shouts as he approaches.

'Leaving? But I thought we were getting married!'

'We are, but not here. Come on, let's go. I've packed the case.'

Blown by the wind, I stagger after him, completely bemused.

'Where are we going?' I call, but Michel cannot hear me, or he is not listening. He has a scheme afoot, and it involves settling the bill, organising someone to collect our case and

ringing for a taxi to take us to a strip of the airport reserved
for private inter-island aircraft. Amid the scramble I have to
bullet back to the room after the taxi has pulled up because
we realise that the bellboy has not collected the didgeridoo,
and then scurry to the lobby loo to change from bathing
suit and sarong into shorts and a top dragged from the case.

So it is only once we are seated, squashed together at the
back of a plane loaded with sacks of unripe bananas, do I
receive an answer to my question.

'Aitutaki. I telexed yesterday and have just received a
reply. A representative from the hotel there will collect us at
the airport and we will be married in their garden later this
afternoon.' He puts his arm around me and draws me
towards him. 'I have told them we would like something
special. So, we'll have our Polynesian wedding after all, and
because the storm has not touched that island, we'll have
sunshine, too. After the service we'll drink New Zealand
champagne and swim in the crystal-clear lagoon. It's the
most magnificent I have ever seen.'

Aitutaki.

Stuck in our Rarotonga hotel, I have been reading a
bunch of South Pacific guidebooks I picked up in Sydney. I
know that Aitutaki is one of the most northerly of this
southern group of Cook Islands. Other facts I have learned:
the Pacific Ocean is larger than all five continents put
together; its depth is deeper than all other oceans; reef
sharks and plentiful other more dangerous family members
inhabit these waters; sharks have not evolved in many hundreds of thousand of years, which is proof of their perfectly
proportioned form; coral is the fastest-produced structure of
anything created by any living beings. Some of these fascinating if not terribly useful bits and pieces I have gleaned
while trying to keep myself sane during the interminable
rain, dreading a dismal beginning to married life, which I,

with my acutely superstitious Irish nature, might have read as a bad omen.

The pilot arrives, apologising profusely. He is in his early thirties, has lustrous, bleached hair and a thick Aussie accent. There will be a short delay because the wind is too strong to take off, but once we are airborne, he assures us, it will be a smooth and pleasant ride.

I cannot deny a silent moment of scepticism.

The engine of our plane drones like a snoring bee, the air in the cabin is stifling, the bananas, green when we left Rarotonga, smell so fruity that I think they must have ripened during the two-hour flight. My head aches from the lack of fresh air and because I haven't eaten a thing all day. But I am thrilled by what awaits us below.

Michel is filming our approach to Aitutaki through the window on the left-hand side of the plane. Occasionally I lean against his sticky flesh and gaze down upon what he sees. It is little different from what I am looking at: tiny, sand-banked atolls, *motus*, in turquoise water so clear you can almost see the fish swimming. Here and there a lone, dark-skinned fisherman leans out from his canoe to draw in his net. The triangular-shaped lagoon is fringed with small, white waves breaking against the coral reefs which, in turn, are ringed by deeper, greener waters, winking and sparkling in the sun like precious stones. There are lagoons within lagoons. Turquoise, white, green, aquamarine smudged with golden shafts of sunlight: a sultan's jewellery casket.

I hear the shift in the engine's whine and the plane inclines to the right. Bags of bananas slide heavily against my feet as we swoop and then dip gently seawards. The pilot calls to us from the cockpit to get ready. 'Landing in ten,' he shouts. And then I catch sight of 'our' island. It slides into view as though from the other side of the curvature of the world.

Aitutaki, a slug-shaped mass of pale honey sand peppered with sparse patches of one- or two-storey shacks and buildings buried among forests of palms whose fronds are waving and flapping in the wind like happy dancing girls.

'Yes!' I turn and press my head into Michel's chest and kiss him hard. 'Thank you.'

A short, fat, local woman holding a page torn from a notebook which reads, 'Carol and Michelle' awaits us in the shade out of the broiling afternoon sun. I step into and immediately out beyond airport customs, which is little more than a corrugated shack, home to no more activity than a dozen flies buzzing in circles. Sealing-wax red flowers are in blossom everywhere in large, square-shaped tin cans. A Cook Islander, wearing a straw Stetson and chewing, sits patiently in an open Jeep, the only vehicle in sight. I wave and hurry towards our female guide while Michel remains busy with the pilot. Our case is unloaded; dollars exchange hands; the pilot gestures his thanks and climbs aboard his aircraft. Aitutaki is not his destination – he has made the stopover only to accommodate us. I introduce myself to the woman, whose name is Gladys, and point to Michel, who is approaching. Gladys frowns, looking confused.

'Who's he?' she asks, in an unexpectedly accusatory tone.

'Michel,' I repeat.

'Michel? But we thought Michel was a woman! We thought Carol and Michel were two women!' She rocks with hammer blows of laughter, pulls two garlands of sweetly scented white frangipani flowers out of a raffia shopping basket and hangs them like necklaces round our necks, then waddles to the Jeep, gesturing us to follow. 'Well, that's a relief! The minister was shocked. Come on, climb on in.'

Gladys and Harris, her tall, robust son, the driver of the

Jeep, Michel and I are now floating towards our hotel aboard a raft ferry. Gladys uses the ten-minute journey to inform us that because the plane was delayed by the winds and it is now half past five, the wedding will have to take place tomorrow.

'The minister is keen to talk to you,' she says. 'He hopes to meet with you after his service in the morning which you will, of course, attend, and then, if he finds everything in order, he will perform the holy rites a little later in the day. But you're not to worry, he'll see you at the church hall this evening for the singing.' I am admiring the lush vegetation and listening to the creek water slapping against the raft, aware that Michel at my side has also cottoned on to the fact that the minister she is referring to, as well as herself, her family and probably ninety per cent of the inhabitants of this corner of the island, is clearly either a member of the Cook Islands Christian Church or a Mormon. As far as we are concerned, both faiths, as practised here, lean towards zealous. I have been reading during our rainy sojourn in Avarua that since the missionaries left these islands the American evangelists have moved in and have found great success here.

Everyone disembarks. Harris, carrying all our cases, plods forth, leading the way to reception, which is hardly difficult to find because the hotel and complex, even with its dependencies, are compact. Well, tiny. The resort consists of the main reception building with its dining room and eight guest huts, the *bures*. We sign the register and are escorted to our *bure* by Pururangi, a pretty, if rather beefy, black-haired Polynesian woman in her early twenties who informs us gaily that she has been chosen to be our bridesmaid and witness.

'I love weddings,' she trills. 'What a special weekend. We have the Pearly Stars for two days, too.'

I look heavenwards and see no stars – it is still light – and then out across the lagoon in both directions. This vista is mind-blowing. Black herons are stalking about in the sand or wading at the shore's edge like cautious holidaymakers mindful of what they might step on. Our hut is the very last between land and Pacific Ocean. There is nothing else except a comma-shaped sandbank and one rather round-shouldered palm between us, the shimmering lagoon and the distant blue horizon. A few yards from the shoreline, I spot shoals of tiny, slender fish leaping up out of the water. They leap as one, an arc of silver, a platinum rainbow, and return to the unseen leaving shimmery ripples in the limpid ocean. Michel suggests that our wedding take place under that very palm. Married on a shelf of sand surrounded by lapping lagoon water, with palm fronds as bower? Too romantic – everything I have dreamed of – but will the minister agree?

Later, when we stroll back to reception, we are greeted by the New Zealander, Tony, who runs the place and his local wife, Bundy. They invite us for a beer, which we readily accept.

'Never had a foreign wedding here before,' remarks Tony. 'If it goes well I might start advertising the idea. Get the tourists in. One of our guests caught sight of you earlier,' he says to me. 'Claims you're a TV star. Is that right?' Before I can answer he goes on to tell us that they have another celebrity staying. 'Mabel Burt.' He stares at us wide-eyed, awaiting our reaction.

We shrug.

'Mabel Burt, mate, the Maori singer from New Zealand. You haven't heard of her?' We shake our heads apologetically. 'She's here with her husband and her trio, the Pearly Stars. Funny thing, tomorrow's her wedding anniversary, so it's all go here this weekend. I could advertise in the *Cook Island News* and the *New Zealand Times*: "Aitutaki: the wedding of your dreams – live like the stars".' I am smiling to myself, wondering if Tony is referring to the Pearly Stars or to myself and Mabel Burt who, I calculate, is probably about as internationally celebrated as I am. The idea that anyone would cross the world to play out the same wedding fantasy as Carol Drinkwater or Mabel Burt strikes me as highly amusing and I burst out laughing. Tony is nonplussed by my reaction and, as if to compensate for my irreverence, his wife announces that the minister will interview us later at the village hall after the community singing, and then finalise the arrangements for the wedding after his service in the morning. It is then that Michel deals the blow that almost changes our fortunes on the island. 'We are neither of us regular churchgoers. We were hoping for something a little less conventional. A tropical wedding, Polynesian-style,' he states warmly and with great grace. 'Obviously, we are looking forward to meeting the minister and arranging the ceremony with him, but I doubt that we shall be attending the service in the morning.'

The silence that follows this announcement is as heavy as lead.

'Well, I'll pass on your remarks to the minister, but I don't know what he will have to say about it,' states Bundy curtly, and with that she rises as though the very idea of dallying at a table with beer-guzzling heathens is an affront to her faith.

What the minister has to say about the matter is perfectly straightforward. He refuses to marry us. In fact, he refuses to meet us at all. As far as the hotel and the church are concerned, we are no longer suitable candidates for the holy sacrament of marriage.

'Funny, it seemed OK to them when they thought we were both women. Oh, well, now what?' I ask Michel later, after the community singing in the village hall which we have dutifully attended, and where we have been introduced to the renowned songstress Mabel Burt, who is an affable, broad-faced New Zealand Maori and about as glamorous as her name suggests.

'We'll find another solution,' replies Michel.

I am spreadeagled across the iron bed in our *bure*, an open book on my stomach, listening to the cadences of the hot, dark night. The air is thick and still. There is no air-conditioning. Instead we have a metal ceiling fan which creaks and spins erratically but does little to shift the lethargy. Beyond the open window the blackness is irradiated by brilliant constellations of Southern Hemisphere stars and by the moon, which is an apple peel off being full. I am mesmerised by it, glowing like a topaz in the ultramarine sky.

It's daytime in Europe, back at the farm. I wonder how our dogs are getting on. 'There are no dogs here,' I murmur. 'None of that incessant yowling and barking one hears so frequently on remote islands.'

I shift over on to my hip, feeling deliciously at peace, south of the equator, in the tropics, where the towering vegetation barely stirs in the sweltering darkness and where I close my eyes for a second and drink in the rhythmic lapping of the waves. I am toying with the idea of a midnight swim, so invigorating to immerse myself naked in the water's phosphorescence, when Michel interrupts my reverie.

'Look at these guys.'

'What?'

He reaches for his camera, directing it at the flaking white wall where two large shiny-brown cockroaches, the colour of the leather sandals worn in Fiji, are butting up against one another like stags in combat.

'Jesus, Michel, I hope they don't bite!'

The following morning at breakfast in the deserted dining room – everyone else is at church – Pururangi serves us eggs. Back and forth she plods with plates, pots of coffee and

Carnation tinned milk, looking very downhearted. Eventually, she owns up to her disappointment. She had been so looking forward to attending a *papaya* wedding and, even better, to have been chosen as bridesmaid, that instead of accompanying her family to the singing at the village hall she had spent her Saturday evening weaving garlands for her hair.

'Papaya?' I repeat.

She giggles and explains shyly that *papaya* is the Maori word for foreigners.

'We would still love to have you as our bridesmaid.' Michel asks her if she knows anyone else on the island who might agree to marry us.

The question perplexes her. She furrows her brow. 'I think,' she pronounces, and trundles off to the kitchen.

We take a small boat out on the lagoon. I want to do some snorkelling and there is precious little else to do to pass the time if we are not now getting married. Michel rows while I watch the gorgeous, technicoloured angel fish darting playfully to and fro before disappearing beneath the hull of our skiff. 'Coming?' I ask.

'You go ahead. I'll swim in a minute and then I'll wait here for you.'

I dive overboard, slip on my flippers and scud off towards deeper waters out by the coral reef, hoping to see sharks.

It is a while before I am aware of the sun's rays burning into my wet, salty back, at which point I turn like a porpoise to cool my flesh and to gauge how far out I have travelled. I catch sight of Michel instantly. He is upright in our bobbing boat, waving and gesturing to me to come back. I flip over on to my stomach and crawl fast back towards the shore. 'They've found someone!' he shouts when I am within earshot. 'Let's go!'

Sand crabs run for cover, vanishing with the agility of

liquid into tiny holes as we haul the boat out of the sea and secure it to a tree. An egret circles overhead. The sun is high in the sky. It must be about noon. According to Michel, Pururangi's husband has gone off on his scooter to one of the neighbouring villages to search out a man he knows who would be more than willing to help us out.

'Is he another minister?'

Michel has no idea. All he understood from Pururangi's cries from the shore was that we are to be ready for two o'clock.

We shower and dress. My brightly coloured wedding dress is shoulderless and sleeveless but has a whale-boned bodice and a full, short skirt plumped up with yards of netted pet-ticoat. Within seconds of climbing into it I am perspiring and the netting is scratching my tanned-raw skin. Michel attempts to adjust the speed of the fan at the wall switch but it whines a complaint and beats on at the same monotonous pace. It is half-past one. He suggests we go to reception and find out what the plans are but I cannot face the blistering sun in this frock and wait on the bed. Sitting proves too uncomfortable because the whalebones are pressing into my sunburned buttocks, so I lie back and count the cockroaches. There are seven. At home, geckos, not cockroaches, hang from our whitewashed ceilings and walls. When we return we intend to keep bees.

A short while later, I am woken by excited male voices beyond the window. They are chattering incomprehensibly in what I take to be their local language. Cook Islands Maori is rather similar to the Polynesian languages spoken in Tahiti and Hawaii, or perhaps they are discoursing in a local Aitutaki dialect. I haul myself back on to my feet to take a look. Four burly men are transporting two trestle tables, which they place in the sand alongside 'our' palm tree. An island woman, not Pururangi, carrying a pink plastic laundry basket stacked with champagne flutes, brings up the rear.

Who are they expecting? We have no guests.

I see Michel hurrying along the beach. One of the natives who has deposited the table and is returning to the hotel greets him with an enthusiastic handshake. They exchange a word or two and then Michel hurries up the steps to our hut.

'So, it's finally happening, is it?'

'Well, there's no sign of Pururangi's husband. According to Tony, it's nothing to worry about. However, it's unlikely the ceremony will take place promptly at two. Mr Pururangi rang reception from a callbox a few miles away to say that the man he had in mind has left the island, so he's going to find another fellow who has been recommended to him.'

'Right.' I pad back to the bed. 'Maybe I'll take this frock off for a while. It's killing me. And have a shower.'

'There's no water. The generator's off for a couple of hours. Tony said to apologise. It'll be back on around four.'

I lie down again, convinced this wedding will never take place.

I am wrong.

At almost five o'clock, Pururangi's husband pulls up with a male passenger on the back of his scooter. The other man is a Maori chief dressed in shorts and muddied boots; he was working in his garden when Pururangi's husband called on him and explained the *papayas'* predicament.

'Why are you telling me?' the Maori asked.

'They would like you to marry them. I've been everywhere, can't find a soul.'

'Good Lord! Well, why not?'

Our chief is a jolly sort, if a touch confused about the wording of the vows. We settle to discuss it but are interrupted by Tony and Bundy, who have come to warn us that we had better get on with it or the light will fail and it won't be possible to have the ceremony outside. Darkness falls swiftly in the tropics.

'Quick, then. Do you want "obey" left in in the sentence to love, honour and obey?'

I decide against obey and, with that, the proceedings begin.

I am rather amazed to find, as Michel takes my arm and solemnly walks me to the tree, that a modest crowd has gathered. Mabel Burt and her trio, the Pearly Stars, each with his ukelele, who have offered to provide the wedding music and entertainment; Mabel's husband who, it turns out, is a cameraman employed by a New Zealand television station and has agreed to film the occasion with Michel's camera; a lean, handsome Danish couple and their two naked children who are more taken up with their seashell-hunting than paying attention to our nuptials. The guest who apparently 'spotted' me is present with her husband and another middle-aged couple also holidaying at the hotel. All four are originally from England but emigrated to Australia in the late fifties, when the £10 single passage to a new life Down Under was on offer. The first couple are now living in Wellington. They moved to New Zealand, I learn later, because they found that they were less homesick there; its landscape felt more familiar to them. The second are based in Melbourne. They are a curious-looking quartet. Each is sporting a safari hat woven out of freshly cut coconut fronds made especially for them by Pururangi, who stands in splayed bare feet looking solid and resplendent in a brilliant pink shift dress. Her thick, black hair has been plaited with garlands of purple and yellow flowers.

I have slipped a virgin-white hibiscus into my own curly locks.

Mabel and her group strike up the music. A little ditty entitled: 'She Wears My Ring'.

'Ring! Oh, Lord!'

It is only then, as we – I in slingback heels – are sinking into soft sand, stepping towards our Maori chief, still in his shorts but now wearing reading glasses and a very serious expression, that it dawns on Michel and I that we haven't thought to organise a ring. I swiftly slip off the little emerald-encrusted engagement ring he bought me three years ago and shove it into his trouser pocket.

'We'll have to use this,' I whisper. My hands are trembling and I fear I will drop it. 'Turn it the other way up so you can't see the stones and don't, for God's sake, lose it in the sand.' My voice is quavering, nagging almost, because I am horribly nervous.

There is little reason to be. The ceremony goes off without a hitch, and even though we cannot claim this to have been an authentic Polynesian wedding – for since the Christians and evangelists have got hold of these islands, what is a Polynesian wedding? – the register is signed and witnessed by plump, dark-skinned, hugely warmhearted people with unpronounceable Polynesian names. All this once our Maori chief, in his khaki boy-scout shorts, has pronounced us man and wife. (No one, not even us, notices that the date on the marriage certificate is incorrect – it still bears yesterday's date.)

In the waning light of this gloriously bizarre and unforgettable day, as the sun is sinking and pinking a benign gathering of clouds, Michel makes a speech which so guts me that when it comes to my turn to say a few words I cannot utter a sound. Tears are streaming down my face. I hastily toast absent family and friends and hand over to Mabel and her trio, who hum and strum and croon while many bottles of the hotel's NZ bubbly are quaffed and this motley gathering of complete strangers begin to acquaint themselves with one another.

Our Maori chief, champagne flute in hand, is smiling merrily now. He raises his glass, wishes us years of enduring happiness with many healthy children running about our olive farm, and then thanks us both for inviting him, before admitting shyly that he has had 'such great fun, far better than spending the afternoon gardening' and continues: 'I never thought when I got out of bed this morning I'd be here, performing a *papaya* wedding. But if the chance comes along again, I'll do it like a shot.'

It is only then that he owns up to the fact that he has never performed any form of marriage service before.

'Are we legally married?' I am on the point of whispering to Michel, but then I look about me, marvel at the colours streaking across the ocean from the setting sun, feel the squeeze of a hand wrapped around mine and decide the question is irrelevant.

Back in our *bure*, we discuss the possibility of lingering a while longer, having a honeymoon. But we have so much to crack on with back home. We are still awaiting the final decision about whether we are to be awarded the coveted AOC award for our virgin olive oil. We settle for an overnight stop in Tahiti, where we hire a red Jeep and drive out of town to the Gauguin Centre. The following morning, after a starlit night in a wooden-stilted house built out in the ocean waves, we catch a dawn flight to Los Angeles, change planes at breakneck speed and land in Nice, exhausted but thrilled to be home.

Fruits of Spring

I am alone in my book-lined den, enclosed within the century-old, metre-deep stone walls of our villa standing at the heart of our hillside olive farm. Above my head, a newly installed fan is gently spinning. Its breeze flutters the papers strewn across my desk while I continue to make notes: research for a new book.

Unfortunately, my work, though well-intentioned, is faint-hearted. My concentration is erratic, my brain befuddled, my thoughts swimming all over the place. I rise and sit and rise again, toking on swigs of Badoit mineral water direct from the green plastic bottle, attempting to allay both nausea and the torpor that has taken hold of me. Why can my mind not settle? Why must it whizz off in incoherent directions? I smile at my foolish questions, knowing the answers; chuffed to bits.

Beyond my sheltered refuge, the sun is beating down out

of a cloudless, forget-me-not-blue sky. It is May, the final weekend of the Cannes Film Festival, and the temperature is unseasonably hot. I rise once more, then, tossing Biro, notes, mineral water and intentions aside, I walk to the window, fling it wide open and loll listlessly against the casement, inhaling the scents of the season. Heavenly drafts from the flowering lavender bushes – such an intrinsically Provençal perfume – reach into me, clearing the heaviness in my head, alleviating the sickness in my stomach. We have planted dozens of these canescent shrubs up against drystone walls and along the borders of the tiled terraces where we spend so many hours of our days. Aside from the pleasure of its perfume, according to Frédéric at the garden centre, lavender is a wasp deterrent, but nothing, as far as I can see, not even meshed netting, seems to disenchant the carnivorous little blighters who gatecrash our meals and drill into our hams and cheeses, brazenly gorging themselves. Many of the lavenders are coated in a carpet of bees. These furry gatherers are dipping and rising as they pollinate, winging from one purple cluster to the next.

Our lavenders are of the *Lavandula dentata* variety, more commonly known as French lavender. It is drought-tolerant, has a longer blooming season and is the species most frequently found here along this Mediterranean coast.

I should be jotting this down, but I stay put.

I stick my head out into the afternoon and my ears are assaulted by the zirring and zinging of male cicadas busy with their friction-driven mating call. Stretching and straining beyond the casement, I lean to survey the land. The herbage has grown knee-high and is shot through with lofty, lipstick-red poppies. Come evening, I love to roam these grasses, these endless stretches of soft, breezy greens and audacious scarlets; to canter a passage through and feel their caress and tickle, their lick against my calves. The scene puts me in mind of a Gustav Klimt painting, *Poppies Amongst the Poplars*. Though of course, we have olives, not poplars.

Returning from our wedding six weeks ago, we roved the garden by starlight, wine glasses in hand, rediscovering our terrain, making love in the spring grass, recumbent on the earth; flushed embraces beneath sprays of apple blossom. Might that have been when . . . ? I smile at the possibility.

Turning my head to the left, I sight our two cherry trees, groaning with shiny burgundy fruits, so ripe their skins are splitting. We should have harvested them a week ago but now it is almost too late; the fruits are falling or have been pecked at by my enemies: the magpies.

Nature at its diverse work of propagation. Yes, indeedy.

I reach for the bottle on my desk once more and knock back another mouthful of the mildly fizzy water, but the reeling sickness remains.

In between the late wistaria and the bougainvillaea seasons, perhaps beneath the apple trees, I have fallen pregnant. Six weeks is all I am gone, but the being inside me, not yet the size of a snail, has me in its grip. My body's rhythms are being shunted about by its minuscule presence. Mostly, I feel drained and, like today, spaced out. I hide away in this writing room attempting to immerse myself in study but the days pass, I remain unfocused and my condition leaves me with zero tolerance for this unseasonably early heat.

But I am over the moon.

To date I have borne no children of my own. This little being will be my first. I have two stepdaughters, twin girls from Michel's first marriage, Clarisse and Vanessa. They visit us regularly but they do not live with us. In any case, they are growing up fast and taking charge of their own lives. I am late to be starting a family and this pregnancy was not planned, but it has long been hoped for. I have miscarried more times than I care to remember.

The pregnancy test, which is three days old, remains in the bathroom. I have left it there, in its plastic casing, next to the soap dish on the side of the old porcelain bath that was in this long-abandoned house when we found it. When Michel comes home he will not be able to see the result of the test because its reading has faded, but I have kept it anyway. The soft pink which turns to blue in positive cases, such as mine, looks like nothing more than a used square of blotting paper. He will probably ask me why I still have it and I won't be able to explain, except to say that I wanted to relive the wash of delight I felt when the discovery was actual.

I haven't breathed a word to him yet, about having his baby, and I won't until he arrives. I won't blurt out such special news on the telephone. I won't write it in an e-mail. I want to be there standing in front of him – the best seat in the house – to watch the smile break across his face. I want to share the joy of that first moment of knowledge, of all that this baby will mean to our lives. I feel jealously possessive about this moment to come. He arrives this evening and, impatient as I am, I am hanging on, savouring the scene, playing it out in my head, over and over again.

In the meantime, when I am not horizontal on the bed, victim to physiological changes, my days are taken up with research for my new book as well as with our projects here on the farm. We are still grappling with the unfathomable bureaucracies involved in gaining the coveted AOC – the Appellation d'Origine Contrôlée, the highest accolade given for fine quality produce – in our case, our excellent olive oil; the green-gold olive oil that we press from the drupes of our venerable *cailletier* olive trees. Olives of Nice, the fruit is known as locally, harvested from the variety that prospers along this stretch of Mediterranean coast. We had hoped for a letter on our return, but still nothing. Michel is chasing.

Quashia, our loyal Arab gardener, is building us a fine

new woodshed constructed from honey-toned stones and locally fired terracotta tiles. I hear him shovelling and hammering as I write. We could not run this place without him. Due to our frequent absences, he has taken charge of the vegetable garden and planted it up for us. The only snag is that he has failed to create variation and our beds are now swamped with big-leafed, yellow-flowering courgettes that have grown into monstrous-sized marrows, great green appendages that won't fit into the fridge, and tomatoes, the vines of which are bending and breaking under the weight of the pappy red fruits – more than we could ever eat or cook with.

And I, when I am not scribbling, am locked away indoors studying the nuts and bolts of beekeeping. We have decided to find ourselves an apiarist who might be interested in placing half a dozen of his hives on our hills and sharing the honey harvests with us. Michel wants us to strike up an arrangement with a local bee farmer along similar lines to the relationship we have built up with René, our olive-tree guru. René assists us with the pruning of the trees and the gathering and pressing of our fruit and in return he keeps two thirds of our olive produce. We were lucky to find him. Our little farm, this most unexpected enterprise of ours, has got off to a fortunate start. Quite by chance we have fallen upon a plot of land that yields first-class olive oil. But we have much to learn, a long way to go, if we are to honour the AOC we have our hearts set on and gain a deeper understanding of the Provençal way of life.

I know nothing whatsoever about beekeeping, or *apiculture*, and in order that I do not present myself as completely ignorant in this complex business, I have bought myself a textbook, a hefty tome in French, that claims to tell me everything I will need to know about hive construction, the rearing of the queen, extraction of honey and royal jelly, the nutritional value of pollen for humans, manners, the social activities of worker bees and the husbanding of the whole. These stripy little insects are arthropods, as are butterflies: species with bilaterally symmetrical bodies divided into segments. Fascinating reading, but it grows exhausting during my bouts of morning sickness, which last well into the afternoons. They will pass, I know, and are a small price to pay for the joy of the child to come. Still, I am unaccustomed to lethargy and thankful it won't endure for months.

When I arrive at the airport to collect Michel I see that his Paris flight has been delayed and is not scheduled to land for another hour. Instead of hanging about the crowded, Friday-evening concourse, where the noise, cigarette smoke and film-festival hullaballoo will put me in a grumpy humour, I decide to drive to Nice where I can while away the time at a beachside café, watching the sea and quietly studying my *Beginner's Guide to Beekeeping*.

Sitting alone outside the café-bar in the soft evening light, engrossed in my manual, I am only vaguely aware of the arrival of a moustached man who settles himself and his newspaper at the small round table right alongside mine until he shouts loudly to the waiter – 'Henri!' – and lights up a Gauloise. The waiter brings the man a pastis and they chat animatedly together. His exhalations of smoke drift my way and draw my attention. I feel a sweep of nausea wash over me and decide to move, but before I can scoop up notepad, pen, book and bag, my neighbour – a middle-aged, leather-skinned, fubsy Mediterranean with the florid complexion of one who lives out of doors, victim to winds and sun – makes a totally bizarre comment which stops me in my tracks. 'Have you seen them dancing?' is what he asks.

I assume that he must still be talking to the waiter, and glance behind me to see if Henri is standing close by. This provokes my neighbour, who grows noticeably hot under the collar and begins waving his hand at me. Before I know what's happening, he is leaning over my table and rapping his finger (one of the two holding the burning cigarette) hard against my manual.

'The bees, madame,' he says. 'The dance of the bees.' He repeats his words in an emphatic way, as though he considers me deaf or simple. 'Danced till they were stunned. So, you're wasting your time.'

'*Excusez-moi?*'

With a bulging-eyed nod, he raises both hands, fingers heavenwards, 'You won't find such matters in books. Books won't give you the truth!' And with that he downs the remaining swig of his pastis, tosses a few coins on his table, calls *bonne soirée* to Henri, picks up his *Nice Matin* and struts off.

I am left feeling both irritated by this bumptious individual and curious, and as soon as he is out of sight I riffle through the pages and then flick back to the index in search of a chapter or heading on Dancing Bees. There is no mention of any such activity. Stupid of me to have bothered to look. I dismiss his comment, laughing at myself for having paid him any attention at all.

Once we are back at the house, Michel busies himself in the kitchen chopping the parsley, chives and basil I have collected from our maturing herb beds. During these last days I have been planting baby lollo rosso salads and rocket, which have shot up so fast that I am able to harvest some of the tender young leaves for supper. We are having *loup*, sea bass, which I have marinated in five tablespoons of Bourgogne Aligoté white wine, generous dribbles of olive oil, pepper, ground sea salt, sprays of fennel, a sprig or two of celery and slubs of freshly picked lemon, ready to bake in tinfoil on a bed of sliced onions and tomatoes – our own, of course.

I prepared everything earlier so that we would have little to do this evening. The plane's delay has meant that we are eating late, but the temperature is heavenly and we can dine by candlelight beneath the stars.

I have said nothing yet to Michel about my news. Still savouring the moment. While the oven is heating I walk round to the big old fridge we bought second hand and have installed in the garage by the stables, where we store our wine and keep our washing machine, and draw out a bottle of champagne. Once I have uncorked it and placed it in a cooler, I take it, with two long-stemmed flutes, to our wooden table to await Michel, and set it down next to a plate of small, round toasts generously spread with a creamy and very garlicky *crème d'anchoïade*, anchovy paste, which is made locally and which I buy at the *épicerie* in the village.

The cicadas have given up for the day, but the dogs have awoken, no longer beaten by the heat. They smell dinner and have begun pacing the terraces, marking time until we sit down to eat, at which point they will settle under the table in the hope of being thrown the odd morsel, even though they know I refuse to indulge them in this. Presently they are barking, demarcating their territory, warning off intruders, most especially the wild boars, those great hulking beasts who scour our hill in search of roots and acorns.

One evening, during our very first summer here, while I was alone – Michel had returned to Paris – occupied in the garden, watering the first of the plants we had purchased, geraniums, a passiflora, some herbs, I was frightened by strange gruntings and heavy breathing. I turned my head fearing a burglar, but found myself staring at a huge, hirsute wild boar. She was a female, the more dangerous of the species, foraging for food. An awesome sight, she stood her ground, eyes fixed on me, until I crept stealthily but deter-minedly away.

Although we are aware that they have not abandoned these ten acres of ours, since that evening there have been no more close encounters with these strapping pigs. We assumed the dogs were successfully keeping them at bay until we began to notice damage to our renovated drystone walls. This is usually a clue that *les sangliers* are about. They leap and stamp from one terrace to the next, displacing the stones which, as they loosen, sink into piles of rubble. Months of Quashia's work destroyed with the careless kick of a hefty hoof.

They enter our holding from the rear of the hill, approach-ing us from its summit – up there, we are not fenced in – and, as they gain courage or grow hungrier, they shuffle ever closer to the house. A few nights back, Quashia spotted a family of four stalking the land, tearing up the grass.

'Are we celebrating?'

'Mmm?'

'I see champagne.'

Lost in my boar concerns, I had briefly forgotten. Michel is at my side now. He sits at the table, looking at me quizzi-cally, then leans forward, lifts the bottle from the cooler and begins to pour. He hands me my glass and raises his. '*Santé*,' he says.

I lift my flute and gently trace it against his. '*Santé*. Here's to us and – our baby.'

My eyes prick with moist emotion and I rub at them, attempting not to be a softy.

Michel is on his feet and draws me to mine. '*Chérie! Félicitations!*' Arms around my waist, he seeks my lips. '*Je t'aime*,' he whispers, holding me tight. 'That's wonderful news. The best.'

Later, when the bottle is empty and we are laughing sense-lessly with joy and a surfeit of champagne, the scent of

burning from the upstairs kitchen arrests us and reminds us
that our delicious sea bass is still in the oven. I rise to hurry
up the newly tiled steps that skirt the side of the house to
retrieve our supper but Michel presses me back. 'No, you
don't. No overexertion.' And off he goes, returning a few
minutes later with the barely recognisable remains of our
fish, charcoaled and bubbling inside the scalded tinfoil.

It is half-past ten on Saturday morning. The sun is already
high and the temperature is mounting. I am crouched on the
ground observing a minnow mayfly resting on the stone surround of the pond. René was meant to be coming by at
half-past eight. We had arranged with him that he would
accompany us to the farm of an *apiculteur*, 'the best beekeeper in all Provence', who happens to be a dear friend of
his. 'I've known him since we were lads.' But not for the first
time there is no sign of our silver-haired olive master and no
news, either. I go inside and ring his mobile, but it is on
answer machine so I don't bother to leave a message. Instead
I take the opportunity presented by his tardiness to prepare
myself grilled tomatoes on toast as a second breakfast, which
I tuck into out on the terrace.

'What are we doing about this beekeeper, then?' Michel
refills our coffee cups. 'I've never seen you eat that before,'
he adds.

'I know, weird, but I really fancied it. There are a couple
of other names on my list. The first is M. Manneron. He has
a stall at the Forville market in Cannes. I met his daughter
there when I was buying our poor sea bass. The other I contacted after reading his details on the label of a honey jar.
They both live further afield than René's pal, but we could go
anyway, make a day of it.'

Both beekeepers are expecting us, but both live in the distant hills, one inland towards the mountains and the other in

the Var. Michel thinks that we may have left our outing a little
too late in the day. It will be a long and sticky journey in his
ancient, non-air-conditioned Mercedes, we have tickets to see
a film at the festival later and he is concerned that I should
not wear myself out. We argue the point in an amiable way,
because I am determined not to allow a little nausea to spoil
our plans for the day or stand between us and our modest
farming ambitions. In any case, I have been looking forward
to the outing while poring over my bee tome.

'Think of it, Michel, beehives standing in rows the length
of the terraces.'

'Steady on, we're only talking five or six hives.' He laughs,
picking up the phone, still expressing misgivings about the
taxing nature of such an upland reconnaissance in my condition.

The first apiarist informs him that he cannot wait in. '*Je
suis très occupé*,' M. Le Beekeeper advises us, and goes on to
voice the view that we live too far; the journey would be
unprofitable unless he were to install a minimum of seventy
hives. Undeterred, Michel replaces the receiver and rings M.
Manneron, who is less dismissive and assures us that he will
be waiting for us.

'If you're not feeling up to it, we can postpone this,'
Michel reasserts, but I shake my head.

Within the hour, we are heading off in the direction of Digne-
les-Bains, leaving the Alpes Maritimes behind us, taking the
Route Napoléon, where the roadsides are buttoned with
summery white and yellow wild flowers, heading towards
the Alpes de Haute-Provence.

Once we are through the chaos of modern day Grasse,
with its commercialised perfumeries and overconstructed
high-rises housing most of the region's bureaucracy, the traffic begins to thin out. At 600 metres we pass glowing,

bald-pated men dressed in shorts, walking purposefully. Here, in the environs of Grasse, there are dozens of *maisons de retraites*. Even today it remains a fashionable place for the French to retire to, and many of the ornate *belle époque* buildings have been converted into luxurious nursing homes or apartments, standing high on the hillsides looking out towards the distant sea.

Succulents grow everywhere out of the rocks, their sharply needled fronds reaching heavenwards like wailing women or the tentacles of giant octopuses. It was the British who brought succulents to this side of the world, transporting them from their distant colony of Australia. Also from Australia came eucalyptus trees. Their heavenly perfume always reminds me of home, because it is the first to greet you when you exit the arrivals hall at Nice airport and walk towards the *parking*.

Alice de Rothschild had a vast and very fabulous garden here in Grasse at her austere Villa Victoria (now converted into flats) to which Queen Victoria paid a visit in 1891. As was the custom with all Mme Rothschild's celebrated visitors, Her Royal British Majesty came bearing a gift of a tree which she was invited to plant in the grounds herself. Unfortunately, in the execution of her task, our Queen, who never tripped lightly on her feet, trampled all over one of the flowerbeds, destroying several rare plants in the process. Madame de Rothschild sent her instantly packing.

'I like the idea of inviting guests to plant a tree,' I say.

Continuing our climb inland in this solid yet ancient car, we reach the mountains, the most southerly of the Alps. Here the views plummet into lush, emerald-green valleys and sometimes, through a break in the ranges, we catch the sparkling blue of our own doorstep Mediterranean. The vegetation is not yet alpine; there are still the occasional reminders of hot lands. No palms at this altitude, but tall, willowy eucalypts perfume the air. Cork oak, *chêne liège*, is growing profusely everywhere – an indigenous tree to this region – but there are no more olive trees to be seen. We are saying a temporary *au revoir* to the land of baking sun and beloved *oliviers*, leaving them behind as we ascend towards a cooler clime. Herbs spice the wind. We turn a corner, a delicious scent hits our nostrils. Juniper. It grows wild up here in the scrub. As does the aromatic broom, with its tightly clustered butter-yellow blossoms, now in full flower. The altitude begins to slacken the heat. I breathe deeply, more easily. This old car burns oil, exhaling clouds of navy fumes which make me dizzy, so I am grateful for this milder climate. It clears my head, offers comfort to the journey.

Eight hundred metres. The landscape is changing. The dense, chocolate-red earth, so evident at sea-level along the Esterelle coast, is in sharp contrast to the stark white stone at this elevation. Clefted white rocks loom all about us, runnelled with tracks which resemble fingernail scratches across naked flesh. Small furry blue flowers at the road's edge. Forests of pines, not the generous-branched *pin parasol* which so elegantly shades the coastal diners, but the pointy-tipped Christmas ones that put me in mind of rows of paintbrushes. Even the buildings up here have an alpine look to them. Wooden homes with slanted roofs that resemble Swiss wall clocks. I half expect little hand-carved people to pop out, twirl and disappear again. Their shutters are solid, workaday wood. None are painted the electric colours ours are; here they are varnished to protect against the fierce climatic changes. The artists' hues for which the Côte d'Azur is so renowned have been bleached out at this altitude, all but erased. We are travelling through a world of dun brown, white stone, deep conifer evergreens, softwood forestry tones, with dashes of russet. It is a less audacious, less vibrant palette. Bare nature, no livestock. Little activity.

Swinging the *lacets*, the hairpin bends, we begin to encounter another breed of tourist: the cyclist with his trim, busy buttocks in brilliant blue Spandex body and hard hat, pedalling for all he is worth.

And turning my attention to the left side of the road, I spot a sign with an engraving of an eagle and the letter 'N' beneath it. 'La Route Napoléon.' 'We are following the tracks of Napoléon Bonaparte, Emperor Napoléon I.' As I speak the land takes up the eulogy. Everywhere we see Café Napoléon, Camping Napoléon, Parking Napoléon.

On 1 March 1815, having fled incarceration on the island of Elba, Napoléon landed at Golfe Juan – his escape had been financed by his doting sister, Pauline, who, the year before, had sold her jewellery in Nice and, as he was escorted through St Raphaël, a heavily guarded prisoner en route for Elba, she had slipped him the cash needed 'to make flight possible'. Today Golfe Juan is a buzzing resort, sandwiched with beachside cafés, boutiques and clubs thumping with the beat of popular music; a playground for the young and trendy. But when Napoléon set foot on that shore with his 1,200-strong army, it was a humble fishing village. From there he marched on Cannes, conquered it, and the very next day began his trek northwards.

Keen to avoid the Rhône Valley, where he knew he would be greeted with hostility, he chose this mountain way, the route to Sisteron, which today is more famous for its deliciously tender lamb. By the time he arrived in Grenoble, throngs of people had amassed and were waiting for him. He marched into their city to the resounding cries of: '*Vive l'Empereur!*' Like the soaring eagle on his insignia, he must have felt invincible. His triumphal return to Paris, the seat of his omnipotency, must have seemed reassuringly secure.

Roadside shacks are in evidence now, selling kilo pots of honey, predominantly lavender. And lavender bouquets advertised at two for 10 francs. Signs tell us that we are at 'La Source Parfumée'. Rather splendid, I remark, to know that one is living at the source of a perfumed world. It cries out to be the setting for a fairytale.

We pass though a hamlet with a garage offering all manner of repair work yet chock-a-block with rusting husks of vehicles, a spattering of houses and a trim whitewashed *auberge* decorated with a faded hand-painted advertisement. It reminds me of those Dubonnet commercials I used to see on television when I was a small girl and the perfect universe they depicted: tranquil summer lanes in the heart of the French countryside. In my own childhood I rarely knew that warmth, that peace and sunshine of mind and I have some-times asked myself whether, somewhere deep within, I wasn't seduced by those commercials. In my search for happiness have I sought a world where jolly French workmen in jaunty automobiles motor about with not a care in the world? The *auberge* we are approaching displays a less genial image, however. It is a larger-than-life silhouette of tricorned head and shoulders. A haunting, black shadowy figure stencilled against a white wall. We draw close and I see that the adver-tisement is for cognac: Cognac Napoléon, of course. A small man enlarged to many times his own dimensions.

I think of product placement and the fortunes certain stars are paid for lending their names to merchandise. 'I wonder what our Corsican hero would have been paid today for all this,' I laugh. 'He's a bankable icon, that's for sure. And there's no copyright to stop anyone from reproducing his image.'

As we pass through Castellane, heaving with tourists and the only traffic jams we encounter throughout our journey, we see signs everywhere for the Grand Canyon du Verdon –

the largest gorge in Europe – which I have never visited. But no time for that today.

I return to the purpose of our outing – honey – and share with Michel what I have been studying. '*Apis*, a genre of bee that collects pollen for honey-making – not all do – has been around for somewhere between ten to twenty million years. Incredible, eh? It seems that bees and honey have been on this planet longer than man as we know him. *Homo erectus* dates from the Newer Pliocene period. The earliest bee fossils found date back to the Miocene period. There is a fossil in the Smithsonian Museum in Washington which is nine million years old. Man was already consuming honey somewhere between three to eight thousand years before Christ. An ancient industry, on a par with olive farming.'

I fall silent, stunned by the beauty of the nature around us.

Winding through one of the mountain passes, *les cols*, a coach approaches, driving fast, blasting its horn like a demented beast. The sound alone might sweep you away, send you spinning into the ravine that plummets more than a thousand feet beneath us. The rush and drama of the coach whistling through the mountain pass has sent a flock of rather large swifts scattering, screaming, regrouping and sweeping in and out of the clefts and crevices of the carved limestone alongside us. Are they swifts? Yes, alpine swifts, with white underbellies. In winter these *cols* must surely be impassable.

Our journey takes us through a lush valley where we drive in and out of a pretty and inviting town, Barêmme. A fertile oasis where Napoléon spent the night of 3 March 1815. We pass fields of apricot trees, cherry, bamboo.

Bamboo. I had thought that the origins of bamboo were in China, but I have read that its early history includes India, America, even Africa. In the Mediterranean, the Romans cultivated it as a decoration. Indian bamboo, which grows to great heights, encircled many of their temples. There are over 200 different species. Its cane was believed to carry the magic of the Orient within it.

The fruit trees prompt thoughts of lunch; I am hungry again. Michel suggests that we eat after our rendezvous with Manneron. 'I'm sure we can find a mountaintop restaurant in Mézel serving delicious local produce. What do you fancy?'

I consider his question as a steam train comes puffing along a track that flanks the road. Written the length of its three carriages is '*Nice à Digne*'.

'Something with tomatoes,' I answer.

There are maybe a dozen passengers aboard, all peering from the windows. It resembles a blue and white Dinky toy, a lithe Thomas the Tank Engine from a world of children's literature which precedes Harry Potter. We watch it rock and sway and then the signal goes down on the track in front of us and the train steams across the street.

The signalman's house to the right is green and shiny, with a carapace of ivy. Cut into it are red oblong window-boxes crammed with scarlet geraniums and, in the garden, two crooked tables dressed in red checked cloths.

Matisse wrote: 'Red becomes a sound like a note escaping from a musical instrument.' When I look upon the ruddy richness of these flowers, I see what he was getting at. And our poppies in the garden; so hot is that colour, I hear the heroin-cracked voice of a jazz singer, scarlet lips flush against a silver mike, crooning the blues.

The signal goes up and on we go. Now the train is to our right until it disappears into a small tunnel, chuff-chuffing cheerfully out of sight.

We have reached 1,200 metres above sea-level and the out-skirts of Mézel, where the air is heady, knife-sharp and spicy.

It is fragranced with the scent of wild lavender, which cannot grow so easily closer to the coast: it needs an altitude of over 900 metres to survive.

The sky, the light, the land are a delicate chromatic tapestry; the chalky earth is as pale as faded butter or goat's cheese, the sloping fields are a deep, inviting amethyst and the cloudless blue sky seems almost within reach. My head out of the window, hair blowing freely, I inhale the piquantly aromatic herbs, brush plants and trees known collectively as *garrigue*.

La garrigue Méditerranéenne includes a vast selection of wild and sweetly scented bushes and plants. What a paradise for bees . . .

As we close up the car to ask about Manneron and stretch our legs, I hear the echo of our footsteps on the dry, empty pavements. There is a hint of wind for which, after the length of the journey, we are very grateful. I crane my neck to release the stiffness and sight an eagle drifting effortlessly on the windslip.

'*L'aigle volera de clocher en clocher jusqu'aux tours de Notre-Dame,*' said Napoléon, the returning hero. The eagle will fly from belfry to belfry until it reaches the bell towers of Notre-Dame. Flushed with early success, his dreams must have soared with those overhead birds as he and his retinue marched northwards, cutting a celestial route through these Haute-Provence Alps. Above him, the lords of the domain, swooping, hunting, killing. He would have been watching those raptors, living in proximity with them, planning his campaigns, inhaling rushes of their potent power, hell-bent on his own resurrection.

Looking out across these mountains, where the natural peaks rise sharply skywards, not dissimilar to bell towers, I can picture where his image might have come from. Today, over a thousand birds of prey are executed every year by the power lines the EDF, the electricity board, have installed in these ranges. If their wingtips brush against two lines at once, they are electrocuted instantly. Others are wiped out by forest fires, pesticide and fertiliser poisonings or illegal hunting.

Napoléon would have had the opportunity to observe nests built in treetops on the cliff faces and to hear the broad, flapping wings of a variety of diurnal and nocturnal raptors hunting between one range, one peak, and the next. Instead of the sombrous tolling of church bells, he would have been listening to the eerie, resonant skirls of those mighty predators echoing through the stillness, cutting across brittle streams of light.

Nearly two centuries later, numerous birds of prey have become a rare sight. Bonelli's eagle is now an endangered species. Probably no more than fifty pairs survive in France.

'I think it's a young Golden,' murmurs Michel. I tilt my head and fasten my attention on the mighty bird. From this distance it does not look golden at all. Its underbelly is a dark, chocolatey brown.

'Why do you say that?'

'It has a golden head and nape. See how it glides, the "V" of its wings? See, it has white markings on its wings and tail.'

A tractor purrs by in the main street of Mézel and draws me back to earth, to this friendly little mountain town, where I notice chamomile growing in stone pots at the road's edge. This is a very different Provence from our coastal strip. It is far removed from the glorious *belle époque* splendour and glitz of the Côte d'Azur. The tourists here are in handfuls; they pass in dribs and drabs or sit in the roadside cafés studying maps. Not the roasted packs shuffling about by the coast, stuck in traffic, gorging despondently on ice creams and cola, or the film festival crowds. Here they are fresh-faced and purposeful, walkers in sensible sandals and batik shorts, no-nonsense haircuts or hippy-long curls, swinging woven swagbags from their shoulders.

Beyond the town, crossing a rather unattractive bridge, we go in search of the Manneron holding. An umbrous-featured local points out the route. 'But you can't walk it,' he warns. 'It's too far. It's way up there,' is the sole indication we are given.

Back in the car, we begin to scale a track, a *sentier muletier*, probably once trodden only by mules and *les bouquetins*, the splendidly horned goats that used to roam freely in these southern Alps but are never seen these days outside the national park. Slender-trunked trees rise up all around us. The higher we climb – and I thought we had reached the summit – the narrower and more perilous the path grows. The ground has turned to a shade of bleached nutmeg. There are numerous butterflies: minuscule citrony ones and larger, darker fellows and then another, a rich, creamy butterscotch. I am sorry to say that I cannot identify any of them, though the small ones could be Clouded Yellows which are habitués at this altitude. I dare not look down; the verticality makes me giddy. So I zero in on what is aloft and catch sight of what looks like a *village perché* hidden high above the trees, squeezed between bouldered rock formations.

'Look!'

I cannot believe the car will make it. It whines and wheezes as we snake our way round the mountain until eventually we reach the tiny hamlet, which bears no sign to tell us its name. We pass a man and boy leaning together against the wall of a house. They stare at us as though we have come from outer space, intruders to these dizzying heights. We park in a square, the only square, at the end of the road. Literally. The only way out of here is retreat. We must have climbed a hundred metres since leaving Mézel. The view is stupendous. One lone man is tinkering with his car, which has a Paris registration plate. I ask directions to a café or bar. He laughs. 'There's no bar here. There's nothing. Eight houses. Not even a baker. If you want bread you must return to the town.'

Does he know where we can find the beekeeper, M. Manneron?

He shakes his head. 'I'm *en vacances*, sorry,' and off he goes, up a narrow cobbled lane, the only lane, to one of the other five properties – we have already passed three that look out over the view. I glance at my watch. It is minutes after midday and I hear the echoing clatter of plates and the chime of voices behind semi-closed shutters. It is baking hot and there is the familiar zirring of cicadas which I haven't been aware of since leaving the coast.

A dog barks, and then another. Within seconds a cacophony of howls and barkings has broken out. We sight one rather dusty-looking hound chained in the square behind several rusting, wheelless trucks and then a second further over in a pit of earth. Both are dun-brown. Why would anyone need a guard dog here? What's to steal? Who is there to steal it? Beyond the yowling mutts is a small walled cemetery. We take a look. Neat graves adorned with plastic flowers. The family of—. Sadly missed mother of—. Shiny enamelled photos, oval-shaped like cameo brooches; pre-war portraits of severe-looking men and women in starched collars and swept-back hair. I am suddenly fascinated by the history of this place. Who left? Who stayed? Who married whom? Every villager turning out for a birth, a marriage, a burial. Who went to war, who came back? To live so intimately with one's neighbours. No secrets. Or might the entire hamlet harbour a dark secret? The Parisian tourist is calling to us. He has enquired after our apiarist and the news is that he doesn't live here. He lives in Mézel.

'But we have just come from there.'

'No, his place is outside the town. There's a hillside, an escarpment, where he has a holding with many hives.' Yes, that sounds like him. We thank the young Parisian for his trouble and begin to stroll the few yards back to the car, making one more stop to take in the magnificence of the location and its utter isolation. It is then that I see the sign.

La Réserve Géologique de Haute-Provence est une Réserve Naturelle Nationale, spécialisée dans les Sciences de la Terre. Sa mission est de protéger le patrimoine géologique. De la fin de l'Ere primaire au Quarternaire, ce sont, trois cents millions d'années que roches et fossiles nous racontent.

Dans ce territoire de 145,000 hectares, immense musée en plein air, les géologues de la Réserve Géologique de Haute-Provence font revivre ces époques disparues.

. . . découvrir et d'aimer le monde des roches.

The notice is informing us that we are gazing upon 145,000 hectares of a natural, open-air museum. This is a geological reserve. We are standing smack in the centre of one of the oldest inhabited regions of the world, where the rocks are impregnated with fossils and prehistoric signs of life. For 300 million years these rocks, these mountains, have been telling their stories, or so claims the Haute-Provence Geological Reserve. History written in stones; in their wrinkles, folds and eruptions. Every curve, every hollow is a language in granite. Michel tells me that among the fossil deposits found in this vast region are hundreds of examples of ammonites as well as footprints of prehistoric birds. Footprints of prehistoric birds who circled these mountains, landed, fed, procreated here.

Hills, valleys, forests of green folding one into the next, far-off mountains, distant crickets, all beneath the crystal midday sky. It is as though time has stopped and we are gazing into the memory of an ancestral brain which is both stupendous and terrifying. The world revealed, omniscient, staring back at us across the ages. I feel my heartbeat quicken.

'But Paris is a very old city and we were very young . . .'

Why, suddenly, do I recall and find myself mouthing these words of Ernest Hemingway's from *A Moveable Feast*? I cannot say. Perhaps because this place *is* so very old and we, by comparison, are still young. Our future is undrawn. Our love is young; this baby within me certainly is. And in the earth's stillness and age, its continuity, its witnessing of time, its wisdom, I sense a warning – the distant echo of an ancient haunting.

Hemingway was referring to the temptations outside his own marriage, an adulterous affair which damaged for ever love's trust. In that sense our love remains shining and untested. But it is not invincible; what if it all goes wrong? What if I should lose this child, too? I slip my hand into Michel's and he squeezes gently on it. A bird high above screeches. I turn my face up towards the light, scrunching my eyes to close out the noonday glare. The buzzard's shadow crosses over me, darkening the day. My head begins to swim and nausea returns; the height grows vertiginous and I turn and walk silently to the car feeling as though I have travelled a great deal further than two hours' distance from the coast, from our farm and from the happiness I seek to create.

As we return towards Mézel, Michel warns me that M. Manneron will probably consider our site too far for him.

But still, he may have good advice for us. 'You are not to be disappointed, *chérie*, if he refuses us. It is a great deal further and a more arduous drive than the map suggests.'

Manneron's stock farm is situated in an isolated backwater in the Alpes de Haute-Provence, and although he and his family live *en ville* in Mézel, the beehives are some distance out of the town, and off the beaten track. When we eventually find the narrow, grass-rutted goat run that leads us to his holding, the beekeeper is leaning against the gate clutching his mobile phone – which is how we have finally tracked him down – waiting for us.

He greets us with a shy shaking of the hand. His pebbled glasses are so thick I am surprised he can support the weight of them. A taciturn individual who has been awarded the Red Medal, the highest honour in France, for the quality of his honey, he speaks impossibly softly in response to our questions and otherwise not at all. Accompanied by M. Manneron, who strides with the ease of a country-dweller, one who spends his days negotiating rugged terrain, we climb a steep incline and then follow him, in single file, along a trail crossing an escarpment. 'Any special tips you might share with us on the husbandry of bees?' asks Michel.

Manneron does not reply. I am uncertain whether he has heard. He pauses to catch his breath or to give us the opportunity to do so – Michel is discreetly watchful that the effort is not too much for me – and then we continue our ascent in silence. Now the path has widened and we are walking side by side. The view in every direction is simply magnificent. I glance furtively at this myopic man striding with his head bowed, deep in thought, and I am curious to know what is going through his mind. From here we descend the scar, moving into an alpine valley, a shallow plateau scooped out between two peaks, and keep moving through windblown grass until, eventually, we reach the hives, *les ruches*, which are laid out in two long rows. Large, white, square boxes standing on short wooden legs amid the tufty mountain grass. A quick calculation tells me there are approximately one hundred.

'Where exactly are you based?' he asks Michel, who pinpoints our location. Manneron nods, contemplating it.

'I understood you had many more hives?'

'Ah, yes, but they are not all here. These have been gathering lavender honey. I have others at work on the *sapins*. These little girls collected from the *romarin* before I brought them up here. And a good season they've had, too.'

'So you move the hives to the flower sources?'

'Transhumance. Most *apiculteurs* practise it.'

'Have you heard of bees dancing?' I ask awkwardly. 'What I mean is . . . might there be a dance of the bees?' I am not convinced that the activity exists but, if it does, Manneron strikes me as a man who might know of it, and I am keen to find out. Besides, the memory of that fellow at the beach café has stayed with me. Our beekeeper leans towards me, peering so close I feel as though I am wearing his glasses. 'They have two routines, but it's only the workers who dance,' he confides.

'Two?'

'Yes, there's the waggle and there's the round. Each dance is a different configuration and communicates a different message. Sometimes, early in the mornings, I open up the hives and there they are, dancing away.'

I am amazed. 'What's it all about?'

'A means of communication. A way of informing the foraging bees where they can find a good source of pollen, of notifying the others of a change of address, you might say – the repositioning of the hives. The language varies slightly between one geographic race of honeybees and another, and thus resembles birdsong and human languages in having local dialects. Looked at that way, you could say that my little girls dance in Provençal.' He grins, pauses and frowns, as though trying to recollect something, and then smiles before continuing in a thickly accented English: 'A swarm of bees in May is worth a load of hay; a swarm of bees in June is worth a silver spoon; a swarm of bees in July is not worth a fly!'

'Did you write that?' I venture.

'What? *Mon Dieu*, no. I think it's a load of nonsense! Folklore. My wife found it on the internet this morning. Listen, I won't be able to help you myself. Your farm is too far. *Desolé*, but I'll lend a hand in finding you someone. You can count on that.'

Silver Side of
the Coast

Parking in the town of Cannes during these fifteen days of the film festival is a nightmare. The Croisette, the internationally famous lido that borders the seafront, is cordoned off. All general traffic must make circuitous detours and sit snarled up for hours on end in narrow lanes and back streets. Only official film-festival cars have access to the Palais, where they disgorge stars and filmmakers of every nationality who pose for the paparazzi while climbing the red-carpeted stairs, watched by thousands of attendant stargazers, eyes agog, alongside the old port. During these days in May, Cannes metamorphoses into a beargarden, and, frankly, the only way to negotiate it is on foot.

But how to get from our farm in the hills to the coast without finding ourselves lumbered with a vehicle that we cannot arrive in or park? Michel has come up with a rather natty solution. We don our evening clothes and fly down the hills on a scooter he has bought for me, but which I don't dare use without him, because the first time I took it out I drove it slap-bang into our neighbour's wall, buckling the front mudguard and smacking my nose so hard I was left with a bruise the colour of winter pansies. I have been behind the wheel of cars since I was sixteen – it is illegal to drive in England at sixteen, but that's another story – yet when it comes to two-wheelers I seem to lack the aptitude. I have no sense of balance and I fear the exposure; I have grown used to the security of the metal carapace of a car and believe myself to be protected, but on a bike I panic and wobble all over the place, like someone's granny after several whiskys. Still, for the festival, the scooter is the ticket. We park and lock it up in one of the back lanes of the old town and from there we stroll to the Palais, our coveted film invitations at the ready. At this time of the evening the back streets of the *vieille ville* are relatively quiet; the action is taking place around the Palais, known to the local Cannois population and those who work in the film and television industries as 'the bunker' due its consummate ugliness and desultory ergonomic values.

Arriving on foot rather than in a chauffeured limo provided by the festival for official guests of the festival – this honour is reserved for those who have a film in competition – means that we must push and shove our way through the crush of crowds as plentiful as spectators at a Premier League football match. What an assault to our senses after the tranquillity of Appassionata and our day out in the mountains with the shy beekeeper, M. Manneron. As we approach the glaring lights, music – as usual a well-known film score – blasts from the humungous loudspeakers while the glitterati shove and kick like fishwives to get to the front of the queue, for once inside the huge cinema, the seats are not numbered; it is a first-come, first-served affair.

Everywhere people are begging for spare invitations, hopefuls in makeshift evening dress whose dream it is to walk those red-carpeted steps and maybe, just maybe, have their photograph taken by one of the paparazzi who flank that stairway to fame. Between street level and entrance to the Palais, there are twenty-four steps and then, if you are up in the grand circle and not at auditorium level, which we are, another eleven to climb. I know because I count them regularly – it gives me something to concentrate on, helps me feel less shy. The attention of the world is spotlighted here: every television station, every international newspaper and magazine have sent representatives. Each May, approximately 25,000 people converge upon this coastal resort, amphitheatred by its deluxe hotels, to partake of the mayhem and madness that is this festival.

Cannes is about this moment. Ever since 1946, when the first film festival was inaugurated here to celebrate the town's liberation after the Second World War, it has become its raison d'être. Every other festival, every other season, is a pale reflection of this glitz. The buzz, the hype and, it has to be said, the tackiness. Spot the celebrity. The photographers are everywhere, pointing lenses, flashing cameras at well-known faces, sequinned, fishtail frocks, backless gowns and plunging cleavages, any trick in the book or fashion accessory to grab the attention of the thousands of snappers congregating the length of these hallowed steps. Stunning women hanging from the shoulders of drop-dead gorgeous men pose and pout before the strobe of flashbulbs and the blinking, adoring crowds.

As we negotiate our way through the scrum of overexcited people, Michel wraps a protective arm about me. 'How are you doing?'

'Fine,' I smile.

'Ready?'

I nod.

He takes my hand and we begin the ascent.

It is important to look cool, composed and, above all, to smile. It is no good concentrating on one's feet in an attempt not to trip or hitching up one's frock or frowning like a sourpuss. Smiling and swanning are all part of the show, the parade, the masquerade. The music is 'Thus Spake Zarathustra'. Up we climb, arm in arm. No selfconscious rictus grin this evening; I have the best reason to be gleeful and I am sailing up the stairs, savouring every minute of it. I turn my head and glimpse my husband, the father-to-be of my child, at my side. Flashes explode around us. I barely notice them; I am fathoms deep in my own happiness, our happiness. Michel squeezes my wrist, a tiny recognition of the swell of joy within me. The paparazzi always snap him, not because they recognise him – they don't – but because he looks magnificent in his black waistcoat and white *smoking*, which enhance his imposing, Prussian good looks and that long curly hair of his, and I am chuffed to be the woman on his arm.

Once up the stairs, we are jostled inside, huddled and shuffling like a colony of emperor penguins, and directed to vacant rows of seats by one of a dozen uniformed girls. Tonight, just as we are about to take our places, someone yells out Michel's name, bawling it across the rows of chairbacks. Coiffured heads turn. We spin around to see who it might be and catch sight of an eager, middle-aged man elbowing his way through the shimmering crowds to reach us, all the while shouting and waving. He seems to know us well and is almost jumping for joy to find us here. His stomach is straining in his outdated dinner jacket, he is flushed and perspiring, but he seems thrilled to see us, if the huge smile animating his shiny-complexioned face is anything to go by. I know we know him, but I cannot place him.

'Who is he? Have we worked with him?'

Is he a business associate of Michel's from Paris? But his accent is Provençal. He presents his chunky wife, who is clearly overcome to meet us both, particularly me. 'Now I can put a name to that English accent, madame,' she teases. 'And we love that television series of yours.'

And then it dawns on me. We are in the company of M. Di Luzio, our sooty plumber-cum-chimney sweep, and his wife. Tonight, as spruced and scrubbed as a newborn baby, he is quite unrecognisable. What is clear, though, is that he and his wife still insist on believing that I am Emma Peel from *The Avengers* – a series in which I have never played so much as a guest role. Even here, amid the madness of industry posturing, M. Di Luzio slaps his thigh like a principal boy in a pantomime, wiggles his hips and winks at me triumphantly. Then he turns his head and, through the assembling crowds, roars to another couple, friends of theirs, apparently, seated high up at the back of the upper auditorium. 'It's her!' he bellows in his thick, Provençal twang. 'Her off the telly!'

Later, after the screening and before going for supper, Michel and I stroll the Croisette arm in arm. It's fun to gaze, to miss as little as possible and to bear in mind that as far back as the late nineteenth century this famous lido has played host to the rich, the royal and the famous. Along its waterside arena an astonishing aggregate of destinies has become interwoven.

Prince Leopold, Duke of Albany, the youngest son of Queen Victoria, died here in 1894 after an accident at the Villa Nevada. Her Royal Majesty, his mother, paid a visit to Cannes three years later, with an entourage of over a hundred, to mourn her son and to visit the church of St George which had been built in his memory. However, much as she loved the French Riviera – the name was bestowed on the place by the visiting British – and was a regular visitor to these shores, she quit Cannes after only four days, declaring that she strongly disapproved of the immoral carryings-on here.

'I would be fascinated to hear her opinion today,' I say to Michel as we weave our way through blasting horns and autograph-hunters.

In 1949, the glorious, flame-haired film star Rita Hayworth married the Aga Khan here and lived out most of the rest of her sad and lost life in a villa in Le Cannet, which overlooks this renowned bay. It was the management of the Cannes Carlton Hotel who suggested to that same, now deceased, Aga Khan, head of the Ismaili Muslims, that they would be happy to bottle his bathwater to sell to his faithful as an elixir of life. In 1953, a seventeen-year-old nubile French girl, the daughter of bourgeois parents, posed on these golden sands (the sand is imported) for the paparazzi and caused such a sensation that from that day onwards her rise to fame as world sex kitten was assured. Brigitte Bardot. In some ways, she did as much for the perception of women in the fifties as her feisty suffragette predecessors, because of the new attitude she displayed to sex. BB was portrayed as a woman with carnal values who cared more for her own pleasures than for the men who partnered her. These days she is pretty much dismissed by the French. Though reaching sixty is not a setback – in France, women *d'un certain âge* are revered – she has not aged with the grace or poise of Catherine Deneuve. Pictures show her looking plump, wrinkled and rather vulgar, and I suspect that her marriage to a senior assistant of Le Pen, the leader of this nation's extreme right, has been the final nail in the coffin of her image.

In 1955, just a couple of years after BB's explosion on to the world scene, a very different breed of woman, the American model-cum-actress Grace Kelly, met Prince Rainier of Monaco here and, in marrying him a year later, renounced film-star status for that of Beautiful Princess endowed with Kingdom and Untold Riches – the ultimate escapist fantasy.

And that, it seems to me, is what Cannes is about. This fringe of Provençal littoral remains the land of make-believe, but what fascinates me is, at what cost?

Occasionally, a fellow producer from Paris or London, some industry person, waves to us, or a harassed American executive, here for the market rather than the festival, stops to say hi to Michel and to enquire, 'How's business?'

While they exchange news, I take the opportunity to drink in the scene.

Although it is almost eleven at night – the second competition screening starts somewhere between 10 and 11pm – this famous beachfront drag is jam-packed with people. All along it, folk are sitting in cafés or restaurants or at tables on the pavements doing business, a few rather too ostentatiously. Others are acting chic, being famous, spending money, while others still are talking serious film. Many are sporting black tie. These tend to be the professionals who, like us, have just attended a screening or are about to sit through the later performance, for *smoking*, evening dress, is de rigueur here during the festival. You cannot climb those renowned red steps after 6.30pm unless you are attired in evening dress. Michel and I both rather enjoy this custom. These days it's about the only occasion I drag out the glad rags, and it adds a certain elegance to proceedings which, after all, purport to be about the celebration of filmmaking.

Beyond this nucleus, looking keenly and hungrily about them, are surges of star-spotters, wannabes, tourists, and make-believers and, to keep these motley swarms controlled, there are police at every corner, lining the streets, whistling at and redirecting the noisy streams of traffic.

*

This evening the weather is perfect. Balmy with a lilac sky as clear as a bell. Constellations of stars light up the night. Yes, it's the season for stars, but the terrestrial ones won't be spotted here. No, they are to be found hanging out in heavily guarded villas, attending exclusive parties in châteaux hired by distribution companies desperate to promote their latest multimillion-dollar extravaganza, or they are staying at the Hôtel du Cap, where the management refuse to accept payment by cheque or credit card, where attendance at one breakfast meeting at least is essential if you are to be hailed as a member of that most exclusive of all clubs, the A list, and where you can lose yourself in the sumptuous grounds, *le parc*, play langorous tennis in diamond-studded *baskets* (plimsolls, to those of my generation) and where, it has to be said, the view from that strand of the Cap d'Antibes out over the Mediterranean is truly breathtaking. But we are not members of that A list, and nor do we particularly wish to be. Well, if I am honest, I have hankered after that fame – I began composing that dreamed-of Oscar speech when I was ten years old – but not Michel: he is far more grounded, far less Hollywood-oriented. Or, as the French might say, '*pas très 'ollywoodien*'.

So here we are, strolling contentedly along the Croisette, hand in hand, enjoying the brush of palm trees soughing lazily in the hint of breeze – palms, by the way, were yet another British legacy to this coast. They imported them here in the nineteenth century along with the fluffy, sweet-smelling golden mimosas that are today celebrated at dozens of Provençal mimosa festivals in late January – when, suddenly, from out of the huggermugger of people, looms an unshaven, scruffily dressed journalist. He calls my name and I try to recall his. Jacob. Yes, that's it. I became acquainted with him in Madras, India, when I was a guest at the annual film festival there. I introduce him to Michel, and without further ado he gets straight to the point. He is here with his girlfriend, he explains, covering the festival for a German magazine, but the girlfriend, Barbara, of whom he spoke frequently in India, is at a loose end and not feeling well. He asks for our phone number and enquires whether she could come up to the house, use the garden and pool, hang out with us?

'Where we are staying is pretty grotty,' he moans, 'as well as being horrendously expensive, but it's in a good position for me. Still, Barbara can't sit in all day and she hasn't managed to find tickets to any films because she doesn't have any accreditation. Any chance that you guys could dig up a festival badge and a few tickets? Or if you have a spare room, maybe we could move up to your place?'

Before I can open my mouth, Michel tells him, '*Desolé,* it's not possible.'

We say our goodnights and he hurries away. I turn and glance after him. I am remembering an occasion several festivals back when I went into my bank and witnessed a scene that quite distressed me. A youngish but balding Englishman with an air of down-at-heel desperation was at the front of a rather long queue attempting to cash a cheque for the princely sum of £30. The teller refused him. He became loud and upset and an assistant manager was called to the scene. He begged her for the money, regaling her with his hopes for his first film, while the rest of us waited patiently. Eventually, the assistant agreed to telephone his branch in London, but while she was away making the call, he turned on his heels and fled like a hunted rabbit.

I recount this tale to Michel and then reflect on the fact that, whoever you are and no matter what your reason for being in Cannes during these fifteen glittering days in May, there is one thing you can bet your life on: it's costing the individual or the corporates an arm and a leg.

'The town of Cannes must be so rich,' I say.

'I am not at all sure about that,' replies Michel. 'In fact, there are whispers of financial problems.'

'Really?'

Smiling, he leads me off the Croisette into a side street. We are making for a friendly, family-run Italian restaurant he favours.

'I'm starving,' he says. 'Let's eat. What do you fancy?'

'Stuffed tomatoes. I'm dying to know what you've heard.'

'Didn't you have tomatoes for lunch?'

'Yes, and breakfast.'

Our Sunny Surroundings

After early-morning coffee, while the sun is rising into honeydew clouds that drift out of sight to reveal a clear blue sky, Michel begins a full day's work, even though it is Sunday, while I swim, shower and beetle off to Cannes.

The first performance of this, the last day of the festival, is due to screen at the Palais at 8.30am. The dress code is casual, seats are marginally less fought-over and I will find space for the ancient Merc in a *parking* we use above the historic fruit and vegetable market. From there, it is a pleasant stroll to the Palais.

Here lie aspects of Cannes I relish. It was at this hour, in this season, that I discovered this seaside town. Michel and I, sleepy off the first flight in from Paris, drove by hire car into the washed winding lanes of the *vieille ville*. Everywhere was amber-lit with the warm glow of early sun and the euphoria of newly tasted love. Little did I guess on that heady spring morning that this southern coast of France was soon to become my home.

Today, the promise of the sun's eternal heat caresses my flesh anew. There are handfuls of festival people abroad. The street cleaners have been at work, and few signs of last night's revels remain. From a dozen smoky cafés, bustling with Cannois locals, freshly brewed coffee tempts my taste-buds. At the water's edge, rows of yachts, rented at fall-over-backwards prices for this festival, sway gently in the harbour wash, sheltering sleeping guests, heavy-eyed from a surfeit of champagne and partying. Alone, I climb the hoovered red steps, not a photographer in sight, claim a seat and yield myself up to my first and original love: the magic and illusion of cinema.

After a rather disappointing film, I decide to stretch my legs. Strolling in the sand along the seafront, kicking my toes into the curls of waves, I pause to observe the comings and goings as the town swings into action, rolling its cam-eras on a whole new hard-bitten day. Everywhere along the Croisette are signs of the film festival winding down. Fleets of taxis are parked outside the hotels, preparing to depart for the airport carrying sales executives. All films in com-petition have been screened. Tonight is *la clôture*, the closing ceremony at which the winners are announced and the coveted Palme d'Or, the golden palm, is awarded by a jury of professionals to the film of their choice, the equiva-lent of the Oscar for Best Picture. I spy two police officers moving along a pair of beach dossers with sleeping bags and a tawny-haired mongrel. Cannes cannot afford to expose the fissures in the image, cannot reveal itself in a less than ideal light. There is too much at stake. Contrary to what I had believed, the town is not accruing wealth. Michel was right. It is in a great deal of debt. This has been a revelation to me. In my naïveté, it had never occurred to me that towns, municipalities, are obliged to balance their books just like the rest of us, and it certainly never occurred to me that a glitzy and expensive resort such as Cannes would not be rolling in spondulicks, lolly, palm oil. But Cannes is indeed up against it.

Michel Mouillot, the mayor, a man we once lunched alongside, before he was elected, at the Hôtel du Masque de Fer on the island of Ste Marguerite, is being leaned on from every direction. Shops along the beach strip and the streets and lanes to the rear are closing down at an alarming rate, while those who are managing to hang on are struggling for dear life to pay their rents and taxes. This is all very unfortunate for the local *commerçants*, and it puts the town in a difficult position vis à vis its traders.

So it tickles me to scout this illustrious beach parade and peek at the methods the town is adopting to keep up its illusion of wealth. The Côte d'Azur sells itself on its image of open-top sports cars speeding, carefree, along the Corniche, the cliffy coastal road between Nice and Monte Carlo; movie stars and princesses in darkly shaded sunglasses; palm trees swaying in the barely discernible but welcome breeze; champagne on the terraces of hotels and villas with linen-white façades and, at the pinnacle of it all, the advertisers' ultimate dream, fairytale romances, such as Diana in love with Dodi, holidaying on his playboy yacht. *La jeunesse d'orée* living out their brief days of bliss. Cannes cannot risk even a sniff of bankruptcy when what it is about is selling lifestyle, especially when it is the lifestyle of movie stars and international playboys. I see the windows of several empty shops are togged out with development projects. The displays include photographs, cuts of green and blue plastic representing golf courses and miniature swimming pools, all flanked by plastic models of homogenously designed apartment blocks bearing such names as Bougainvillaea Park or Sunset Haven.

A rather garish ice-cream parlour has opened up where a designer dress shop has gone under. Billboards harnessed across the façades of several buildings bear gigantic posters promoting films that will never see a movie house, possibly not even the video stores. A new Hilton has recently been constructed. And there are plans for extra gambling facilities: tongues are wagging at the prospect of another casino in Cannes and its boost to the economy. A rather splendid *belle époque* hotel has been torn down and replaced by a sugary-pink block of flats. This has caused a *petit* scandal, but Michel Mouillot stands his ground. His interests are the interests of Cannes, he declares brazenly.

The strip remains dominated by high-priced restaurants, cafés and estate agents, even while the price of real estate, *immobilier,* is plummeting. The rich and famous, or the rich and unscrupulous, bought in here at top-dollar prices, invested further fortunes in renovating their villas, equipping them with every modern amenity, installing Jacuzzis and state-of-the-art whatnots, and then, when they came to sell again, found that their properties were worth less than fifty per cent of their disbursements. Not surprisingly, the local community, shopkeepers, hoteliers, agents, are growing jittery.

It's a crisis. We await the outcome.

It was Somerset Maugham, who lived for many years on the luxurious and lushly verdant peninsula of St Jean-Cap Ferrat, who described Monte Carlo, the small tax-free kingdom between France and Italy, as 'a sunny place for shady people'. In his day, I am sure it was an accurate and witty observation of those who took up residency on that tiny horn, but today, Maugham's phrase could be applied to a broader area: it rings true everywhere along this palmy littoral. The French Riviera is a magnet for hopefuls and no-hopers in equal proportion, in the same way Hollywood draws the would-bes and wannabes to the world of celluloid. The south of France, predominantly Cannes, promotes itself as the California of Europe, the multilingual film centre of the world, at least for the fortnight when this, the most famous film festival in the world, unveils its latest package of stars and stars-in-the-ascendant. In the hills above Cannes, a kilometre or two away from our crumbling farm, there is a residential quarter named La Californie, twinned with Hollywood, which boasts some of the most expensive real estate in France, much of which is hidden behind tall, thickly fronded palm trees and equally tall, electrified iron gates. To rent a villa on that strip during the film festival can set one back something in the region of £5,000 a day.

Aside from this film festival, there are two television festivals held in Cannes, one in the spring, the other in autumn. There is a music festival in January, as well as festivals for the worlds of multiactive media, young aspiring actors, short films, advertising, television commercials, antiquary, clairvoyancy, yachting, parlour games, real estate and, for the town of Cannes, the most lucrative festival of all, the Duty-Free Festival, which is held in the late autumn. Yes, festivals are big business here. International companies fly in chairmen, presidents, vice-presidents, any and all executives by the planeload, and they are all on generous expense accounts.

'A duty-free festival?' I asked incredulously when I first heard mention of this one. Particularly since Europe is now a united body whose duty-free borders have been dismantled and across which travel no longer offers this perk. But that has made little if any difference, it seems, to the thriving duty-free market elsewhere. This festival is heavyweight money for the town. Prices escalate during that autumn week. For anyone who is not a card-carrying duty-free merchant, a hotel room is an impossibility at any price. These traders are the guys who call the shots. So much so that Cannes has been warned that if it does not build two new five-star hotels, providing every amenity required and desired by these visiting sales people, the organisers will move the whole shebang to Barcelona.

A few years ago, when I was in Fiji researching a novel, I pulled out a six-page supplement which had been slipped beneath my hotel room door, delivered with my daily copy of the *Fiji Times*. The entire leaflet was devoted to a Fijian Indian lauded in the headline as 'the Duty-Free King of the World'. Perfect. I was looking for such a figure for the novel I was there to research. I telephoned his office to request an interview. Thrilled and totally puffed up by the notion that his ideas and opinions should be of interest to any foreigner, he invited me to dinner at his home. During the course of the meal, learning that as well as earning my living as a writer I am also an actress, he bragged: 'I won the golden palm at Cannes.'

Naturally, this claim puzzled me. I must have shown my disbelief because my host hurried away from the table and I heard him rooting away in one of the many other rooms of his palatial bungalow. He returned clutching a statuette which indeed announced him to be the International Duty-Free Palme d'Or winner of the previous year. I was highly amused but duly congratulatory, and have taken a far more active interest in the flow of traffic in and out of the town ever since.

In the olden days, indeed from 1923, when Coco Chanel made her first summer appearance on the Côte d'Azur, when the first open-air swimming pools were constructed here and the summer season as opposed to the winter season was hailed as a fashionable affair, wealthy families – including, no doubt, Signor Spinotti, the Milanese businessman who

built our villa – or families of *haut standing* from Paris or the
United States would descend by train or motor car, take
suites in the deluxe hotels and occupy them for the duration
of July and August. These days, those who can afford such
luxuries have villas of their own, or have found other equally
fashionable, less tramped-over destinations. Even so, Cannes,
up to the present, preserves those two summer months as
trade festival-free. Hotels do not have to tout for such business while the heat of the sun is at its zenith and the
Mediterranean is milky warm.

Much has changed since Mme Chanel first put her elegant
toes in the clear, blue Mediterranean and trilled, '*Ah, les
délices de la mer!*' These days, during the summer months,
the coast becomes infested with a very mixed bag of visitors.
First there are the jazz and art aficionados who, like us, frequent the Jazz à Juan festival and the Jazz at Cimiez
fortnight held among the starlit olive groves in the Parc des
Arènes, where a magnificently renovated, red-ochre, seven-
teenth-century Genoese villa houses a permanent collection
of Henri Matisse's work. Cimiez, in the hills above Nice,
where Matisse lived, worked and died, and where both he
and Raoul Dufy are buried, in the cemetery of the Monastère
Notre Dame de Cimiez, remains a fashionable residential
area. As well as the jazz-lovers there are the family holidaymakers. Usually they come cruising through in their laden
BMWs and Volvos, making for nowhere in particular just so
long as it is southerly and sunny. The bourgeoisie from Paris
flock here to their *résidences secondaires* to dine on fresh fish
and *crustaces*, jog through the oleander-blossomed parks
and bake themselves on the beaches, sipping Evian and wearing designer next-to-nothing. To these add a whole host of
transients, including troops of coal-black Africans from the
Gabon and Senegal in gloriously coloured batik print *jub-
bahs*, who traipse the beaches and the exteriors of the

fashionable *restos* and cafés, attempting to sell their imitation Louis Vuitton bags and purses, trays of watches, lucky charms and sunglasses galore.

I enquired of one such African how he came to be living here and he told me that he had been brought over from his native village by a *patron* who was housing him and many others like him in two dingy rooms in Nice. It seems that these *patrons* set up these immigrants with their merchandise and if, after a certain period of time, they have not sold sufficient trinkets and earned handsome cash returns, they are kicked out of their living quarters and, if they are fortunate, booted on to the next boat out. If they are not, they are left penniless, without work permits or prospect of employment, to fend for themselves.

Aside from these Africans, whose skills appear to me to be far removed from those required for a heavy sell – most seem far happier whiling away the hours showing me scruffy photos of their kids or chattering about their homeland villages or their uninspiring experiences in southern France – there is a whole host of other, less salubrious, illegal immigrants, in addition to the professional criminals. Crime pays here, particularly during these summer months. Kids on scooters will target a chicly attired tourist. They ride up, ask the time and then, while the unsuspecting stranger, usually a woman (it has happened to me), has her arm raised to check her watch, they snatch her handbag and make off with it.

And thieves in vans descend from other *départements* of France. It is a busy season for them. They cruise the hills and case the villas. A practised eye tells them when holidaymakers are in situ and when they are out, and holidaymakers are renowned for failing to lock away that extra bit of cash and jewellery in a safe.

During our first penniless summer on the farm, before we had gates and fences and dogs, a procession of tired-looking men on motorbikes or in Citroën vans ascended our hill at regular intervals. Armed with catalogues and brochures, they attempted to sell us one of a selection of the alarm systems they had on offer. Many of these blokes looked completely unscrupulous and we both agreed that we would not trust them with our shopping lists, never mind our modest and pitifully empty farmhouse.

A Dutch producer friend of Michel's bought a villa in the neighbourhood of La Californie and paid exorbitant sums to have an alarm system installed. A few months later, the company telephoned to inform him that the equipment was antiquated and needed to be updated at a further cost of something in the region of 20,000 francs. The Dutchman refused. A salesman from the company telephoned again when his wife was there alone. He talked her into allowing him to send one of his representatives over to either confirm their opinion or find some way to modernise the present system. The woman agreed. She let the man in and, busy with her own chores, left him to his work. After he had spent a tedious amount of time fiddling with and readjusting various clocks, he informed her that there was nothing to be done and that she and her husband would be obliged to invest in the company's newly modernised equipment.

When Michel's friend returned from his business trip in the Netherlands, his wife recounted to him the latest development in the affair. He hit the roof and telephoned the company to make clear that in no circumstances would he pay them another sou to install a new system. The very next day, the couple were burgled in broad daylight. When they returned from their lunch on the beach and walked in to find their house in disarray, he checked the alarm system and discovered that it had been disconnected. Naturally, the police were called. Their enquiries revealed that the monthly *abonnement* our friends had been shelling out to the security firm to link up their alarm to a twenty-four-hour surveillance service was actually connected to a fax machine. When the couple in question drove to the firm's last given address in search of the culprits, they learned that the *société* had been out of business for eighteen months. The police shrugged and said there was nothing more they could do. Stories of such swindles and rackets have passed into local legend. At this level, they are unfortunate for those who are stung, but we are on the Côte d'Azur, 'a sunny place for shady people', and when the heat is on, there are degrees of shade.

Returning to the house, I potter about at my desk for an hour and then, while Michel goes through a thick envelope of papers that arrived when we were in the mountains yesterday, I whip us up a salad of mozzarella and tomatoes dressed with basil, ground black pepper, our own oil and slivers of fresh mint. And, to follow, plates of fresh vegetables braised in oil, herbs and garlic.

'There is no debating the fact that the French have a mania for bureaucracy,' I remark while tucking into generous helpings of lunch. My observation is borne out yet again by the veritable suitcase-load of forms piled on the garden table in front of us. They come from ONIOL, the organisation we have been waiting to hear from for the best part of a year. It is they who are considering our AOC rating as producers of quality olive oil. Over a glass of Chablis, we set about trying to fathom out the forms, fill in the various questionnaires, which comprise several columned boxes requesting information about the number of fruit trees we have, what sectors they are planted on (our smallholding is divided up into seventeen sectors, *parcels,* of land) and the distance between them and the olives.

'I think we ought to meet up with these people. According to all this, we may not qualify for an AOC at all,' says Michel.

'But Christophe, the mill owner, said our oil is of the finest.'

'That doesn't appear to be the concern. Well, not at this stage, anyway. Formalities first, and these forms seem to suggest that the details I supplied do not conform with their requirements. If I understand correctly, a farmer needs a minimum number of olive trees to qualify as an *oléiculteur*, and unless we are registered as bona-fide olive farmers, we are not eligible for any grants or awards, hence we cannot be promoted to AOC status.'

I ponder this over a mouthful of cheese. 'What is the requirement?'

Michel stares at various pages, frowns and then replies, 'It doesn't specify. I can never get through to these people so I'll have a word with the Chambre d'Agriculture tomorrow morning. We must find out what this is all about.'

The following morning, he telephones the Chambre d'Agriculture in Nice and is informed that he must discuss it with ONIOL, which is precisely what he has been attempting to do for the past year. When Michel explains this, the *fonctionnaire* at the other end of the phone suggests a particular woman at the organisation. 'Ring her, say you have spoken to me and you'll get an appointment.' This Michel does and, miraculously, we are offered an appointment for the very next morning. Michel postpones his return to Paris and we drive to Marseille for our long-awaited interview with the ONIOL representative. I am a tad nervous, for if this body, which regulates olive plantations and oil pressing, does not back us, our request for the dreamed-of AOC will be rejected out of hand before our oil has even been sampled.

I had naïvely assumed that the sole criterion was the quality of the produce.

'*Mais, non!* There are rules,' we are informed as we sit down.

'Ah yes, *bien sûr*.' I should have guessed. How foolish of me to have assumed that here in France it might simply be about the quality of the oil and not also about the maze of paperwork involved at every level of government funding, not to mention union considerations. In this case the farmers' union and the union of *oléiculteurs*, olive-growers. Will we be obliged to join a union of beekeepers, I ask myself silently, when – if – we eventually find someone who is willing to share a few hives with us?

'And they are?' enquires Michel, smiling disarmingly at the young lady in black who, behind the mountains of untidy files sliding all over her desk, sits opposite us smoking furiously. I feel prenatal nausea creeping up on me again.

She sets sail, listing at full rattle a host of must-dos and have-to-bes. I am lost. It takes me back to our early days in Provence. Legal French then and legal/agricultural jargon now: both have me beat.

What I do understand is that Michel's summing-up of the situation was spot-on: we need a minimum number of *oliviers* on our farm, our *verger*, to qualify.

'How many?'

'Two hundred and fifty.'

'Two hundred and fifty! But all we have are sixty-four mature trees and a dozen small fellows I planted last year,' I stammer.

'*Hélas*, monsieur, madame, that is the regulation.' She begins to rise. The interview that has taken us months to achieve is at an end.

'What if we planted another two hundred?' suggests Michel.

I stare at him open-mouthed. Who will pay for them? Who will oversee them? Water, prune and harvest them? Our irrigation system is rudimentary, humping hosepipes and watering cans by hand, and we are soon to have a baby!

'Well, that's a different matter.' She sits again, then rises, lighting up yet another dark-tobacco cigarette in this windowless, airless space. 'But that is not my department. I oversee the *versements*, the funding, for the quantities of oil produced. You must talk to my colleague. She looks after the grants for plantation development. But first, I need photocopies of your passports and your bank RIB.' Michel furnishes our Relevé d'Identité Bancaire, our bank-account identification slip – experience has taught us always to attend official meetings such as this one with these photocopied documents at the ready, because you can bet your life they will be asked for – and she leads us through to an adjoining office where we are introduced to another young woman, also clad in black, with layers of raven hair pinned carelessly into a nest. She appears equally frazzled, rather more vague, and smokes just as furiously.

Half a dozen forms are dug out of drawers to be completed here and now, more photocopies of our passports are requested – this causes a minor hiccup as we came with only one of each, but it is satisfactorily resolved when Michel suggests that the first young woman make copies of the copies we have left in the adjacent room – and then another batch of forms is handed over to us, to be taken away, studied, signed and returned *assez vite*: 'Time is running out. You have left it very late to qualify.'

Her remark is exasperating. Still, I resist the temptation to point out that it is almost a year since we sent in our letter requesting an application form and only a couple of days since we received the rather unhelpful reply.

'You understand that if you decide to plant the requisite number of trees they must be purchased from an ONIOL-approved *pépinière?*'

Officialdom. Small print, large print. I sigh loudly.

'How do we go about finding the nurseries?' asks Michel, unruffled.

'I will send you the list. But first there are regulations to study,' and off she goes again to organise the photocopying of another five pages of bureaucratic stipulations.

As we leave she adds: 'Here is the representative you need to contact at the Chambre d'Agriculture. Without his approval, and it must be his, the file is invalid. Mention my name and he'll see you without delay.'

Michel jots down the details of the gentleman in question, thanks the young woman for her *gentilesse* and *accueil chaleureux* and assures her that we will be in touch again in the near future.

France is a country renowned for the quality of its agricultural produce and, along with its mania for bureaucracy, it requires stringent adherence to the rules. The Chambre d'Agriculture oversees every aspect of French farming, be it beef, rapeseed, cheese, olive oil, horse meat: whatever it is, nothing gets past the eagle eye of this government department. Its designated olive oil *bureaux* are in Nice and Marseille (there are none in the north of France, because it is a southern industry, an exclusively Mediterranean product). When we return home, Michel telephones Nice to make an appointment and is informed that the chief of the department himself will come along to visit us. Fortunately, he is the very man suggested to us by our contact at ONIOL. Might we finally be getting somewhere?

While I am still struggling to make headway with what I am beginning to discover is a most elusive breed, the apiarists, the bee-masters, a delicious piece of scandal is rocking the town of Cannes and sending the waters roiling beneath those gleaming, sleepy yachts.

The snappily dressed, savvy mayor, Michel Mouillot, is arrested. For corruption. A small matter which the local rag, the *Nice Matin*, and restaurant gossip assure us will be ironed out in a jiffy. I take to buying the local paper. It is not a journal which up until now I have bothered with, but it does have its own brand of soap-opera-style 'reportage' which, given the case in question and the subject of my research – the changing face of Côte d'Azur–Provence – I find delightfully appropriate. Watching Mouillot across the salon of the crumbling hotel out on the offshore island of Ste Marguerite several years ago, I had playfully cast him as a leading figure in an American soap, and now, here he is, star of his own scurrilous show, whose ratings are rising as *le petit scandal* gets out of hand. For the scoop is being picked up by the national and, indeed, international press. It seems that these frauds concern dealings in London, in the heart of the City. Rather large sums of money have been changing hands. There is a suggestion that someone is seeking a permit. Briefcases, carried as hand luggage, are stuffed to bursting with cash. *Le marché noir, la caisse noire.*

As the beaches begin to reflect with glistening supine bodies, the scandal escalates. Local folk talk of little else. Meanwhile I, in my den, am yet again on the telephone to M. Manneron. Yes, I tell him, we have understood that he does not wish to commit to the *emplacement des ruches* on our land, but he has promised to pass the word around. Indeed, he confirms, but so far, not one beekeeper has expressed interest. Oh dear.

The morning of the departmental visit from the Chambre d'Agriculture is upon us and I am quite taken aback to find myself greeting a handsome, dark-haired, vigorous young man of twenty-five or -six who arrives in jeans, T-shirt, walking shoes and briefcase. This is the chief inspector. I had been expecting someone a little more sedate, mature and office-bound. While Michel goes off to fetch a bottle of wine and three glasses – de rigueur when negotiating such matters – the young gentleman and I seat ourselves at our wooden table in the garden. Behind him, I see branches of tender fruits: pears, apricots and peaches, and the orange trees decorated with their tiny green balls. I am fascinated to know how, at his age, he has acquired his position but feel that at this stage to comment on his youth might not serve us. However, as usual, my insatiable desire to glean facts gets the better of me. I broach the subject delicately: 'Have you been employed in this line of work for long?' He stretches his long legs, strokes our golden retriever, Ella, who is nuzzling his arm, and smiles.

'The chief before me was retired from the office. I came to it pretty much directly from university.'

'Really, why? Was he . . . ?'

'Couldn't handle the stress. He had a nervous breakdown and nearly went mad.'

I may know little of the demands of working for the Chambre d'Agriculture, but I would have put the stress level of such an occupation reasonably low on the trauma scale, compared with, let's say, air-traffic control, mining or television production.

'Is the appointment so taxing?' I venture.

Michel returns with the tray and begins to uncork the rosé. Our friend leans back in his chair, rocks on two legs, splaying limbs, physically expanding at the prospect of a chilled glass of wine in the noonday sunshine. He looks about him, calibrating the holding. 'Nice spot you have here. Well situated, close to all amenities yet private.'

I am desperate to know why his former colleague nearly went mad. I see little sign of any such infliction damaging this wholesome young man.

'*Santé*,' smiles Michel when the drinks have been poured and served. We all three sip our wine and sit silently relishing the moment.

'I was just hearing from monsieur . . . that the previous chief of the olive department was retired early due to unstable health. And I was interested to know what caused it.'

Michel shoots me a glance, fearful that I may be opening a can of worms we won't want to get into, but our companion seems perfectly happy to discuss the affair.

'It's no secret,' he begins, taking another sip of his rosé, 'that the Provençals, and most particularly the farmers, have developed their own ways and methods and don't take kindly to interference, as they call it, particularly from official bodies such as ourselves. My predecessor was given the unfortunate task of visiting every registered olive farm and informing the farmers that Europe was now one entity, which meant that new standards for agriculture – health, sanitation, farming equipment etc. – were to be enforced. Well, to a man they took it badly and refused to be ordered about. And to make sure that the poor chap understood their sentiments, they fired at him with rifles and shotguns. The second his Renault passed through the gates of an *oliveraie,* he was blasted with bullets. His front windscreen was shattered, his tyres were punctured, dogs bit him, sticks were hurled at him, to say nothing of the verbal abuse. I only encountered him once or twice, when I was still a student and was working in the offices as a *stagiaire.* On both occasions the poor chap arrived back at his desk, clothes torn, shaking and gibbering, reeking of alcohol. It was shortly after that he requested early retirement and I was offered the post.'

'Aren't you afraid?' I ask him.

He laughs. 'No, the farming community is getting used to the changes, slowly accepting the new order, and where they remain obstinate – well, I find ways of gently persuading them.'

Lucky, our Alsatian, comes loping towards us and I fear this may be the day he finds himself savaged by an olive farmer's dog. We should have chained her up. I rise hastily, preparing myself for the attack but, no, she approaches at speed, sniffs at his fingers and settles herself like a docile puppy at his feet.

Before I can ask him what his gentle persuasions might be, Michel suggests a tour of the land and off they go to pace out the distances between the trees which takes them the best part of the lunch hour. When they return, *le jeune monsieur* seems satisfied. We have breached no rules as yet, and as long as we agree to plant the extra quota of trees and maintain the required distances between olive tree and olive tree and olive tree and fruit tree, he sees no reason at all why we shouldn't be given an agricultural registration and, from there, be awarded our AOC.

We are getting somewhere.

A few days later, we receive a letter from one of the unions informing us that an officer will be coming to inspect our land. This is followed by a visit from a serious-faced inspector who needs to interview us and register us as olive farmers. Passports photocopied yet again, we find him waiting, an hour early, at our gate when we return from a shopping expedition. He is in time for lunch which, naturally, we offer him and, equally naturally, he accepts. Then, as coffee is served – *'Un petit noir pour moi, madame, s'il vous plaît'* – out come the papers from the briefcase. 'Which of you is registering?' he asks.

Michel and I look at one another and shake our heads. Does it matter?

'It's up to you. It's a security, insurance for your health.'

'We are covered,' I retort. 'And please can I make it clear that we both also practise other professions? We don't wish to deceive anyone.'

He frowns. 'That's not the point, madame. You have to

register and pay the fee, which is negligible.'

And so Michel signs his name on our behalf, and with this insignificant spill of ink he has been transformed, in the eyes of the French law, French tax offices, social security bodies, and the farming union, as well as the Chambre d'Agriculture, into an olive farmer. Or so I thought.

'Ah, *non*, madame, not the farmers' union. *Non*, that is another matter.'

'But we thought that you—'

'*Non, non*, we are *la mutualité*. I will give you the name of the man you must telephone at the union . . . It is important that you don't tarry in this matter . . .'

And so it goes on, and on and on. Who can blame our poor, scowling postman for his miserable frame of mind? Every morning I am obliged to keep an ear open for his moped, and the second I hear it come putt-putting round the foot of the hill I have to leg it downstairs to the garden, play catch with Lucky, who loves every minute of this frenzied game, up to the point when I chain her to a tree, where she remains sulking and uncomprehending until the traumatised fellow has delivered his load and motored off well out of biting range, and I am left with the large brown envelopes containing magazines and pamphlets all offering assistance with *la culture et entretien des oliviers*. As well as letters informing us that several other *fonctionnaires* from official oil *syndicats* will be arriving; delegations of them, it seems, and they all bear names that sound in translation like mouth-watering delicacies: Mr Lemon (M. Citon), Mr Duck (M. Granard) or Mr Jam (M. Confit). All stride the land, counting aloud the metreage between trees, counting the trees, noting the numbers of fruit trees which have been planted on the same terraces, while I prefer to gaze at the blue heavens, a splendid background to the fruit burgeoning all around us, or to drift off to other more pressing agricultural concerns of my own.

For example, it occurs to me now that I had been intending to research the origins of the cherry tree, and that in all this wooded land of ours I have never once seen a bird's nest. Certainly, none in the olive trees, and I am curious to know why that might be. I am about to ask one of these learned gentlemen when I realise that a very perplexed member of this particular party is addressing me.

His troubled expression has been caused by the sight of my humble pomegranate tree. It has stopped him in his tracks. He is staring at this unassuming sapling as though looking down upon something quite disgusting.

'Mais ça, c'est un grenadier, madame! Pourquoi? Pourquoi?' he demands with extreme gravitas, as though I have committed a mortal sin, which in his eyes, of course, I have. Why, he wants to know, have I stuck a pomegranate in the middle of the olive terraces?

I stare at him, shamed and open-mouthed. I have no satisfactory explanation. Other than the fact that I dreamed of looking down from the poolside upon its vermilion-red flowers, its hard, crusty fruits with skins like a country maid's complexion, there was no deep or meaningful reason except, damn it, why not? I fancied putting it there.

He shakes his head in sorry bewilderment – he is dealing with a foreigner, tantamount to an idiot – and continues with his inventory while I, somewhat humiliated, take heart from listening to the songbirds who are in lusty throat on this glorious day.

I make a mental note to look up the history of the pomegranate, and on we go.

On we go, moving to the age of each of the *oliviers* and their varieties. All our trees are *cailletiers* except for four young ones, which yield larger drupes than our venerables but less fine oil; these are known as *tanches*. On each inspection these saplings also stop the visiting *fonctionnaire* in his tracks. *Mais pourquoi?* they ask dryly, and I am obliged to launch into yet another explanation as to why we have a mere four trees, obviously recently planted, of this other variety. The reason is quite simple. In the early days, when I purchased and planted these babies, I was unaware of such delicate nuances as single-variety farming. Indeed, it never entered my unProvençal head that we might one day be standing here going through this rigmarole at all – all in the hope of gaining one very modest AOC.

Once I have explained about the *tanches* they shrug, note down my faux pas and warn us solemnly that we cannot farm these drupes and press them along with the others.

'Of course not!' we cry in operatic horror, which seems to appease them.

'Marinate them in brine is my advice to you. Use them for serving as *les hors d'œuvres*,' is their suggestion, and we nod colludingly.

'You are probably not aware, madame, that the *tanche* olives were originally from Nyons in northern Provence, though I expect you have noticed that they are very black in colour. They are excellent for making *anchoïade*. Best to pick them when they are slightly overripe. Wait until they are showing signs of paper-thin wrinkles, caused by the first frosts, and for heaven's sake, do make sure to use lashings of garlic. Or you can make a most excellent *tapénade* with them. Now, I have a particularly fine recipe, less well known than most. I make it up myself and it's a personal triumph *chez nous*, even if I do say so. It includes a little cognac. My secret, of course, but . . .'

All that is left to do, it seems, once these men have tracked every inch of our land and given us their opinions, hints and inside information on every last detail, is to order the trees. This will have to be done from a *pépinière* in the Var; there is no ONIOL-approved grower any closer to us.

'You will be sent a list,' we are informed. 'When it arrives, make an appointment, go and have a look at the trees. Make yourselves known to the growers, that's my advice.' Michel assures everyone that if necessary we will hand-pick each and every one of the 200 trees ourselves, which seems to thoroughly delight them. That's the spirit, I hear them mentally declare.

And then we are told by one or other of this endless stream of suited visitors that we will not be eligible for agricultural water rates until we have furnished proof that we hired a *sourcier*, a water diviner, who has come to the farm, tramped the land and confirmed that there are no natural *sources* anywhere to be found. Any, that is, that could be used to supply us with natural water so that we do not have to apply for a subsidy from the Lyonnaise des Eaux.

'A water diviner? You are kidding me!'

But Michel shakes his head. The condition is for real. 'And we'll have to do it, *chérie*. Do you remember when we bought the farm, Madame B. mentioned something to us about a *source* here, the well that we have never tracked down?'

'How do we go about finding a water diviner in this day and age? Do you think they advertise in *Les Pages Jaunes?*' I giggle.

And you know what? After a truly fascinating half-hour trawling through the Provençal Yellow Pages, I come across an advertisement in the 'Water Suppliers' section under the heading: '*Rain Bird, Hunter*'. Could this be what we are looking for? Just for fun I telephone their number, but receive a frosty response. Of course they are not an agency for water diviners; they are suppliers of garden watering systems. Do we need a quote? The answer is we badly need an automated water system, an entire irrigation system, in fact – summer watering is the bane of our lives because it takes so long – but such an installation is way beyond our means right now, and when I admit this the woman hangs up. The whole business is mind-bogglingly exhausting and, with a baby on the way, I confess to being a touch reticent at the prospect of extending our olive plantation to such a degree. With so much extra work, how will we cope?

Still, the more I chew it over, the more I come round to the idea. Our little farm will truly earn its title of olive farm.

And what to do about this water diviner?

Water divining is surely an ancient trade, part of the old order. Its practitioners have been dismissed in a world of modern technology, cast aside as perpetrators of jiggery-pokery. To insist we find ourselves one might well be a novel attempt – and not without a *soupçon* of Provençal cunning – at protecting, reincarnating the local heritage. Well, I'll go along with that. In such a frame of mind, I determine to find us one.

Quashia, who is busy strimming the terraces – felled are the seeding poppies and spring wild flowers – shakes his head solemnly when he hears what I am about. 'There's no water source on this farm,' he pronounces.

'Well, according to the *vendeuse* we bought the house from . . .'

He shakes his head again. 'You're wasting your time and your money. You tell the Lyonnaise des Eaux, as well as all those clowns who've been marching about here sticking stakes in the ground, that if there was water here, I'd be the first to know it. I spend my life scaling and strimming these terraces. No one knows them better.'

A fact that cannot be argued. And I tell him so, while inhaling the scent, borne on the breeze, of newly cut herbage.

Then, to cap it all, Quashia announces his need to leave. 'What!'

'Don't you worry, I'll be back. I won't abandon you. But I must go and marry off my last son. I promised my wife we'd have him wed before the year's out, and it's more than my life is worth to break that promise. Besides, he's given me an ultimatum. He says he'll be married next week without me if I don't get there. That's impossible, of course; he doesn't have the wherewithal. Even so, I'd best get on my way.'

'Why, no question about it, you must go, Monsieur Quashia,' I tell him.

And so he must. I smile and pat him on the shoulder. I cannot allow myself to dwell on the labours that lie ahead knowing that, for the foreseeable future, without Quashia, we will have no one to lend us a hand.

Treating the Trees

The evening before his dawn departure, our loyal farm manager strolls up to say his *au revoir*s. This involves walking the garden with Michel – a male ritual they always play out before one or other leaves for any length of time – and then sitting at the table beneath the spreading magnolia tree to partake of a pot of mint tea with us, sweetened with spoonfuls of coppery Provençal honey. As we watch it plop into the cups, we promise ourselves that this time next year it will be from our own hives. On this occasion, Quashia has also come to collect a salary advance because 'weddings are such expensive affairs'. I am rather taken aback by the sum he has calculated the whole business is going to cost him. Until he explains that, in Algeria, the preparations are the responsibility of the groom's father, as is 'footing the bill for every darn thing', and that involves more than just the protracted wedding festivities.

'What else could there possibly be, Monsieur Quashia?' It amuses me that, considering the length of time Quashia has been working for us, I still address him as 'monsieur' and use the formal *vous*, rather than *tu*, when speaking to him. I never call him by his given name. I have no idea why this is. We are family, in our way. Certainly he has become more precious to us than any run-of-the-mill member of staff, and infinitely more than a hired hand. Still, unlike René, Quashia maintains a professional distance. 'Are you expected to build them a home as well?' He has mentioned in the past that he single-handedly constructed each of the dwellings his other sons and daughters and their offspring inhabit. I had presumed he had chosen to do this out of his profound sense of duty and generosity, but now we learn from him that, yes, he will build his son a house but first, over the coming days, his entire village will be invited to his home and fed at several feastings that take place over a period of days. But, above all else, the bride has to be purchased. 'And this young lady is not cheap!'

'You must buy her, I see.' Again, I had taken it for granted that, if there was a dowry to be paid, it would be the bride's parents who would be shelling out, but in this part of Algeria, north of the Sahara, apparently not. I had also assumed that such customs as the buying and selling of marriage partners had died out altogether. Evidently not, in dear Quashia's case.

'I am still in the middle of complicated negotiations with her family,' he tells us. According to him, they hail from a distant part of the country where the customs are marginally different. It has been agreed that the ten days of feasting for both partners' families, friends and fellow villagers and the building of the marital home are all to be paid for by Quashia. 'On top of which, they're demanding three dozen sheep and a certain amount of cash.'

'Seems a bit tough on you,' I venture.

'My lad wants her, and they know it.'

His son, the very last of his children, is twenty-two. Both Quashia and his second wife (not the boy's mother) have been deeply troubled by the fact that he remains single.

'But he's still young, Monsieur Quashia, give him time,' I have advised on several occasions in the past.

'I was married at sixteen, and it's better that way. He has to get on with building us a family.' Quashia, who is the proud grandfather of close to thirty, is adamant. Whatever the cost, he will purchase this bride. 'If only,' he tells us plaintively, 'to keep my wife quiet. She's such a worrier.'

I am up with the rabbits the next morning to drive him to Cannes to catch the dawn TGV to Marseille. Even before I have downed my coffee, I see him trudging our hill loaded down with presents trussed up in cardboard boxes and squeezed tight into tartan nylon bags.

'*Pour les gosses*,' he grins, as he swings his load of gifts for his grandchildren into the boot.

We say our farewells at the station and off he goes in his checked orange shirt and moth-eaten Panama on his leave of absence which, he has assured us, will last no longer than six weeks.

'If you need anything, I have left the number of a good friend of mine, a Monsieur Halaz, in the pocket of my work clothes in the garage. Give him a ring. He's a decent sort.'

Brandishing fistfuls of cash, he bids me a fond *au revoir*. I wave him off, picturing the stages of his journey with all those bags – the train to Marseille, from there a boat to Algiers on the northern coast of Africa, and then on by country bus to the small village south of Constantin where his wife and extended family reside and await him excitedly – and, as always, I feel sadness at his departure.

*

Back at the farm, summer is approaching at a galloping pace. Every living plant is showing early signs of wilting in the heat and for the next two months most will need to be watered on a daily basis. And I am alone here, well, without Quashia and now Michel, who has returned to Paris to resume work on his animation film, but with three newly installed house guests. An actress pal of mine from way back, who I haven't seen since we were in our twenties because she has been working in Hollywood on one of those glamorous, highly remunerative soaps, tracked me down and arrived with two teenage daughters, proclaiming a need for 'peace and retreat, darling' and declaring that our 'sweet home' is the 'dreamed-of haven'. She is in the process of a bordering-on-bankruptcy, highly publicised divorce. The 'ex', many years her junior, is apparently 'poor as a church mouse but mean as a skunk'. So here I am, pregnant, with a house full of hysteria, and no one to lend a hand.

I telephone M. Di Luzio to see what arrangements might be made for a watering system of sorts and to ask if he knows of a water diviner, but his answer machine is on, and he is away on holiday. I leave a message and then call René, because the disease *Cyclocodium Oleaginum*, known as *paon* and caused by the fungus *Spilocea oleginea*, is spreading at a virulent pace and is visibly jaundicing the leaves of the olive trees.

'This malady must be treated with a fungicide as soon as possible,' he tells me when he drops by to take a look.

'Is there no way round it?' I beg, because spraying the olive groves does not fit in with my desire to run this place organically.

He shakes his head solemnly. 'You should have done it at the beginning of the year when you were pruning the trees. I warned you, Carol.'

'Yes, I know you did, but . . . are you absolutely certain that there is no natural antidote we can come up with?'

Again he shakes his head, and I sense a hint of impatience at what he perceives as my romantic approach to farming.

I now learn that our tender young olive drupes must also be protected against, *la mouche de l'olive Bactrocera olae*. This is a fly they are prey to during this approaching season of extreme heat.

'It's rife everywhere this year.'

I stare at them in dismay. Now, more than ever, it is essential the trees remain healthy; we could be visited at any moment by heaven knows what organisation, and infected trees could prejudice for ever our status as olive farmers. But I have dreamed of, and maintained, up until now, whenever possible, an insecticide-free policy, and I am loath to change course at this critical juncture.

'I read of another system being tried out, to combat these flies. Traps attached to the branches that attract them . . .'

'It is not efficient, and far too expensive. Any farmer will back me up on this. Ninety per cent of the olives are attacked anyway, fall too soon and rot. Still, it's up to you. They're your trees. But you'll have to count me out if that's to be your approach,' declares René with an edge I have rarely heard before. 'Trust my expertise. I'll mix the products together, *un seul traitement*. It will lower your costs – the hire of the machine, for example – to spray them together, but I can't manage it without assistance,' he tells me squarely.

Fair enough. He is seventy-six. The fittest seventy-six-year-old I have ever encountered, but still there are almost seventy trees to treat over many terraces and Quashia would have done the lion's share of the work.

'Can it wait until Michel is back?'

But when we calculate the days between now and Michel's next scheduled return we both realise that to tarry would put both this year's harvest and the viability of the trees in jeopardy. René suggests bringing someone with him, one of his chums who would accept a reasonable daily rate – in cash, *bien sûr* – but no one is available: they have all committed themselves elsewhere. I am deeply relieved because, as is so frequently the situation for us here, money is scarce and we are struggling.

We have a baby on the way, a watering system to plan for, a water diviner to unearth and bees to track down. My head is beginning to spin.

'Carol, are you listening?' René is reiterating the fact that he cannot accomplish this job alone, and so I suggest myself for the role of assistant.

His immediate response is to guffaw and then, to cover this rather impolite reaction, he sighs, coughs and mutters incomprehensible misgivings which I fear amount to nothing more than the fact that I am a woman.

'I'd like to,' I encourage.

He is mulling it over, harrumphing and breathing at my side. '*C'est vrai,* Carol, that you are always willing to learn, and the truth of the matter is that I have no alternative. All right, I'll hire the machine and see you at half past seven on Saturday morning. Or is that too early for you?' He asks this with just a hint of sarcasm, the insinuation being that show-business folk, *les artistes,* such as myself don't get out of bed till noon.

'René, you know me better—'

'Yes, yes,' he mutters. '*A Samedi.*'

Artiste or no *artiste,* nothing alters biology and I *am* a woman and, to René's way of thinking, this is no job for a female. I shall have my work cut out to prove to him other-wise. What I have avoided disclosing to him is my condition. If he were wise to the fact that I am pregnant, he would never agree. But I have telephoned my local GP and con-firmed that there are no risks involved. In any case, my share of the workload will not be taxing, and I will take care.

Saturday rises warm and bright; it threatens to be baking.
I am awake and out of bed before six. Dogs fed, coffee made,
e-mails answered, I head off down the drive to wait for him.
I fear that the noise of René's diesel-powered Renault, plus
the petrol-generated machine for the tree-treating, might
wake my house guests, who demand their beauty sleep, so I
ring my silver-haired olive guru to warn him and we decide
to begin at the bottom of the hill and work our way up.

As soon as he arrives I see that he is in a business frame of
mind. I am no longer Carol, but the lowly assistant. The
first task, he orders, almost the moment he arrives, is to mix
the products in with the water. It is unusual for him not to
greet me with the customary double French kiss on both my
cheeks and I am aware that he has not got his head round
doing this job with a female.

'Fill this with water, please.'

The plastic container he is referring to, which fuels the
machine, holds 150 litres of water. Machine and water container, along with hundreds of metres of piping, are in a
trailer – *la remorque* – hooked up to the back of his Renault.
The length of hosepipe in the cottage garden will not extend
to his car but we have plenty more rolls up at the house. I
offer to run up and fetch one.

'No, no,' he dismisses, and I sense the early signs of his ill
humour. 'I have a plastic bucket in the car. You can use that.'
And so here I am, in the lane at the foot of our land and
alongside our caretaker's cottage, empty because Quashia is
away, sloshing and carting buckets back and forth, filling
them from an outside tap.

The cottage garden has one olive tree, an ancient one and
fairly laden with ripening fruit. René decides that we'll begin
with that. He barely needs my help because he can reach it
easily from where his car is parked. I stand back and watch,
paying careful attention. There appears to be little to this

tree-treating business and I cannot think that, as assistants go, I will prove to be a disaster. What could possibly go wrong?

Once inside our grounds at the foot of the hill, his car and its trailer strategically parked off the driveway on the grass, he begins to instruct me in earnest. 'Your job is to keep the hosepipe supplied. It needs to remain flexible at all times, do you understand?' I nod. 'Don't let it get snarled up on any of the drystone walls, and don't let it curl back on itself or the flow will be restricted.'

Yes, I nod again. It sounds simple enough. He trots off along the lowest terrace to the farthest trees, holding the spraygun from which trails the hosepipe, or part of the hosepipe, which in turn is attached to the giant water container. The rest of the piping remains unfurled in the trailer. Five hundred metres of it. To me it looks like any other garden hose, but René has told me that he drives kilometres into the hills to borrow this specific one for us.

'Couldn't we just buy our own? Then it would be here whenever we needed it,' I have asked on several occasions.

'No, it is special.'

'Really? In what way?'

'It is lined and protected, so that it won't easily wear. It needs to resist the force of the product flowing through it, and it costs a pretty price. The amount you need for here would make it prohibitively expensive because you can't get near the trees with a tractor. There are too many terraces and no accessible routes up and down the hill, nothing but mule tracks on this property. No, you must walk it and haul the piping by hand, which is time-consuming. On top of which, you need hundreds of metres of piping.'

All this sounds a touch fantastical to me but I acquiesce, silently plotting that the next time I am at the Co-operative Agricole I'll acquire a few hundred yards of the stuff, and we'll hear no more about it.

'Switch on the machine,' he shouts to me bossily, 'and hold the hosepipe the way I've shown you. And make sure it doesn't rub against the trailer, or the piping will get damaged and spring a leak and then we'll be in serious trouble.'

I signal my assent and loop a few metres of the pipe loosely over my shoulder, creating some slack. I am watching René at the far end of this lower section of our land; he is staring up into the branches of a gnarled old olive tree. Beneath it, he stands no taller than a matchstick and resembles a small sentinel insect. I switch on the machine, which starts to make a rather disgusting slurping sound, like an old man drinking soup, and then the solution starts to feed through. This sends the hosepipe into dancing gyrations.

René is circling the distant tree, spraying up into it, and I am trying to keep an eye on him as well as concentrating on the line of pipe which is skittering through the dry summer grass. It weighs heavily against my shoulder, twisting and turning against me like a snake in pain, or in love. Still, I have it under control and I own up to actually rather enjoying myself. It is a beautiful morning. The sun is shining through the trees and the water mixed with the blue fungicide powder – which I am assured is the next best thing to organic but which looks worryingly lethal to me – is rising and falling through the branches and creating streaming rainbows. It is quite lovely. Our silvery trees are streaked with cold, sharp colours.

There is a very light wind, indiscernible really, but it is sending the spray whorling downwards. René signals to me to switch off the machine, which I do as he strides bow-leggedly back in my direction. 'I need my mask.' And into the boot of his Renault he disappears.

'It's like a factory in there, René,' I tease.

'What is?'

'Your car. No matter what is needed, you have it to hand.'

'It's not a factory. I am an artisan; it is my *atelier*.'

'Yes, well, that's what I meant.'

He reappears now from the trunk of the car with what looks indisputably like a Second World War gas mask and a floppy desert hat. He pulls the mask over his flushed face and plonks the hat on his head.

I stare at him, amazed. 'I'd love to take a photo later,' I grin.

He says something in reply, but I don't understand a word through the mask. The sight of him on this hot morning, a little man standing with a spraygun in his hand and this out-moded military equipment covering his whole head, is quite ridiculous and I burst out laughing.

He pulls off the hat and then the mask. 'Start up the machine. I told you once, why aren't you listening?' And off he trots. 'And I will need more pipe.'

'Yes, René.'

We have a good rhythm going. René does occasionally wave a frantic arm at me, signalling me to clear out of the way, but before I can run for cover, my hair, face and sun-glasses are rained upon and I am speckled in blue liquid. To protect against fumes, I have tied one of Michel's handker-chiefs over my nose and mouth. My shorts and T-shirt are filthy. Dog turds decomposing in the grass, dust and bits of straw-like weed have fouled the pipe and are now stuck to me, too, but otherwise I am performing my role without too many hitches and we are making good progress. It is hot and tiresome work. The further we go, the more piping I am obliged to lift, negotiate and release. I must look like Houdini, or a snake-charmer, with coils of the whirligigging stuff wrapped around my waist and hanging from both shoulders. I am sticky with perspiration from the effort, and covered in bits of twig, but I don't really care. It's farm work, and I enjoy mucking in and learning and I feel sure that

René must be just a little impressed with his female sidekick. Until, all of a sudden, when my silver-haired friend is at the farthest point in the garden, I am caught off guard by a cry coming from above me at the swimming-pool terrace level. 'Darling! Darling!'

Ali, my actress friend, is out of bed. She descends a step or two, clumping in stiletto-style mules. I turn my head to acknowledge her. 'Sleep well?' I shout through the handkerchief, aware that I must not be distracted.

'The girls fancy hamburgers for supper,' she cries. 'Shall we have that, or would you prefer to do a barbecue, darling?'

The pipe in my now gloved hand – the speedy movement of the rubber had been burning my palms – is being tugged, unbalancing me, and I need to release some slack. 'Whichever.'

'Do decide, darling. The girls and I want to go shopping. We can pick something up on our way back.'

I don't want to deal with meals and menus now. 'You can't get out,' I shout up to her.

'Why not?'

Can't she look? I am thinking. Can't she see that there is a car and trailer blocking the driveway? I gesture with my head and turn my attention back to my task. I am now being dragged across the new stone path Quashia has laid on our Italian staircase, beneath the rose bower which shades a part of it, my arms being scratched by thorns, heading generally, and inelegantly, in René's direction. He must be getting impatient, wondering what I am doing.

'How long?' I hear from on high.

'An hour, maybe two.'

'Oh, that's all right, darling. We'll have a swim and make a pot of café-o-lay. Oh, that looks like fun! You're like the baddie in a Western. How are you getting on?' But she wanders away without waiting for my response.

René is approaching, trotting towards me, bowlegged but still agile, tearing off his ridiculous mask to reveal a flushed, rather cross, stiff-lipped face. 'What are you doing? I can't reach the farthest trees.'

'Sorry.'

'I want to have this finished before the sun gets too hot. Please give your attention to the job in hand!'

I nod, and he stomps away.

'Actually, Carol? Darling!' It is Ali again.

I untie the hankie and sigh. 'What?'

'I think we'd like to go out now. The girls fancy a cappuccino in the village.'

'You can't!'

'Surely someone can move that little van?'

'Carol!' Now it's René calling.

Wouldn't I rather be somewhere else? Wouldn't I rather be back sitting in a make-up caravan on location somewhere divine, being pampered, running through lines in my head, concentrating on the scenes to come while chatting amicably with the likes of drop-dead gorgeous Hugh Grant, or in London drinking champagne with pals at the celebrated Ivy restaurant?

'Carol, please ask the little man to move his car.'

I pull the handkerchief away from my face. 'I think that might be difficult.'

'Well, the girls are getting restless.'

'Carol! Carol!' René is marching towards me again. Now what? 'I have no pressure. What's happened to the pressure?'

'I don't know. I haven't got a clue,' I squeak. As far as I can tell there still seems to be liquid running through the Michelin suit I have wrapped around me. I can still feel it agitating against me, as though I am dancing a rumba with an invisible partner.

'There must be a leak somewhere. We'll have to turn off the machine and then look for it.'

René is shaking his unmasked head from side to side. Chastened, I follow him back to the car and we discover that where the pipe is resting on the back of his trailer, due to the fact that it has not been properly protected – my fault, undoubtedly – and to the hours of vibration it has endured, it has worn through and sprung a leak. The water container is empty. Our carefully mixed (and rather expensive) blue, foamy liquid is gushing like a special-effects river down the hill. René sighs loudly and begins rummaging in various toolboxes in the boot of his car. 'We'll have to cut it and rejoin it.' He glances up towards the sun, which has risen high above the tallest of the towering pines. My head is swimming with heat and exhaustion and, although I haven't suffered from morning sickness for more than a week, I am beginning to feel woozy.

'Ah, good, is he moving?' Ali has arrived, dressed to the nines. She introduces herself to René with a beaming and slightly pert '*bonjour*'. He is instantly entranced. All the irritability written across his face disappears in an instant.

'*Quels beaux yeux*,' he croons. '*Beaux yeux bleus*. Tell her, please.'

'René, this is Ali. Ali, René has asked me to tell you that you have lovely blue eyes.'

Ali simpers and then asks if I could persuade 'the nice man' to move his car. This I do and René agrees in a flash. Seconds later, the trailer is temporarily disconnected and all vehicles are being shunted and moved as the girls file by.

'*Diable*, what a family! Please compliment the mother on the breathtaking beauty of her daughters.'

I do as requested and the trio of bronzed females swans off down the drive, waving and giggling at our olive guru. I have rarely felt less feminine as we trudge back to work.

An hour later we are sitting on the terrace enjoying a well-earned beer when my house guests return with cartons of ice cream and suntan lotions and glossy magazines and disappear into their rooms. Within seconds they reappear, three lean, creamed bodies in skimpy bikinis, and begin splashing and frolicking in the pool. René swigs at his beer, watching them.

'Wait a minute! That's not . . . ?' He gazes at me pop-eyed, as though he has just been visited by the Virgin Mary. 'From the series . . . ?'

I nod and smile. He slugs his beer.

'*Mon Dieu*,' he mutters. 'Fancied her ever since I first saw her on the box. She's smaller in real life. Even so . . . Man, I love women. You know, I haven't changed. I'm still . . .' he pauses, looking wistful. 'It's the years that have changed.'

I smile. He may be seventy-six, but those sharp blue eyes of his are burning with desire.

'What's she doing here?'

I shrug. 'A friend of mine.'

'*Diable*,' he mumbles, still transfixed by the dripping-wet vision of Ali. 'By the way,' he continues, finally turning his attention to me, 'you worked well this morning.'

'*Merci*.'

'You know, you work like a man.'

I roar with laughter, a long throaty outburst. 'Is that a compliment, René?' I ask.

'*Mais, diable,* of course it is.'

Our tomato vines are producing fruit that is ripening so quickly and in such abundance that this particular section of our vegetable garden looks vaguely like an advertisement for Red Nose Day.

'Why on earth did Quashia plant so many vines?' I ask Michel when he returns for the weekend and we are occupied with watering, traipsing buckets, feeding hoses back and forth.

'I think that, aside from the dozen plants you picked up at the garden centre, he must have taken seeds from the garage and thrown them into the soil. Don't forget he can't read French. He may have confused the labels on the packets and mistaken them for another vegetable. We will have to find ways of using them or they'll go to waste. Have you ever made chutney?'

I shake my head and suggest instead that, as we already have plenty of courgettes – marrow-sized – I should invest in an aubergine plant. 'Then I can try out a recipe for home-cooked ratatouille, prepared with fresh, garden herbs and our very own olive oil.'

'Great idea,' says Michel.

I take a quick peek in the garage to check where all the seed packets are stored. It is difficult to find anything in there amid the chaotic clutter: chainsaws still spattered with wood shavings, strimmers covered in tufts of dried grass, petrol canisters, flagons of oil, brushes and hoovers and tablets for the swimming pool, a zillion tools and con-trivances of every conceivable shape and size, chunks of old rusty iron that Quashia is saving for a rainy day, boxes of Lord knows what that came with us from London or Paris and have never been opened or used. I sigh. It is a miracle Quashia planted tomatoes and that nothing more lethal has ended up in the ground. This space should be put to better use, I am thinking, as I move next door to the stables to feed the dogs. Only then does it occur to me. We will be needing quarters for our baby. Not in the early days, but once he or she has been weaned. This is the perfect place.

'The garage and the two stables could be converted into a two-bedroom extension. I know we don't have the money to do it now, but what do you think?'

Michel laughs, drawing a cork for our evening glass in the garden. 'It's exactly what I had planned to suggest to you. I will make up some rough sketches and we can get some estimates.'

A day or so later, I make a trip to our hand-made tiles man in Mouans Sartoux to begin the approximate costings.

''My word, you look well!' he exclaims.

I smile shyly and then regale him with our olive and bee tales.

'I know a bloke, bit of a toff, but he's a farmer and his sister keeps bees. I'll give him your number. They might help you out.'

I nod gratefully, choose the tiles I fancy for our proposed extension, give him the measurements I have drawn up, and he promises to post us a *devis*.

On my way home, I spot a sign I haven't noticed before. It is advertising a nursery, right off the roundabout, a short drive towards the old Grasse road. I pull over, turn off the main intersection and there, to my utter delight, I discover a splendidly equipped garden centre. I make directly for the vegetable plants, which are outside in a spacious yard that vaguely resembles a miniature rainforest. Fully grown tropical trees shade me where the air is damp and cool. Water is falling in crystal sprays from strategically placed pipes and there is that vibe here which I adore, of silent, lusty growth. I stare skywards through the cupola of fronds, trawling the alleyways, smelling and touching, intoxicated by the scents of the damp roots, earth and leaves, until I come across the aubergine plants. I choose two, both of which look robust and have several small, pendulous fruits hanging from them. As soon as I get back to the house, I plant them.

Although my pregnancy brings serenity, it also rules my every waking and sleeping hour. Few physiological changes have taken place yet and the morning sickness has finally abated, but cravings and dietary predilections are taking an uncontrollable hold over me. I am developing an aversion to meat, I cannot sit within a mile of anyone who is smoking a cigarette and I have developed an obsessive craving for tomatoes, preferably raw and straight from the plant, though I fear this is because I do not have the patience to wait until they are cooked. Given that our garden is chock-a-block with the red beauties, if a craving must take hold, this is a rather convenient one. Still, I find myself at whatever hour of the day or night clambering through vegetable beds protected by green netting – Quashia has pulled out some of the roll stored for the olive-gathering, attached it to bamboo canes and hung it in sweeping swathes to protect against scavengers, though not against me – searching out the ripe tomatoes; the riper the better. This is unusual. In normal circumstances my preference would be for fruit a tad underripe, green even. Not now. The redder and the mushier the better. As soon as I have picked them, I stuff them into my mouth, gorging on them. Juice and seeds run down my chin and along my arms. I feel sure that I am a disgusting sight, but I simply don't care; I know no shame. The need is beyond my control. I devour until the craving has been sated.

One night I wake, in the grip of a craving. I sigh, knowing that I will not sleep unless it is satisfied, so I steal from our bed. Michel does not stir. I slip on some sandals, grab a sarong and trek off to the vegetable garden. It is a lovely clear night with sufficient light from the moon to guide me. I roll away the stones used to pin the green netting against the earth, lift up the cloth, clip it to the bamboo structure, climb in among the caned plants, sit on the stone surround and begin to feed. Ah, such exquisite joy!

Although I appreciate good food, I would never have

described myself as a glutton, not until this evening. Now I am well cast for the role. It is brought home to me when I hear a shuffling in among the cedar trees and I turn to see two of our dogs, Lucky and Bassett, staring at me in the star-lit darkness. I try to picture what they must be seeing. Their mistress, a sarong tied about her waist, slip-on sandals, seated in the centre of the vegetable patch, hands full of tomatoes, munching greedily, sticky with dripping and spilling seeds and fruits. Even the presence of these two bemused and silent mutts is enough to mortify me, and I decide that as soon as the aubergines are ripe, I will find a more elegant way to calm my feeding frenzy. Over the fol-lowing few days, the aubergine plants fruit half a dozen shiny mauve-black gifts, lovely as dark African breasts. With these I make our first dishes of home-cooked ratatouille. Everything required for this recipe has been grown in our own garden, the herbs and garlic as well as the crateloads of tomatoes and the oil. It is the first season we have grown garlic and I am thrilled with the results. I love the piquant sap it leaves on my fingers when it has been freshly picked.

This homespun dish is a huge success, hot or cold. The plates are emptied and cleaned up with soft, freshly baked, hand-torn chunks of baguette *à l'ancienne*. Even Ali and her two teenage daughters who, aside from consuming generous helpings of ice cream, spend their poolside hours counting calories and preening their skinny-as-maypole figures, lift their plates for seconds. I am delighted and picture lengthy summer days ahead with groaning dishes of ratatouille, as well as an end to our tomato surplus. But not with our trio of English beauties. Ali's divorce calls for attention. The fol-lowing evening I wave them goodbye at Nice airport and return to a sky shot through with coral.

Beekeeping. Archaeologists have discovered in certain

regions of the western Mediterranean representations of hives that date back to 2500BC. Might some have been found here in France?

An Egyptian mural from around 1450BC shows a man carrying a tray full of honeycombs.

During archaeological excavations at Phaistos and Knossos, on the island of Crete, hives made of earth dating from 3400BC were discovered. At that time, the husbandry of bees was already practised there. The mythology of Crete contains many references to bees, honey and wax.

In Greek mythology, Aristée, son of Apollo and Cyrene, was kidnapped by Nymos, who taught him the fundamentals of beekeeping. Legend has it that Aristée later introduced the art to the inhabitants of certain regions of Greece as well as to the islands of Sardinia and Sicily.

After an hour or two of reading through notes in my den, I make my way to the vegetable garden to pick two aubergines for supper and find, to my amazement, that the twin plants are now sprouting *tomatoes*. But how can this be? I track the length of the plot, convinced I am going mad. Has someone dug them up and relocated them without saying a word? No, these are definitely the aubergine plants. I glare at them. They are green and healthy and growing precisely where I planted them, except they are bearing tomatoes. And not just any tomatoes, but the Tom Thumb variety, with a soft hue of pale ochre-orange. I am stumped, stupefied. I return to the house to recount this bizarre episode to Michel and discover him at his desk in his office, his head in his hands, holding a sheet of flimsy paper. 'Michel? Are you all right?' He appears not to have heard me, which sends a cold chill through me. Some tragedy has struck. Or rather, one of life's truly extraordinary twists of fate, which will take several years to unfold in its entirety, begins today with devastating news. Michel was due to return to Paris tomorrow to continue work with Serge, a colleague of many years and director of the animation film Michel has been developing since last year. Not only is it a project dear to both their hearts, it has created a bond of deep friendship between them.

Without a word Michel hands me the crumpled fax clutched between his fingers. Sent from Paris, it is handwritten by Serge, whose wife was due to give birth to a child any day now.

It reads: 'Please don't contact me. Give me a few days. Lost Melissa and the baby. Don't call; I cannot work.'

I am silenced. 'What can we do?' I manage eventually.

'I'll leave him be for a few days and then I'll invite him here. I think he might appreciate that. What do you think?'

I met his wife only once, a few months ago – she was already pregnant – and I, as a pregnant woman, am speechless.

'What happened?' is all I can ask.

'I have no idea.'

The notion of losing both mother and child in this day and age in a city such as Paris, with medical facilities second to none, is too incredible to entertain. I am numb with shock for them all.

'Shall I fetch you a drink?' I ask.

Michel shakes his head. With a brush of his shoulder, I leave him alone and continue on to the upper part of the house to lie down.

Later, while I am dozing, Michel comes to tell me that, due to this devastating turn of events, he has changed his plans and will stay home for a while longer. I am grateful for his company because I cannot deny that I am shaken by what has happened.

*

We are invited to a party at a villa on the outskirts of an inland village, pitted with homes owned by English expats. Neither of us is really in the mood, but we accept. Perhaps it is simply to seek diversion, to get out and be among people, albeit strangers – our next round of house guests are not due for a bit.

Although it is early summer, it rains. A short, swift downpour that lets up as we arrive. We park in the grounds and approach through a wooded garden where cyclamen-pink strobe lighting sweeps in arcs that make me giddy and paints the faces of the guests fuchsia. Heavy-metal music pounds out an unrelenting bass. Young women in skimpy frocks with exceptionally tanned flesh are gyrating awkwardly. Brits in denim shirts, clutching cans of lager, are hollering at one another. The music thumps on. Lumps of cheddar cheese attacked by everything but a trowel are resting on paper doilies, soggy from the downpour. Rows of empty wine bottles litter the sodden grass.

Michel and I falter. I suggest we leave, or perhaps he does. We turn on our heels and shove our way back through the swell of smokers and revellers as the strobe illuminates and darkens our path by turns.

Somewhere in a nearby clump of trees, I hear a deep and menacing growl.

'What was that?'

Then we notice the dogs: green eyes set in thick heads. Three Rottweilers, tightly leashed, panting and growling. Behind them are two security men dressed from head to toe in black uniforms with knee-high, black leather boots. Their presence is disquieting. We continue on round a corner and come face to face with four more dogs accompanied by a quartet of uniformed men. I am wondering if we haven't stumbled upon something kinky when a woman I was once introduced to in an adjacent upland village comes running breathlessly towards us. She is followed by a very young woman whose mascara is staining her face and who is exceedingly drunk. She is staggering all over the grass.

'I know you. You're on telly,' slurs the drunken girl loudly.

'Where are you going?' enquires the other. She seems unnecessarily overwrought at the prospect of our impending departure.

When Michel explains charmingly that we are going home, she wails, 'You can't leave!' And, assisted by the inebriated girl, she begins, quite literally, to drag us back. The young girl is now shouting and squawking.

My desire to get away has both heightened and lessened. I am curious to know why there are so many dogs here and what the villa might contain that requires such heavy-duty protection. I discover, as we are pulled back towards the heaving mass of desperate celebration, that the drunken girl is the hostess and is hell-bent on acquainting us with her partner, the host. She then proceeds to confide that he beats her. She lifts what little skirt she is wearing and displays a shocking bruise on her sunburned thigh.

'He did this,' she mewls.

My curiosity has waned and, like Michel, whose impatience I feel beating at my side, I simply want to go. Unfortunately, at that moment, the host, who bears the look of a fifty-year-old trying to pass for thirty-something – bouffant hair, gold chain nestling against hirsute chest, pink shirt slit to the waist, tight trousers – comes searching for his sweetheart. She folds herself against him as though he were Prince Charming, and then points at me. He claims in a thick Cockney accent to have recognised me and attempts to lure us back. We shake our heads. He offers to escort us to our car. 'You can never be too careful,' he reasons. The girl hangs from him like a bell, humming to herself; he completely ignores her.

I have taken such a dislike to this man that I can feel my flesh horripilate. Evil is the adjective which springs to mind. We pass kennels of dogs, Alsatians this time, and two more men: uniformed, shaved heads, built like bouncers, dandling rifles. John, that is the host's name, pronounced 'Djo', as he speaks it, informs us that he is 'in security'. He whisks a card from his shirt pocket and passes it to me.

'We 'eard you'd moved to the neighbour'ood' – in fact Michel and I live a fair distance from John's neighbourhood – 'an' knowing your line o' work, you'll be needin' someone like me. Givvus a ring.' And with that he winks at me, shakes our hands and heads back to the party, shrugging the poor dozing doxy from his arm as he retreats.

Sporting a large, floppy hat, white streaks of suncream on my shoulders and nose, I am well armoured against the rays of the sun, but what of the plant life struggling beneath this unrelenting sky? The earth is showing signs of cracking. Every shrub, every blade of grass, is wilting, gasping for water. What impression will this give to any official bods, should they arrive here unannounced and find nothing cared for?

I haven't the time, or the stamina, and Michel won't hear of me carting buckets and hoses across acres of ascendant terraces, so he takes on the task for a day or two, but we must find help from somewhere. Michel is also attempting to locate a particular woman working in the *urbanisme* department at the local town hall. He is having little success. We have received notification from an officer at the Chambre d'Agriculture to say that we are obliged to file our intention to plant new olive trees with the local council and gain their seal of approval.

'Why? We still haven't even received the list of approved nurseries.'

'Because we are living in a green belt. Didn't Quashia leave the name of one of his comrades in case we needed help? Why don't we ask him to come and water the grounds for us?'

'Yes, you're right. The number must be in the garage. But surely by planting trees we are enhancing the green belt? I don't understand their logic.'

'I wouldn't try,' says Michel, and I trundle off in search of the phone number for Quashia's friend M. Halaz.

I have just learned that 'John', the Brit whose party we looked in on, is an ex-convict who served a six-year sentence at Pentonville for armed robbery. When he was released from prison he changed his name and relocated to the Côte d'Azur. Now he is making a lucrative living keeping a watchful eye on clients' villas while they are away visiting family in dear old Blighty. I have no idea how well circulated this information is, but the fact that he beats his elfin girlfriend appears to be common knowledge, which I suppose, given her frankness on the subject, is hardly surprising. I have also been told that a certain number of the Englishwomen who move in that particular expat circle find him 'masculine and sexy', and several claim to have had an extramarital affair with him while their husbands were away on business.

A swindler or a conman in French is an *escroc*, and *escroquerie* is the act of swindling. The petty crook is a very familiar figure here on the coast. Bloodshot eyes, Gauloise pressed between nicotine-stained fingers trembling from a nervous system shot to hell, voicebox husky from a surfeit of *vin de table*, he is quick to size up any situation and create his chance. He can smell good cash pickings and is expert at securing those cash-in-hand deals. Once paid, he is not seen for dust, seeming to disappear off the face of the earth, until you hear his name, that Côte cowboy or Midi maverick, mentioned in connection with yet another ruse perpetrated on yet another trusting individual. Foreigners are the *crème de la crème* in this regard. Those who dream of a home on the Côte d'Azur, but who don't speak the language and, rather than taking the trouble to learn it and to mix with the 'natives', prefer to spend their time drinking gin and tonics alongside the pools of neighbouring residents with whom, back home, they would not pass the time of day. *Escroquerie* is woven into the fabric of living here. How could it be otherwise when money is the god? It is the yardstick by which worth is judged and valued.

I return to the garden centre, chugging along the pretty country lane that hugs the rear side of our hill. Families of *sangliers* are breeding in the thick mass of woods here. This is the herd which, when there is a shortage of food, emerges from out of the thicket, ascends the back of the hill and steals on to our land. Perhaps they consider it their territory. Occasionally, I see hunters here, armed with rifles and packed lunches. Quashia wants me to call a hunter in to shoot the boars who destroy his walls, but I can't bring myself to do it.

Before reaching the main road which will take me inland, I pass through an area of open parkland backdropped by the Alps. Here, I see a discreet sign which reads 'Chapelle de Notre Dame de Vie'. Picasso spent the final years of his life in a 200-year-old farmhouse right by here. The house, Notre Dame de Vie, named after the chapel, evidently, where the painter died of a heart attack in 1973, has been vacant since the suicide of his second and last wife, Jacqueline.

Once upon a time it nestled among fields and hills; these days there are elegant properties in enclosed estates – *domaines* – constructed all across the plain and the hillsides. Still, the house remains apart; unsold, abandoned, almost forgotten. A decaying *mas* and a neglected treasure trove on the borders of the *commune* of Mougins.

I have secret ambitions of passing a moonlit evening there, communing with the ghost of genius. To fulfil that dream, or at least get a gander at the place, I have been trying to find it, but no one I ask seems to know its precise location. Several have never even heard of Pablo Picasso.

Arriving at the nursery, I make my way through *salles* of fishtanks, perfumed candles and garden furniture, stepping to the rear, where it reeks of damp soil, lavender and murmuring growth. I seek out a salesperson.

Leaning against a pillar in Potted Vegetables, arms crossed, I come upon a frowning, pale-faced adolescent who answers my enquiry with: 'Don't speak French.' She is here from Scotland on a temporary basis, she tells me, revealing too that she is exceedingly lonely, not having a very agreeable time and knows nothing at all about plants.

'How is your French coming along?' I ask, attempting to encourage.

She hangs her head, mumbling tearfully. 'I just wantae go home.'

My instinct is to invite her over for a swim, but I dither. I have a beekeeper to find, a water diviner to hire, ten acres to irrigate, weeding to catch up on; I have almost given up on achieving any writing this summer, and I have a baby to prepare for. Lord.

The girl begins to sniffle. I hesitate, caught in the dilemma. 'Would you like to lend a hand at our place, water our plants? You'd be out in the sunshine. You could stay on and swim.' This sounds relatively inviting to me, but she shakes her head, scuffs her shoe against the earth and repeats that she wants nothing except to go home. I leave her with a pat on the shoulder and go off in search of someone who might furnish me with an answer to my puzzle. I find a young man shunting dustbin-sized black pots of ferns from one spot to another. He rises, sweating. I explain my predicament.

'Bring them back and we'll change them' is his solution.

'But why would aubergine plants fruit tomatoes?'

'Bring them back,' he repeats crossly.

'I can't. They're in the ground and have shot up to five or six feet tall.'

'Well, what do you expect me to do?' he asks impatiently.

'I just thought that you might explain why, what we can—?'

'I haven't got a clue.' And he bends back to the pot at his feet and drags it away. I toy with buying more aubergines, decide against it – God forbid, they might also turn into tomatoes – and return to the car park, where I accidentally drive Michel's dusty-blue Mercedes into a wooden gatepost. No real harm done – the car is built like a tank – but it adds to my growing frustration with it and how it smokes and fumes and splutters like an ageing, ill-tempered dragon.

Back at the house I find a message from a farmer with a Welsh accent: Lord Harry, the brother of the woman who keeps bees. Their estate is situated between our address and the Esterel. He would be happy to meet with me and help in any way he can. I jot down the details, intending to call after a short rest. Michel brings me tea and I learn that Serge, deep in grief, does not feel ready to accept our offer of a sojourn here in the south. Later in the season, perhaps. This means that Michel must return to Paris. If Serge is not able to work, Michel will use the time to hunt out investors for their film. I smile encouragingly. I know that he must go – our work always involves these arrivals, departures and separations – but it never gets easier. I have been enjoying his daily presence around the place. Particularly with our baby on the way.

He strokes my cheek. 'I'll be back at the weekend, *chérie.*

And, shortly after, we will be together for leisurely weeks of summer here.'

The next morning I drive him to the airport, or rather he drives, because the old car has no power steering and is such a bloody bus to manoeuvre. We promise ourselves that, with the next contract either of us secures, we will invest in a tuppence-ha'penny runaround, rather like my much-mourned Renault 4, the Quatrelle, which sank in mud when the river that abuts the airport burst its banks, flooded the car park and drowned every stationary car in silt and water.

Towards late afternoon, René drops by, as he is wont to do, for no reason other than to while away an hour or two and drink in the view across the sea. He delights in watching the sun go down, chilled glass of beer in hand, with me at his side, an enraptured audience for his tales. This evening he comes bearing a wine made from walnuts. I have never tasted walnut wine, which tickles him. He is in a jolly frame of mind and I suspect that the bottle is a peace offering but, of course, he makes no mention of his tree-treating humour. I walk him over to my aubergine plants. He nods as though he knows the mysteries of the universe. 'They have been grafted with tomato plants,' is his diagnosis.

'Really? Well, what would cause them to return to their grafted source?'

He merely shrugs.

'Might it be an act of survival? Rather as a reptile changes colour or sloughs its skin?'

Whether the explanation is too complicated for the likes of me or he doesn't know I cannot say. What he does tell me is that it is not uncommon to graft one plant with another of a different species. He practises it himself, and has been intending to suggest such a graft to one of our *agrumes*.

'You produce so many oranges that I thought you might fancy a yield of *pamplemousses*.'

'Grapefruits on an orange tree?'

'Or tangerines, if you prefer.'

I am amazed and ponder the proposition. One tree, two fruits.

'*C'est pas la peine à se presser le citron*, Carol,' he grins.

'One mustn't press the lemons?' I repeat, bemused.

'No, no,' he roars with laughter. '*Se presser le citron* means to rack your brains. But if you don't fancy grapefruits, leave the tree to its oranges and I will continue to harvest them. I have made a dozen litres of *vin d'orange* which I will bring you once it's bottled – the wine needs to ferment – and I have two dozen jars of splendid marmalade. All from your oranges.'

More than sixty kilos he gathered in the spring while Michel and I were far across the seas getting married.

'Is it your wife who makes the marmalade, René?'

'Lord, no, it's me. A secret recipe, all stirred up in an ancient copper pot. You'll never taste better.'

'How about harvesting our tomatoes and making us some chutney?'

'I certainly will. I'll gather them at the weekend. But dry some in the sun. Dried tomatoes – delicious!'

I marvel at the capacity this septuagenarian has for life and its earthly pleasures, which puts me in mind of Picasso. I mention to René that I have been looking for the great man's house. 'Have you any idea where it is?'

René is surprised that I have had difficulty locating the artist's home.

'Some people I've asked have never heard of him.'

He shakes his head. 'The property's not hard to find. I was there. I paid him a visit. Years ago, of course.'

'You are kidding me, René! You were at Picasso's house?'

'Yes.'

'Was he there?'

'*Mais oui.* Of course, there wasn't the fanfare about him then that there is now. As I say, it was years ago. I was still young. My sister wanted to meet him, so I agreed to go along. She was interested in his pottery.'

'You amaze me, René.'

'Why? He was just a bloke selling paintings from his house. Making a living like the rest of us.'

'Hardly! He was already world famous by the time he reached that address, exhibited worldwide, hailed as—'

'That may be, but he still had groups visit him *chez lui* to see the *tableaux*, and that was why my sister wanted to go.'

'Did you actually set eyes on him?'

'Yes, we shook hands. He welcomed us.'

'René, you are making this up!'

He stares at me as though I am the one who spins tales.

'What's to make up? He lived here and we visited him.'

'I read that after his death the house went to rack and ruin. His wife committed suicide, tired out by the loss of him and the *heritage* wranglings. It is still empty, I believe, which is why I'd like to find it.'

'Just like Maurice Chevalier.'

'What is?'

'His house, up behind La Bocca. He left it to the state for the use of impoverished artists. They didn't look after it, and now it's overrun with gypsies.'

I prefer not to engage in conversations about gypsies and Arabs with anyone from Provence because it usually leads to a diatribe about how the country is being overrun with foreigners, so I return to Picasso. 'What was he wearing? You know, in all the photos, he's in shorts.'

'Lord, no! He was dressed correctly. He had guests – us. Short bloke. Handsome, though.'

I giggle. René is five feet two. Upstairs, the telephone begins to ring.

'I'll let you answer that.' He kisses me on the cheeks and as he climbs into his shooting-brake he points to several cedar branches extending towards the electricity wires. 'You should get those cut back. They're dangerous. You don't want them brushing those cables. If the EDF see them, they'll have something to say.'

'Don't worry, Michel has already spoken to Quashia. When he returns he'll prune them.'

'I'll take the wood off you; give you a fair price.'

I nod, waving him off without tarrying.

'By the way,' he calls as his diesel-powered Renault sputters in the drive. 'I almost forgot why I dropped by. I've found you a water diviner.'

'No!'

'Yes. But don't tell anyone.'

I shake my head in amazement. Why shouldn't we tell anyone?

The call is from Michel, in Paris. He sounds tired, but he has met up with Serge.

'How is he?'

'Silent. I think work is his best antidote. We'll plot the storylines, then I'll leave him to make draft sketches while I go to Australia. I've found a co-producer there.'

'Australia!'

I have no time to register my dismay; the instant I put down the phone it rings again. The female voice enquiring after me is British, pukka and unfamiliar. I assume it is the apiarist sister of the Welsh farmer, but no. The woman announces herself as Lady Edwina —.

I have never heard of her, but she is inviting me to dinner. The invitation is for the following evening, a midweek night.

'We do so hope you can come,' chirps Lady Edwina.

'We're frightfully short of gels. Rather too many single men drifting about these days. We're a wee distance inland from the village of —, but not difficult to find. Take the Vence road and follow the signs to —.' And she proceeds to give me rather complicated directions. I accept the invitation, partly out of curiosity, but principally because I am assured that Lord Harry, the Welsh farmer, will be attending.

The address turns out to be more than a 'wee distance inland' in a locality quite unknown to me, and not shown on any map we own. But as dusk begins to fall, close to an hour after setting out, driving along a meandering lane cut through Provençal brush, I eventually find the sign directing me left by an impossibly remote petrol station Lady Edwina told me to keep an eye out for. Once I have turned left, I assume that I have arrived, but no. I discover as I crawl through dusty scrubland that I still have another five or six kilometres to go. I begin, ever so slightly, to panic. This can't be right. Michel's old Mercedes grinds on, carrying me with it.

Should I turn back?

It is then that I sight a distant twinkling of lights up ahead and, as I approach, an alarmed gate. I dig about in the glove compartment for the code Lady E. has given me. The gate swings open on to another deserted dust track. I look back and see the gate swing shut. I begin to grow anxious, as though I had rolled smack into a David Lynch film or, worse, one of Cronenberg's. Who would choose to live out here? I ask myself. And why?

On I go until I reach a pocket of recently constructed salmon-pink villas and, beyond, another secured gate. This requires another code, which has also been furnished by my hostess. I roll down the car window but the codebox is not within arm's reach and I am obliged to get out to punch in the figures. Nothing happens. I try again. Still nothing happens, aside from the arrival of a small dog who growls and yaps beyond the wrought-iron gates, warning me away. Its insistence would alert anyone to the presence of strangers, but there is no one to alert, no sign of habitation. The dog scampers up some steps and then down again. There is a hut up there, presumably for *le gardien*.

I call. No response. I boom with my actress's vocal cords. Still no response. I go back to the codebox and hammer in the numbers again, to no avail. By now, I am frustrated, furious and hungry. I have started to turn back when a light finally goes on in the caretaker's office. The spill reveals a narrow gate alongside the main one, which is ajar. I push my way through, skip round the snappy dog, climb the steps and beat on the door. A sleepy-eyed man opens up. I explain my situation, who I have come to see, repeat the numbers of the code and, before I can finish, he presses a button and the gates glide open.

'The house you want is the last. You can't miss it. About three miles up the track.'

'Three miles!'

When I eventually pull into the pebbled drive of what, from this aspect, looks like a very modest modern house, I park up behind an electric-blue Bentley convertible with its roof open, two Porsche Carreras, an old banger – probably a staff car – and a sports Jaguar. All, except the banger, display Swiss plates.

I pull on the bell. The door is opened by Victor, husband to Lady Edwina, a Russian who speaks English with an impeccable accent. He pours me a glass of champagne and leads me directly to an exterior terrace.

Behind us icing-pink, mock Palladian colonnades. We are gazing down upon a capacious pool and beyond, across bosky hills and valleys cascading towards a fingernail glimmer of opalescent sea. I must be facing south-ish; I am staring at the Med, but where, in actuality, I am, I haven't a clue. In some obscure, human fabrication of Wonderland.

Victor has made 'his pile in realty'. He buys up thousands of hectares of scrubland, *le maquis parfumé*, for next to nothing – these sylvan acres are designated *nonconstructible* and therefore deemed worthless. He then proceeds to 'sort out' the permits at the local Mairie and, once these are acquired, he builds residential parks, *domaines*, on the land. These consist of several dozen uniform villas, fenced in with oleander bushes and other local shrubs surrounded by electrified fencing and well-fortified gates. Foreigners are his market. They holiday at these second homes, buried away in the pine-covered hinterlands of the Riviera. Here, the enormously wealthy and overly paranoid can vacation with peace of mind, secure in the knowledge that armed guards and coded gates keep the rest of the south of France out of sight and at bay.

More to change the subject than anything else, I ask him about Lord Harry. 'Both the sister and the brother are a little eccentric, but salt of the earth. Still, if you go to visit them, good luck. He'll be here later so you can see for yourself.'

Lord Harry is the last of the guests to arrive at what turns out to be a birthday bash for Lady Edwina, a point overlooked on the telephone, which means that I have arrived empty-handed and inappropriately attired. Everyone else is in black velvet evening dress. Thankfully, I thought to pick up a plant at one of the villages I drove through. Edwina accepts it graciously, though my less than soignée appearance does cause a look of horror to cross her face. But it is only a nanosecond before her well-bred smile saves the day and almost camouflages her shock. 'My dear, you look absolutely charming. Victor, pour Carol some champers,' is her response to my apology.

My glass is refilled while I am introduced to Colin, who I recognise instantly. Colin is an attractive, thirty-something thriller-writer who began life in the east end of London and now resides in Geneva. His is the convertible Bentley out front.

We are nine, including our hosts. Lady Edwina places me between Victor and Lord Harry, a convivial, lobster-faced aristocrat who is puffing and perspiring from the word go. As we sit for dinner, he already looks the worse for booze. His rotund stomach is threatening to explode through his shirt as he unbuttons his velvet smoking jacket and pours himself a glass of wine. I watch as he dabs his streaming face with a handkerchief and I cannot help feeling that I am in the company of a steaming kettle.

'Cotty top-up?' he bellows at me. I panic, assuming this to be a British expression I don't understand.

'Excuse me?'

'Cotty de Ronnie, dear.' And he serves me a brimming tumbler of a Côte du Rhone red and pours another for himself. I notice that he has several glasses on the go. A Chardonnay in one hand and a 'Cotty' in the other, and he has already polished off the rest of the magnum of bubbly.

By now we have dealt with the foie gras, which, for a reason I have missed, seems to have caused a minor fracas between host and hostess, and we are getting stuck into steak and kidney pie served with peas. I feel as though I have walked on to the set of a Noël Coward play. Three seats away, across the round table, Lady Edwina is lolling tipsily against the breast of the writer, strategically seated to her right. They are engrossed in what appears to be a very intimate conversation about matters of the heart. I catch little more than the general drift because Harry is bellowing and huffing alongside me. I turn my head to my left where hubby Victor, blithely disinterested in his wife's table manners, is attempting to prise details of my marital status out of me. I confirm that I have a husband who is in Paris on business, but I divulge nothing of my pregnancy.

Copious amounts of 'Cotty' are being sloshed into tumblers and poured down throats at a rate that simply amazes me. I am surrounded by the cream of Britain's élite class. These men, save for the Swiss-resident writer who hails from the back streets of London, claim education at the finest of English public schools. Lord Harry's accent has now become thick, lilting Welsh. He leans close, swaying, and whispers with the breath of a dragon some furtive secret which I don't quite catch about his daughter, a svelte English blonde dressed in gold seated opposite, the youngest by far at this Mad Hatter's dinner party.

I frown, confused. 'I thought Lydia was Edwina's daughter?'

'Yes, with me! I married her first! Lydia's mine!' he rages wildly, his eyes bloodshot, but with neither rancour nor venom. His yelling seems to be more of a flailing in the dark.

Next to Lydia is seated a flamboyantly turned-out gentleman in black velvet *smoking* with yellow silk cuffs, red embroidered slippers and full, if discreet, make-up. He puts me in mind of Somerset Maugham. The poor man looks profoundly bored. Moments later, he leaves the table never to be seen again, but it is of no consequence because his disappearance goes unnoticed.

The fact is, our hosts are plastered, and I fear we might be shifting gear here, moving from Coward to something less frothy: the second act of an Edward Albee, perhaps? It is time to leave, but before doing so I am keen to arrive at an arrangement with my neighbour, Lord Harry, about his sister's bees.

'It might be Mummy's birthday today but I have just had *my* birthday and Daddy must buy me a Cartier watch!' wails Lydia.

'Ah, but which daddy?' quizzes her stepfather, the Russian, nudging me in the ribs and winking at me as though he's nobody's fool.

I smile gamely.

Victor decides that it is time to change the mood with a little music. He staggers to his feet and chooses a smoochy tune by crooner Julio Iglesias. The others seem to find this 'just the ticket' while our host, a well-preserved, regularly exercised, bronze-skinned, lizardy fellow of sixty-odd, begins circling the table and gyrating his hips. He is grinning rakishly at me as he embarks on the tale of a past conquest. In lurid detail he describes how he had his way with a nubile 'thing' called Julia. Only at the tail end of the monologue do I learn that Julia was Harry's girl. Before or after Edwina is not clear to me.

'Are you just remembering this now, old boy?' asks Harry with a sigh. I turn to him and see not the blustering drunk who has been bellowing in my ear all evening, but a sad and defeated individual. Perhaps he is actually the most interesting soul at the table. Still, it is definitely time to be on my way, but first the question of his sister.

'About your farm,' I begin. 'May I pay you a visit, Harry? I would like your sister to place a few hives on our land.'

'Of course,' he sniffs. 'Any time you like.'

I offer my thanks and wend my way.

Trekking back in the dark is no simple exercise but the time passes and, surprisingly, I find my route with relative ease. All the while I am contemplating the evening – a madcap affair, to say the least. What a crowd I have fallen upon. The new Côte d'Azur. Shoving aside centuries of history, digging up the earth, sectioning it off into profitable plots with no thought for the old business of farming the lands. Except perhaps Harry, whose sister, with luck, will become our long sought-after beekeeper.

The name Côte d'Azur comes from a book published in 1887 by a Burgundian lawyer-poet, Stéphane Liégeard. He settled happily in Cannes and decided to write a guide which covered the coast from Menton on the Italian border to Hyères, near St Tropez. He named it la Côte d'Azur as a celebration of the inky blueness of the Mediterranean waters. The book was an instant smash hit, and the name stuck.

I yawn, changing gear, as my thoughts are requisitioned by what lies ahead. Irrigation systems. How will we ever channel water up to the summit of the hill where there is plenty of good earth for planting new trees? It will require new piping – sections of what is laid and in use are metal, have rusted and sprung leaks – and possibly a second electric pump. Costly.

We will need to clear terraces everywhere ready for the planting and this will involve more than just the strimming away of the brush which Quashia and Michel have achieved so admirably. A myriad mountainside stones will have to be removed, the decomposing remains of ancient roots from fallen trees still clinging in the earth will need to be pickaxed out, holes dug, compost and fresh earth supplies brought in. I must find out what fertilisation, if any, we should use for all those olive saplings. The soil will need analysis. And the treating of the trees? If the traps, *les pièges*, I suggested to René, used to attract and kill the flies, are not viable, then surely there must be another organic alternative?

I arrive home to noisy greetings from the dogs, who are busy about their starlight guard duty, catch the distant hoot of an owl as I climb the outside steps and fall into bed exhausted, determined to wake early and, albeit singlehandedly, set to work.

Hives of Inactivity

Over the weekend we find a note left in our mailbox, hand-written in a spidery calligraphy. 'Pedro et Maria', it announces, '*touts mains*'. They are offering themselves for tree-cutting, housework, pool-cleaning, *gardiennage*, dog-sitting, painting, decorating, rewiring and car maintenance, among other things. There is a telephone number at the foot of the list of their advertised accomplishments. Michel is impressed, not only by the diversity of the tasks to which they seem willing to put their energies, but because he always admires anyone who goes out to find work, who shows signs of ambition. 'We should call them,' he says.

I agree that they might be capable of executing these chores – though secretly I am always rather on my guard with those who claim the ability to turn their hand to whatever you will – but, I point out, we are not planning on any painting, decorating or wiring, not at any time in the near future; not until we decide whether to convert the stables into bedrooms. 'And we don't need a pool-cleaner, we have Thierry. We have Quashia to look after the land, and the car is way beyond the help of any form of maintenance.'

'Perhaps I'll ask him to prune back those overhanging cedars in the driveway. They really are dangerously close to those electricity cables.'

I am less than enthusiastic about this suggestion. 'Let's wait till Quashia returns, or ask René. It's a risky business, Michel, and we don't know the extent of this man's skills. One slipshod cut and we could end up with lop-eared branches that bring the cables down.'

Michel reminds me that we have a pair of towering pines leaning precariously over two of the lower front terraces and stealing much-needed sunlight from four of our olive trees; they really should be pruned back.

I cannot argue this point.

'If he's reliable, we'll keep him on to water and tend the garden till Quashia returns.'

And so, at Michel's behest, Pedro drops by: a gaunt, wiry middle-aged Portuguese with a face as lined as a latticed gate and a voice as hoarse as a damaged squeezebox. He smokes like a chimney and infuriatingly chucks the butts in the flowerbeds, which does not endear him to me, but Michel seems set on giving the man a chance. I sigh. It is true that he is friendly and certainly eager for the few days' employment; he is equally eager for his wife, Maria, to be engaged as our *femme de menage* on a more permanent basis, which Michel agrees to. After Pedro has left I protest, but to no avail. Michel insists. He rarely puts his foot down but, on this occasion, he is adamant. 'I have been watching you scooting here and there and it is time for you to take it easy. We are having a baby, *chérie*. I don't want to see you lifting or carrying anything, not even shopping, and certainly not cleaning this big old house. I won't discuss it.' And with that he returns to Paris, and Pedro and Maria are taken on as our temporary workforce.

On the morning Pedro is due to begin the pruning of the trees, four Portuguese cronies come barrelling up the drive. They park up and descend from the oldest, most shambolic Peugeot I have ever set eyes on, armed with chainsaws, manual saws, wicker baskets, hammers and an arsenal of useless, ageing tools in their kit, plus a stack of rather heavy lunchboxes which they ask me to store somewhere cool. I am reminded of the mechanicals in Shakespeare's *A Midsummer Night's Dream*.

'*Bom dia*,' I say. 'Where's Pedro?'

'Pedro arrives last,' they inform me, as though it were an acknowledged rule.

'Show us the trees, *as arvores*, to be cut down, madame, and we will get to work,' one says in a French injected with Portuguese where Js are pronounced as heaving Hs.

'Not cut down, monsieur, pruned.'

'*Sim, sim*, madame, *bom*,' he nods vigorously.

'Down there, towards the foot of the land.'

The men stare at the trees and then at one another with stupefied expressions. This is followed by an explosion of the foulest of Portuguese swearwords, silenced by the arrival of Pedro. He parks his equally rusty banger – thank the Lord we didn't decide to take him on for car maintenance – on the lower terrace by the trees in question and climbs out, cigarette between his fingers, hacking and spitting. The men rush as one, hats waving, tools like sabres, down the drive and lunge at him. I am puzzled as to what is going on but when Pedro yells, literally yells at them, before dissolving into a fit of coughing, they hang their heads shamefacedly, gather up their assorted tools and say no more, and I go inside.

Oh dear, I am thinking, this is not Bottom and his merry

men, it's the Marx Brothers. But no doubt they will settle their differences and attack the job. I am at my desk, lost in a world of my own. A wasp is catapulting itself at the glass of the closed French windows, trying to find a way out. I rise and unlock the door and the insect flies free. It sets me thinking about our beekeeping ambitions. I must telephone Lord Harry.

Outside, the day is hot and still. The cicadas crack on, but little else stirs. It is that, the silence from the grounds, that nudges my attention. I haven't heard the whirr of a chainsaw since the Portuguese arrived. On the pretext of going to collect the mail, I make my way into the garden and descend the track towards the gate. There I discover the quintet at the foot of the sprawling pine trees, shirts on heads like turbans, rowing furiously about *os troncos de arvores,* pushing and punching and shoving one another, throwing tools to the ground, stamping feet, fists at the ready, without so much as a single pine cone trimmed.

'Is everything all right?' I call out.

They turn, waving and smiling as though at a picnic.

I decide, while I am outside, to scale the hill and reconnoître the disused water basin. It is in a desperately sorry state. The main weight of it appears to be resting on an anterior drystone wall, which has sunk into a pile of rubbled stones. I fear that, due to the force of rain or hungry boars stamping about, the earth could shift and that section of the hill could slide, taking the foundation of the basin with it and cracking it wide open. It needs urgent structural repairs.

I try to look inside to gauge the condition of the interior but the walls are too high. I shall have to leave this to Michel, or Quashia, when he returns.

I descend as far as the house, needing to rest in the shade for a bit. There is still little sign of activity around the pine trees. I am feeling less than sure that this pruning will ever be achieved and conclude that these Portuguese are a disorganised, hotheaded bunch. Thank the Lord we are paying them by the contract and not by the hour.

Throughout the day, they continue to fight and seem to agree only when they down tools for lunch and uncork several bottles of wine, though these merely serve to exacerbate their tempers.

I stroll in and out of my den at regular intervals, more to keep an eye on them than anything else, and to caress poor, tormented Lucky, who is barking and howling incessantly. She has been chained up since this morning and must remain so. I dare not let her loose. I fear that an animal as nervous as she, the victim of early violence, a skin-and-bones vagrant when we found her, will be unsettled by the constant yammering and shouting and swearing.

The gist of the men's argument, it appears, is not about how best to attack these gigantic trees but who should be the one to shimmy up *os troncos*, the trunks, and how come they are being paid such a pittance for a *trabalho* of such monumental danger. They are hardly a hive of industry, but I leave them to it. The heat of the sun makes me dizzy and, each time they catch sight of me, one or other of them attempts to drag me into the dispute.

Finally, in the late afternoon, I hear the dulcet zirring of the chainsaws.

It is amber evening, shadows lengthening, the cicadas silenced, when Pedro comes banging at the door, fag in mouth, sawdust stuck to his sweating face, to announce that they are quitting work for the day but will be back bright and early in the morning. As is my habit, I offer the team a beer, which they accept without a second's hesitation – one of the few decisions they have agreed on since their arrival. I direct them to the garden table and make my way along the covered terrace to dig five chilled bottles out of the fridge in the garage. Unbeknown to me, Pedro follows and, deep in the crepuscular space, pungent with the aroma of dried herbs left uncleaned on the strimming machines, saucers filled with lethal pink flakes of poison intended for the rats, and trickles of *mazout*, oil, leaking from the ancient central heating system, he creeps up behind me and presses himself against me, breathing tobacco and alcohol fumes into my ear.

Shocked, I spin round. 'Take your hands off me!'

Instantly he backs off, making a gesture which I have come across before. Arms in the air like a surrendering soldier, it reads: hey, cool it, lady.

I return to the group, followed by Pedro, and graciously pour out the offered beers. But I am shaking with anger and aware of flashes of pain at the base of my stomach. Silently, I berate myself for having allowed this man to rile me so. As the gang prepares to leave, I beckon Pedro aside, sounding out the sum we owe him.

'But the work is not finished,' he splutters. 'You haven't seen how well we're doing.'

'Yes, Pedro, it is.'

He smiles, and nudges closer. 'The way you say my name, your accent. Pedro. Pedro. It makes me hot.'

I walk away, seething at his impudence.

'You can't fire me now,' he calls after me. 'There's the second tree to prune.' Given the stress and delicacy of Michel's situation with Serge, I make the decision not to bother him with this matter on the phone; we can deal with it when he returns from Paris. As I walk down the hill later, flanked by the dogs, to lock the gate, I see butterflies everywhere – rich, golden wings tinged with buttery yellow, others pure lime like a watered summer juice. Such pleasure. And then I notice the olive tree.

One of the branches Pedro and his crew have lopped has

plummeted to the terrace below and torn away several of the fruiting boughs on the left side of one of our olive trees. I walk over to take a closer look. Ripped from the main trunk, fresh creamy-white wood exposed, the limbs are hanging in the evening light like severed silver wings.

I hurry back inside and telephone René. He is not there. I leave a message, asking him to do what he can to lessen the damage. This careless destruction of our tree and of even a small percentage of our olive yield has upset me. The shooting pains abate as unexpectedly as they arrived, but I recognise the warning sign. I must rest. I decide on an early night, lie in bed perusing my *Guide to Mediterranean Butterflies* and find that the specimens I saw this evening were Clouded Yellows and the lime ones Green Hairstreak. Such a splendidly punk name.

Until this evening, the tiny being inside me has been only that; an energy force, albeit desperately desired, that has been unbalancing my system, changing my eating patterns, tiring me out. Tonight, though, there is a change. I picture a child walking the hills with me, its hand in mine. Scuffed espadrilles, a floppy sunhat, curls, a voice, many questions, a burrowing curiosity. Podgy arms pointing, requesting names of flowers and butterflies . . . My mood is appeased. I am carried into sleep dreaming dreams of a small, emerging person.

A couple of days later, I am attempting to reroute an army of large, black ants that I refuse to treat with pesticides. I don't want to kill them. I want them to get on with their busy lives cleaning up in the garden but to keep out of the kitchen. Barbaric to massacre an entire colony simply because I fear them near our food. My difficulty is that my ploy of leaving bread and jam at strategic distances from the house has not worked: the dogs have eaten the crusts and the ants are back, marching, more resolutely than ever, like a black conveyor belt down a wall from the roof, along a balustraded edge of terrace, and heading in the general direction of the main door of the house. While I am leaning over them, staring at them in dismay, wondering what, apart from insecticide, I can do to make sure they stay out of the house, Pedro's wife, Maria, comes battling up the drive in another rattletrap of a car. I had not been expecting her but I cannot hold her responsible for her husband's out-of-order behaviour, so I put her to work and go about my own.

L'olivier. In my earliest studies, I had assumed that the olive tree, because it is regularly cited in the Old Testament, was possibly the earliest tree known to man. This is erroneous. Think of Adam and Eve and the garden of Eden: figs, apples. I have recently learned of another tree, the bristlecone pine, that does not grow in the Mediterranean basin and so does not concern me here, but what does interest me about it is that there are examples of this species surviving today that are far older than any existing ancient olive trees.

One particular example of this pine, nicknamed 'Methuselah', is believed to be 4,768 years old. It outdates, by a thousand years, the earthen beehives found by archaeologists at the Cretan sites of Phaistos and Knossos.

I hear weeping. I lay down my pen. It is coming from the bathroom; it must be Maria. I deliberate and then choose to ignore her tears, deciding that I should not intrude.

Mimosas and olive trees are not visited by bees. Pollen is not reaped from them; they are not used in the production of honey.

The weeping is unremitting. Maria has shut herself in the

lavatory and is now wailing. I close my notepad, feeling I should offer help or consolation, but it's awkward. I rise from my desk and knock gently on the door. 'Maria?'

'*Sim*,' she hiccups.

'Are you all right?'

The door opens and I find her sitting on the loo seat, stripes of mascara running down a face wretched with misery.

'What is it, Maria? Can I help?'

'It's my Pedro,' she sobs. 'He has another woman.' And off she goes again, wailing like a siren.

The news does not surprise me but evidently it has knocked her for six. In fact, she is so devastated I don't know how to comfort her and eventually murmur something inane like, 'Perhaps you are mistaken.' Trite and inadequate, I know, but I cannot think of anything better.

She shakes her dark head and begins to howl again. 'No, I'm not. He talks of her in his sleep. "*Esto apaixonado por te*," he says. "I love you, your curvacious breasts, your curly blonde hair, your accent when you speak my name. *Esto apaixonado por te*." And look at me, madame!' She is gesticulating angrily now, pulling at her hair. 'Dark, dark, dark!' and, beating at her breast, 'Nothing, *nada* here!'

I step back from the lavatory door, feeling decidedly ill at ease, offering to make tea so that I can slip swiftly away. Infuriatingly, to add to my mood, the ants have made it to the kitchen. As soon as I have a few minutes' peace and quiet, I telephone Michel in Paris, insisting that we put an end to our relationship with Pedro and Maria immediately. I promise to explain when he gets home. Bemused, he agrees.

On Friday, when Pedro drops by to collect his money – I make sure that I am not present – he enquires of Michel: 'What's up, chief? The work we've done is good, *non*?' Michel tells him that the work is not good. He was asked to prune the trees, not hack them. 'And look at the olive tree on the terrace beneath.'

'We haven't hacked the pine, monsieur. We've pruned it real hard so it'll grow faster. That olive's nothing to do with us. It must have been damaged already,' he counters with a shrug, and a drag on his fag.

Michel does not bother to engage in the nonsense of these arguments. 'There are other reasons we cannot continue to employ you,' he says and hands the man his envelope.

Still Pedro does not understand, or chooses not to.

'But what reasons?' he insists.

Finally, Michel, who hates to be forced into any form of confrontation, is obliged to spell out the incident in the garage, at which Pedro stares at him in blank amazement. 'But you can't be upset about *that*, monsieur! I was paying your wife a compliment!'

We are left for months with one over-pruned pine tree and its neighbour listing dangerously. We still have no one to water and, as to the olive, it breaks my heart to see its leaves and tender green fruits withdrawing from life, shrivelling and dying. I cannot reach René.

Later in the afternoon, as I step out of the car, having just returned from the garden centre, where Frédéric has advised me that there is nothing for it but mass destruction of the ants, 'before they wreak havoc in the house and take to biting everyone', Michel comes hurrying out on to the terrace. 'It's your agent,' he calls.

'I bought the dog food,' I yell. 'But I have nothing for the ants. Frédéric suggested some lethal blue powder, but—'

'Telephone,' he shouts again. 'Leave all that. I'll unpack the car.'

I make my way indoors.

'Hello?'

It seems that I have been offered a rather good role in a TV drama for the BBC. In the circumstances my first reaction is to refuse, and then I reconsider. Why not accept? The shooting will only take three weeks, we could most certainly do with the money and, as I need to see my gynaecologist in London, the timing is rather convenient. What is more, the dates coincide almost exactly with Michel's trip to Australia. The only snag is that we have guests, a family of four, arriving any day now and no one to look after the place, no one that is until I finally manage to track down Halaz, Quashia's fellow countryman, who agrees to come up and take on a few daily chores for us until Quashia's long-awaited return. Basically, all that we need is someone to water the plants and sweep the numerous tiled terraces and, during the period when we are both away, to feed and care for our dogs. Normally I would manage these chores myself but the heat and my pregnancy leave me flagging and manual work has become too taxing.

I suggest to Halaz that he comes up before dusk, feeding time for the hounds, and then Michel or I can give him a brief tour of the place and show him what to do.

The man who arrives is a short, bald-pated fellow, partially deaf and totally toothless, wearing a brightly coloured Hawaiian beach shirt, a broad grin and speaking a version of French which surely qualifies as an unidentified language. He shakes my hand enthusiastically and then, clapping his hands as he goes, scampers over to introduce himself to the dogs before I have given the signal. Lucky, interrupted in her evening biscuit and meat slurpings, snarls and lurches at him which sends our prospective help skittering off behind the trunk of the elephantine fig tree, trembling in terror of his life.

'There's nothing to be afraid of,' I shout, running to coax the cowering Arab out of hiding while calling for support from Michel, who is engaged in detaching a small wasps' nest he has found beneath the rear mudguard of the car. 'She's as friendly and faithful as a newborn puppy when she gets to know you.'

'I'm afraid of dogs,' he croaks.

'Then why . . . ?' But I don't bother to finish. Lucky comes loping towards me expecting a congratulatory pat for frightening off the nasty intruder. 'Well, it was kind of you to come. I'll walk you to the gate so that you're not troubled again. Thank you for . . .'

But the man has edged nervously out from behind the tree. 'No, no, it's fine. I'll get used to them. I like animals. It's only that the Alsatian, well, he's rather big. But I promised Quashia that if you called I'd lend a hand, and I will.'

Fruitless to point out that Lucky is a female.

'Truly, it's fine,' he insists, shooting wary glances in the general direction of the stables, where our canine trio are watching on, panting gleefully. Fortunately, Michel arrives about then, wasps' nest dealt with. He calms and charms Halaz, and the two men go off on a tour of the land, which allows Michel to explain the basic workings of our convoluted water system.

Providing our villa and acreage with water involves switching on an electric pump which has been installed in a tiny stone hut in the valley in front of and abutting our land; land that in times gone by was owned by this estate. From there, the water is pumped across the narrow access lane into our grounds and, by means of hundreds of metres of visible black piping, interspersed with the unreplaced lengths of old, rusty, metal piping up to the very summit of our hill and into a gigantic stone basin, from which it freefalls down the hill to the main house, the swimming pool and on to the foot of the land, crossing the narrow strip of lane again, where our entrance gate is situated, to feed our caretaker's cottage. It is a labyrinthine and archaic system but the four neighbouring houses in our forgotten corner of this rather unknown quarter all have exactly the same type of water supply and Lyonnaise des Eaux have no intention of changing it any time in the near future, so we have learned to live with it.

When Michel and Halaz return from their sally round the land, the poor man, who must be at least sixty, is sweating and puffing and looking vaguely puzzled.

'How about we all sit in the shade and cool off with a lemonade?' I offer. I know he won't touch alcohol.

He shakes his bald head, too breathless to speak, chewing pensively, on his gums I think.

'It's a lot to take in, but once you get the hang of it and know what's what, the work will only require a couple of hours a day.' I am trying my damnedest to be encouraging because without him, Quashia's return seems a distant promise and I will be obliged not only to refuse the television offer but, more importantly, to postpone my gynaecological appointment or find another specialist, one I don't know and who does not know me, here in France. Given my unlucky history, I would dearly prefer to be examined by my own doctor. In any case, even if I cancel the trip, I cannot handle this work alone.

'No problem,' he grins, bucking up in the most unexpected manner.

'And the dogs?'

'No problem.'

I shoot Michel a glance and say to him in English: 'What do you think?'

Michel replies in French with a pat on Halaz's back. 'Monsieur Halaz will have it taped in no time, won't you, monsieur? We have the utmost confidence in you.'

'No problem,' the man repeats. 'How much will you pay me?'

'What do you think is fair?' parries Michel.

Halaz stares at his sandals with a frown which seems to carry the weight of the world and then lifts his head and requests a sum which is rather insignificant, tantamount to slave labour, and I think he must have miscalculated. I repeat the figure and he nods nervously.

'I think that's too little,' I answer. 'We will offer you double that, on condition that the tasks are carried out on time and as we have asked.'

He stares at me in amazement and then grins from ear to ear and shakes our hands as though we were long-lost friends. 'No problem,' he says again and again. 'I'll start in the morning, and then you can see how I am doing. I'll be here at quarter to six.'

'Oh, it's not necessary to come quite so early.'

'Yes, yes, it's fine. Quarter to six. No problem.'

At that moment, as matters seem to be reaching a happy conclusion, Lucky comes haring down the hill with Bassett at her heels. They have been off on their early-evening hunt, a recce for rabbits or snakes or stale baguettes raided from some disgruntled neighbour's dustbin, from which they usually return bristling with an excess of triumphant energy. I call her sharply to heel but she heads straight at Halaz, who begins dancing backwards in his sandals while emitting groans of terror. The Alsatian rises on her hind legs, waltzing towards him, and I think the poor man is about to have a heart attack. But she rests her paws against his chest and pants contentedly. His terror turns to an outburst of joy. He attempts to caress her but his contact with her is rather abrupt, the pats almost slaps, and, fearing she will misunderstand, I rush forward. But she seems appeased and remains where she is, front legs now wrapped around his torso.

'See, no problem!' he cries like an ecstatic child. He shakes our hands again and shuffles off down the hill.

'I'm glad that's settled. Did you manage to take a look at that second water basin while you were up there?' I ask Michel as I slip into the summer kitchen and draw out a bottle of Sancerre.

'Yes, it will need shoring up and then some serious plumbing work.' Michel sits down at the table, where I join him, both of us about ready, as the evening draws gently in, leaving the soporific heat of the day elsewhere, to chill out with a glass of wine.

The early-morning sun is rising beyond the rear of the house, beyond the summit of our hill, climbing up behind the tall, narrow pines, framing and transforming their treetops into burnished halos and sending rods of golden light into our bedroom and on to our sleeping faces. I open my eyes to the caress of heat and to the unexpected sound of sloshing water. At first I am confused, and then, glancing at the clock, which reads a little after six, I remember M. Halaz. Michel is still sleeping, which is unlike him. He is usually up with the lark and preparing coffee and fresh fruit for breakfast about now, or already at his computer. Since the conception of our baby I have grown lazier in the mornings and am beginning to revel in idleness. Still, I roll over on to my left flank and clamber out of bed.

Once I have our coffee brewing, I step outside, slip my feet into espadrilles, stretch to scratch the sky and stroll to the terrace's edge to take in the view. The light hitting the distant Esterel is delicate, soft-hued; a purled mist that, later, the sun will burn off. Beneath me, a dusting of dew has alighted on the plants and the grass, which is beginning to turn brown from lack of water, and I am delighted to observe that there are no ants anywhere in the vicinity of the house. I seem somehow to have disenchanted them without needing to resort to killing them. I lean over the balustraded railing and am mystified to see a slender stream of water running down the driveway. To the left of the house, in the *parking*, is Halaz, in a cherry-red shirt, hosepipe in hand, wrestling with its orange plastic nozzle. Suddenly, the nozzle flies off the pipe and a powerful jet of water explodes in his face. He drops the hose fast and the pipe spirals away, seesawing water everywhere. He looks desperate and I see from his lips that he is muttering under his breath. I decide to go and lend a hand. Passing the garage, I notice that the tap alongside the stables has been left running, which would explain why we have a miniature rivulet in the drive. I close off the tap and go to help our man. Drenched, he has taken up the hose again and is attempting to dry himself off with a bright green handkerchief.

'*Bonjour*, monsieur, would you like a towel?' I ask.

He peers round awkwardly, surprised to find me there. 'No, it's fine,' he answers brusquely.

'May I show you how the nozzle works?' I hold out my hand to take the pipe from him but he pulls away, shrugging me off like a child with a prized toy.

'*Jeleconnay, jeleconnay*,' he answers petulantly, in his toothlessly incomprehensible French. '*Cet cazzi*.'

We establish, gently, patiently, that the nozzle is not broken and that it is essential, when one corner of the garden has been completed, before moving on to the next tap, that the other should be shut off tightly so as not to overconsume water, which is mightily expensive. He nods, drags and heaves at the hose and scurries off as though in a race, returning to what he was attempting to do before my appearance on the scene.

Over a delicious breakfast, prepared and served by Michel on the upper terrace – poached free-range eggs and a succulent portion of grilled tomatoes from our endlessly abundant vegetable garden, accompanied by a fresh baguette which he has driven to the village to collect – I express my concerns about Halaz. Michel's opinion is that we need to give the man time to get to grips with the work. As he says this, we spot the very fellow two terraces beneath us, puffing and panting, his red shirt so sodden it clings to his torso as though it had been painted on him, haring from one lilac bush to the next, spraying water everywhere as he trips in his sandals and then heaves and tugs at snake-like whorls of yellow piping.

The next time he appears, hosepipe at the ready and held aloft like an ancient flag of war, he is charging back in the opposite direction, springing from one terrace to the next, as though hell-bent on extinguishing a fire.

'Why is he rushing like that? He'll give himself a heart attack.'

'I have no idea.'

'Lord, I hope it's not because I told him the job should only take two hours!'

The fact is, Halaz explains to me the following day, that he prefers to work quickly so that he has no time to forget what he is doing.

While Michel is at the supermarket stocking up with a mountain of food for my Irish family, who eat like horses and are due any day now, though we have no idea of the precise date because they have not yet let us know, the telephone rings. My cousin's Irish accent greets me warmly. He is phoning to say that they have not managed to get flights and would it be all right with us both if they came later in the year? In fact, the change of plan suits us, but I am surprised by the news about the airline tickets. 'Why not?' I ask.

'Ah, Jeez, I haven't had the time to look,' is the response.

I have to smile.

Through one of the tall French windows, as I put down

the phone, I spy Halaz engaged in what looks like a one-man Aborginal corroboree or a Dutch clog dance. The hose in his left hand is swinging to and fro and irrigating most of the antique terracotta tiles as well as our teak dining table, not to mention feeding the fountain of water rushing down the stone staircase in front of him. Meanwhile, his right hand is flopping backwards and forwards and turning in bizarre circles; all this as he hops excitedly from leg to leg. The sight of these insane gymnastics makes me burst out laughing. What is he up to? I ask myself, and I creep out to take a closer look, but I can find no rational explanation for his performance. What I do observe, though, is that the garden is swimming in ponds of gurgling, bubbling water. We'll be waterlogged before the week is out and I shall be forced into a desperate search for René's elusive water diviner. Where *is* René? I am thinking. Why hasn't he returned my calls? At this rate, Lyonnaise des Eaux will have a shortage if not a crisis on their hands.

Michel returns, laden with shopping, and I greet him with the news that the Irish have postponed their visit. We stock most of the perishable foods in the deep freeze and stack the bottles of wine in the shuttered cool of the summer kitchen. The whites and rosés are left to chill in the garage fridge, and then we begin to address our own departures.

The fly in the ointment could prove to be leaving Halaz here in charge and this does not make my confidence sail. 'I caught him flapping about in the garden like a demented bird.'

Michel tells me not to worry so much. 'He's getting the hang of it, *chérie*.'

But at what cost? I dread to think of the water bill. We will definitely be needing a diviner.

'Do you think we should get a quote from Di Luzio for plumbing that second basin?' I ask.

'Did he call back?'

'No,' I sigh. Summers in Provence.

'Let's wait until Quashia returns. It may be beyond repair.'

I drive Michel to the airport. He is taking a plane to Paris, and from there will be departing in a few days' time for Sydney. We say our heartfelt goodbyes and I weep like a child.

'Please don't be sad, *chérie*. It's only for three weeks, and then we'll be back at the farm and together again. August will be upon us and I shall stop travelling for at least a month. We'll invite the girls down to spend a week with us, and Serge, too, if I can persuade him to accept. I am concerned for him. Think how lucky we are. *Nous avons la chance;* we have a baby on the way and everything to look forward to. *Je t'aime.*' He kisses me tenderly, hugs me tight and then speeds off to his departure gate. I wave him goodbye with a smile but I cannot deny a presentiment that my sadness is not entirely misplaced.

Driving back to the farm I determine to shrug off my downbeat mood. When I arrive Halaz has gone off for the day and I come across two taps at different points in the garden pouring forth. Sun-reflected puddles have collected everywhere and, to keep their coats cool in the increasing heat, the dogs are dozing in them and then transporting the mud and wet all over the place. I rush inside, ruby with rage, intent on calling the man back here right this minute. I intend to give him a damn good trouncing and have the matter settled once and for all but, at that very moment, at the peak of my rage, the telephone bursts into sound.

'*Allo?*' I shout. 'Who? Who?'

It is Jacob, the journalist Michel and I bumped into a couple of months back at the Cannes Film Festival.

'What is it?' I bark at the receiver.

Jacob is calling from the coast. He and his girlfriend, Barbara, have just arrived there, on their way back from another film festival somewhere in Lausanne, I think he is telling me, and are travelling south by car, returning to their apartment in Rome.

'I would love you to meet Barbara.'

'I'm afraid I can't this time . . .'

'She's dying to meet you. She's a great fan. She's read your books, she's seen your films. Would you like to come down and have an *apéro* with us later?'

'Well, I'm awfully tied up today, Jacob . . .'

'Then let us invite you to dinner. Get your work done and then drive down here. "As late as you like," Barbara is shouting to me. But do come.'

My temper has begun to subside and I recall how frequently and warmly he spoke about his girlfriend when he and I were in Madras together.

'Hello, Carol, this is Barbara. Please say yes.'

I have shelfloads to get done before my own departure, which is looming, and I am feeling consumed by misgivings about Halaz but, rather than refuse and be unnecessarily impolite, I suggest to Jacob, who is back on the line, that they come up to the farm instead. I give detailed directions and we agree the hour.

'We look forward to it, Carol. *A plus tard.*'

But my mind is not on this unanticipated rendezvous at all. I am stewing with Halaz's incompetence and determine that when he returns in the early evening to feed the dogs I will speak very sternly to him and threaten to sack him if he doesn't pull his socks up. This I cannot do, of course. At least, not without jeopardising my own trip and my appointment with the specialist, but he does not know that.

Jacob and Barbara arrive earlier than we had agreed, which does not please me, but as it turns out this new acquaintance is utterly enchanting. A late thirty-something, husky-voiced woman with a mane of wild, blonde hair. From her accent it is clear that she hails from one of those upper-middle-class English families who hold themselves in high esteem. The refreshing difference is that Barbara has an air of the gypsy about her. She has healthy, tanned skin and a face as brown as a nut from out of which shine the most mesmerising, soulful green eyes.

I open a bottle of chilled Bourgogne Aligoté, serve two dishes, one of local olives, the other a mix of almonds with pistachio nuts, settle them in the garden, share a few gulped sips with them and then apologise for the fact that I must dash back upstairs and finish the correspondence I was called away from.

'Have a swim,' I suggest. 'There are towels in the spare room. I'll join you later.'

Later arrives all too soon, while I am still buried beneath a mountain of unfinished paperwork, or rather as I am giving up for the moment and leaving it all to go in search of Halaz. Halaz, who, unbeknown to me, has plodded up the drive and paused for breath beneath the spreading fig tree where, in this leafy, shaded corner at the shallow end of the swimming pool, he claps eyes on Barbara, blithely ascending the chlorine-bleached steps, wet, oily as an otter and stark naked. This sighting sends Halaz, whose notion of women is that they should be covered from head to foot, into a state of cardiovascular shock.

Having exited through one of the back doors of the house, I am entirely ignorant of this collision and have no idea, when I find Halaz, what has come over him. All I see is that here he is in the stables, arms outstretched, collapsed against the crumbling ancient wall, fighting for breath with the desperation of an asthmatic, the three dogs' dishes, fortunately metal, having fallen from his grip to the ground and rolled off out of sight. A twenty-kilo sack of biscuits has split open and the contents are pouring all over the floor. In addition to this, three lidless tins of meat chunks swimming in thick gravy have been discovered by the dogs and dragged out on to the forecourt where, heedless of Halaz's state, they are gobbling and slurping with a gluttony which exceeds even their habitual zest. I find them, usually such a harmonious trio, growling deep-throated threats at one another, warning their comrades away from their portion of the stolen provisions.

'What is going on?' I demand of Halaz.

'Where's Michel, where's your husband?' he stammers and pants.

'He left this morning. Why?'

Try as he might, he simply cannot spit out the words. Only the direction of his eyes tells me what has driven him to this state of apoplexy. I turn and observe Barbara, smoking a cigarette, wine glass in hand, spreading her bronzed and naked body out on a towel, luxuriating in the warm early-evening sunshine.

I have to admit that the sight of her does come as a bit of a surprise. I say surprise and not shock, because we have no problem with nudity here at our olive farm, but even so, it is unusual for a guest visiting us for the first time to disrobe themselves so entirely quite so soon after arrival. My first impression of Barbara was that she is a hippy, a free-spirited creature, with a gentle but powerful sensuality. This has been borne out. I only wish that Halaz, an Arab male and a Muslim, had not been the one to discover her, because it leaves me rather on the defensive when I had intended to be stern with him.

'Mr Halaz, you left the taps running again . . .'

He walks away, shaking his head in disgust, deaf to my words.

'Mr Halaz!' I call after him, but he has disappeared. My remonstrations must wait till the morning.

Back in the house, I leave yet another message – a rather bad-tempered one, due to my frame of mind – for Lord Harry's sister, who has not returned my last call. In fact, I have not yet managed to have a conversation with her. I am discovering that these apiarists are an irritatingly cranky and elusive breed, and singularly particular about where their blasted hives will or won't be placed, *l'emplacement des ruchers*. But I shan't be detracted and I say so in my message.

Jacob and Barbara stay for supper. We decide to have a barbecue, but my mood is agitated. Jacob is getting on my nerves, fussing over what he will or will not eat, continuously requesting the use of the telephone, and I am worried about my impending departure. I bury myself in the kitchen, slicing potatoes, chopping parsley and garlic, preparing a recipe of my own composition which I bake with strips of freshly cut sprigs of rosemary in a locally fired faience dish. I am not feeling sociable; I would have preferred to have been alone this evening.

Barbara finds me there.

'I opened another bottle of wine,' she says. 'I hope that's OK.'

'Of course,' I reply, continuing with my culinary distractions.

'And I brought you up a glass. You seem tense. I hope we are not intruding?' Before I can respond, she continues. 'You mustn't let Jacob's neuroses get to you. He can be a pain in the arse, but if you ignore him, he'll stop.' She giggles.

This makes me smile, and I pause to acknowledge her.

'I never take any notice of him and then he shuts up.'

'How long have you been together?'

She sighs. 'Since I was eighteen. I'm forty tomorrow.'

'Children?' I ask.

She shakes her head. 'You?'

'Two stepdaughters from Michel's first marriage and' – I glance down at my delicately protruding, tumescent belly, 'we're expecting one of our own at Christmas.'

She takes a long drag on her cigarette. I have observed that she has been smoking incessantly since she arrived. 'I'd really love a kid.'

'Then why . . . ?'

'Jacob hates children, just as he hates all noise, most music, too much sun, the majority of human beings, red meat, alcohol, smoking – particularly when it's me doing the smoking or drinking . . .' her voice drifts into silence.

I want to ask her why she stays with him, but for once in my life I keep my interrogations to myself. Instead I place my potato dish in the oven, pick up the glass of white wine Barbara has brought me and lead the way back out on to the upper terrace. One level below us, over at the remotest corner, flanked by a quartet of stately cypress trees (*cyprès Florentin*), Jacob is fanning the flames and the narrow column of smoke rising out of our barbecue, and coughing. The air is scented with evening pine and charred herbs. Barbara perches on the balustrade to admire the view out over the sea. To the right of us the sun is moving towards the mountains. Soon it will begin to set, sinking deep beneath the mauve hills, leaving a vermilion sky to decorate the late evening.

'This place is fabulous. You're very lucky.'

'Yes, we are. It needs a load of work and we never have a bean, but in the fullness of time we'll get to it all, no doubt.'

Over supper, aromatically spiced *daurade* lightly marinated in white wine, fresh herbs and slices of lemon from the garden – not forgetting the olive oil, of course – and baked in tinfoil on the open coals, Jacob and Barbara prise out of me the concern I am harbouring about leaving. Almost before I have finished, Jacob suggests that they stay and take care of the place during my absence. The haste with which he has offered, and a fleeting memory of our meeting with him on the Croisette during the film festival, make me dubious. I thank him but assure him that it won't be necessary. Barbara lights up another cigarette, saying nothing. After another bottle of wine, most of which she consumes, they prepare to wend their way back to their hotel on the coast. Before leaving she embraces me like a sister. 'Thank you. I really enjoyed meeting you.'

I notice my watch. It's gone midnight. 'Happy birthday,' I trill, returning her hug. I wait in the drive beneath the clear, starlit sky to wave them off.

My heart is a complex knot of emotions. For Michel and I and our awaited child I carry profound joy and a recognition of our good fortune; for Jacob and his inability to let life in I feel pity, while those green, soul-stirring eyes of Barbara's haunt me, so full are they with fragility and yearning.

The following morning Halaz greets me with the restrained, mistrusting gaze of one who believes he is in the presence of iniquity. My anger towards him, on the other hand, has dissipated. I take him aside and patiently go through all the tasks to be achieved, walking to each and every tap, turning it on, turning it off and then squeezing it tightly shut. I reassure him that he can take his time, that he doesn't have to achieve the work in two hours, that too much water can be as damaging to some plants as none at all, and confide in him that we are counting on him.

He nods gravely. 'In that case, please can I have a new brush?' he asks. 'So that I can sweep to the best of my ability. I'm good at sweeping,' he adds.

'There's an unused one in the garage.'

'No, I don't like those. I prefer the softer ones. The ones you use inside the house.'

Incongruous as I find this, I take the time to go to the hardware store and buy him not one but two new brooms, both of slightly different lengths so that he can have his pick.

When I return our Arab has finished for the morning and left everything in perfect order; not an itinerant splash to be found anywhere. Satisfied, I go inside the house to find two messages, one from Lord Harry, inviting me over later and the second from Barbara, thanking me for the previous evening and leaving a number where I can contact her.

When I return her call, her voice sounds rusty, just-woken-up and unused, and cheerless.

'Have you got something fun planned for today?'

Two Italian friends of theirs have turned up in Cannes and they will get together for a birthday celebration, I learn. 'Sorry about Jacob,' she says, interrupting herself.

'What about him?'

'I don't know, everything.' The line goes silent. I hear a heavy exhalation.

'Why don't you come up here, bring your friends and we'll have a little party in the garden – just something simple?' I suggest. It's a spontaneous offer which I have not thought through. Her sadness troubles me, and for a reason that I cannot quite explain I feel impelled to lift her out of her dejection. In any case, the larder and fridges are bursting with provisions, some of which will not keep beyond my departure, so better to share it all. The idea thrills her.

Just as I am about to shoot off for Lord Harry's, René turns up to rescue the ailing olive tree. 'It's not fatal, but it's a good thing you called.'

'Will the damage affect the tree's performance?' I ask. 'I mean, are we going to lose all this season's fruit from it?'

'Hopefully not, but it will have to be dramatically pruned at the end of the year, and that will affect its yield for several harvests to come.'

I sigh.

He cheers me with the news that he has spoken with the 'finest dowser in the region', who has agreed to visit us. Nick someone.

'It's a drug to him. He has to do it, search for water. He can't stop looking.'

This strikes me as a rather comical claim, but I assure René that we look forward to meeting this gentleman and ask if, given that the man is so hooked, we could please get on with it as soon as possible so that we can settle matters with the Lyonnaise des Eaux who are, in response to Michel's numerous letters, still adamantly refusing to accept our newly endorsed status as local olive-growers.

'We may have to wait until his partner can be here with him.'

'Partner? Oh, I see, I hadn't realised that he might need a partner.'

'Oh, yes. But when you meet him, the partner, that is, you are not to say a word.'

'About what?'

'His identity.'

I suppress a grin. 'Am I going to recognise him?'

'Oh, no doubt about it. Well, *you* may not, of course, but he is very famous in the community. A highly regarded and very wealthy Provençal figure.'

'My goodness.' There are times when I suspect that René is pulling my leg. 'And he does this for pleasure, or . . . ?' I am indisputably his best audience and I cannot help feeling that my keen interest for local learning nudges him towards embellishments that any great storyteller would be proud to have come up with. This might just be one of those occasions.

I scan his robin-red face, those piercing blue eyes, for a clue, but his earnest expression reveals no joshing.

'After he retired he discovered he had the talent for finding water. The pair are old friends; they work well together. One uses a *baguette* – a rod, which is actually shaped like an extended catapult – while the other works with a pendulum. Monsieur— (I'd better not mention his name just yet) is frequently the one to pinpoint the precise spot while young Nick can read to the metre how deep the source is and the quantity of litres flowing there. It's a *vrai* talent. But you will see for yourself. I have no flair for it, *hélas*.'

We have strolled inside now and I see René hovering, hoping for a glass of something refreshing.

'Have you given it a try then, René?'

'Oh, yes, *mais bien sûr*. I hoped it might have become another string to my bow, but it was hopeless. Nothing happened until the gentleman you are soon to meet touched my arm. I kid you not. He literally touched my arm as we were standing over a water source and the baguette I was clutching shot upwards, quivering.'

I listen on with respectful interest and mixed feelings. I am in two minds about what René is recounting. I want to believe that such a talent exists. I am drawn to the mystical element of it; it fits with my vision of the olde-worlde Provençal temperament. But I must admit to a sneaking scepticism. 'Well, I really look forward to it. Can we set a date now, René, please?'

It is essential, with our lovable olive guru, to nail him down, pin him to days and hours. Even so, he frequently doesn't show, but at least then he knows he has let us down. If we leave an arrangement as vague or loose as 'tomorrow', or 'the beginning of next week', it can be weeks before we hear another word from him.

'How about Friday?' he suggests.

'The day after tomorrow? Perfect.'

He takes a sliver of carrot from the dish of crudités in front of him and washes it down with the last mouthful from the glass of Pomerol I have produced, then rises to go. 'Good Bordeaux that, thank you. Expensive?'

I shrug.

'Do you know where the Provençal tradition of serving little dishes of vegetables as appetisers came from?'

I frown, working it out, considering the history of the Greek custom of *meze* dishes, but he is impatient to impart his local knowledge.

'The Spanish Moors. They would originally have been Arab dishes.'

'Yes, *meze*. Turkish and Eastern.'

I have been skipping back through Lawrence Durrell's *Bitter Lemons* and I recall the lovely phrase: 'We sat beside the road in the thin spring sunshine and shared a stirrup cup and a *meze*,' which I do not trouble to repeat to René. In any case, I wouldn't know how to translate 'stirrup cup'. A welcoming glass, perhaps?

'No, Carol, the habit arrived with the Spanish Moors. Definitely. *Ah, oui*,' he insists, nodding triumphantly. I say no more on the subject. I cannot dawdle; I am late for Lord Harry. We have reached the door. 'You do realise, Carol, that you'll have to declare any water we find, don't you?' I shake my head. But I don't foresee any difficulty with registering our find. We have no reason to hide the discovery, should there be one. 'And acquire planning permission to install a drill and pump before you begin excavating. But there shouldn't be any unnecessary delays. Water is the only subterranean product here in France that the state don't lay claim to, did you know that?'

I shake my head again.

'Now, if it were oil, they'd come and take it and you

wouldn't get a centime out of it, apart from compensation for the damage to your land while they tear it up to siphon out the juice. But there's still no law against you keeping for your exclusive use any water found, as long as it is declared and written into the cadastre plans. A *source* must be registered.'

'Please God we don't find oil then,' I laugh. 'Or gold!' I see him to the door and as we peck cheeks I ask, 'What time on Friday, René?'

'Afternoon.'

'Two o'clock, then?'

'No, later. Three or half-past. I'll call you tomorrow and confirm it.'

I realise that I will get no firmer commitment out of him today, so I wave him goodbye and return indoors to collect my car keys. The main thing is that he has contacted the dowsers, and even if they find not a single drop here it won't be serious because, with luck, the water board will be obliged to readjust our price plan. As requested, we will have made the search.

I am running very late when I arrive at Lord Harry's, but I don't want to postpone my visit and miss out on the opportunity to meet his sister and finalise bees with her. I drive through a wide gate, up a winding dust track and into the sweet, tangy scent of freshly picked apricots. There are crate-loads of them everywhere, mostly in an open barn. These, the most recently harvested, are to be dried for use in preserves and *sirops*. Elsewhere, all around, there are fresh, succulent fruits, the main bulk of his crop, which are being harvested now and which will be sold to a supermarket chain. Lord Harry greets me with a robust handshake and then takes me on a tour of the estate, which has been inherited from Baron —, his father, who made his fortune when he came up with the apparently inspired idea to breed prime Angus beef in the Camargue district and sell the meat to the French.

'He made a fortune,' Harry tells me. 'And then retired here to farm fruit, a passionate hobby of his.'

The main house is impressive but needs a fortune spending on it and has a bedraggled air about it. The interior is dark, the curtains left undrawn, and old-fashioned. Empty glasses, used cups forgotten on side tables and dressers. Out of doors, in the dusty yards, it is more animated. There are labourers all over the place, moving to and fro on tractors or on foot, shouting out to one another, up ladders, stacking crates in the barns. Certainly the farm is operating at full tilt, but I cannot help thinking that it has seen happier days.

He drives me to a valley, peaceful and green, with leafy rows of well-pruned trees gravid with ripe fruit, and I am trying to recall what I have found out about the history of the apricot tree.

For many years it was believed to have originated in Armenia, but is now known to have existed long before in ancient China. It reached Armenia via the Silk Route, and from there was transported to Greece and then to Rome. The Romans cultivated it throughout their empire. Today, it is considered a quintessentially Mediterranean tree. It would have been the Romans who brought the apricot to this French coast.

'Where is your sister?' I ask, taking in the expanse of his acreage.

'She's in Geneva.'

'When will she back?'

He shakes his head. 'Your guess is as good as mine.'

I stop in my tracks. 'But you still have her hives?'

'Dozens of them. We can take the car and go and have a look, if you like.' Which is what we do. Standing in a modest orchard of espaliered apple trees, the hives are a sorry-looking sight. Desolate and in need of a lick of paint, they put me in mind of rows of beach huts at an out-of-season resort.

'Where are the bees?'

'There are no bees any more.'

'No bees?'

'Well, there are a few,' he explains. 'Those that have not died or abandoned the hives.'

The few still pollinate Harry's apricots, but the swarms are feral now.

'What happened?'

'Bit of a scandal, as I understand it. I really don't know the ins and outs of the affair, except that my sister lost heart with the whole bloody business and took off.' He offers to let us have a few of the abandoned hives. 'If you want to take them, you can have them for nothing. Help yourself to as many as you like,' he says. 'They are of no further use to me, but you will need to purchase a queen and a swarm of drones of your own.' I would like to quiz him further, but one of his farmhands, a fresh-faced English lad, comes in search of him and Lord Harry needs to attend to other matters. I thank him for his kind offer, explaining that we are not apiarists; we do not have the skills or the time to tend the bees ourselves; we are looking for a beekeeper who might be interested in using our land. He nods sadly. 'Sorry I couldn't be of help. Come and visit me again in any case,' he says. 'My wife's left me, gone back to England, and my sister – well, she's disappeared to the Swiss mountains. Haven't seen her in months. I think she's become a Buddhist. It's bloody lonely here. Just me and the apricots.'

I am now running very late. Thierry, the young bullet-headed fellow who cleans our pool, is at work in the garden when I arrive home with a cake for Barbara from an excellent *boulangerie*-cum-*pâtisserie* on the outskirts of Mougins. He is bursting with some gossip which he cannot wait to share and I am obliged to deposit my bags on the ground while he imparts his news. Because of the spread of residences Thierry works at, he tends to have access to delicious titbits. This one concerns a property belonging to a thirty-something German whose pool he has been looking after for several years. Electric gates, armed and vested bodyguards patrolling the grounds, half a dozen trained dogs, the whole caboodle. Some time ago, while Thierry was at work there, the police arrived in two cars and the German was arrested for drug-smuggling. He has been shoved in jail and the house is now on the market for 36 million francs, about £3.2 million.

'Goodness,' I say, politely feigning surprise, gathering up my shopping.

'No, no, that's not it!' he returns excitedly.

Last Saturday, while Thierry was hoovering and treating the pool – his contract has been renegotiated by the firm of estate agents until the place is sold – a young Russian and his wife came to look at the house. According to Thierry, they liked it, said they'd have it and pulled out a suitcase from the boot of their car containing considerably more than the required 36 million francs in dollars. If French law allowed it, they would have bought the villa right there and then.

'The Mafia are moving in here like the plague,' he comments.

I find my attention drawn back to the scandal down on the coast which has been hogging the limelight since the spring.

'What's the latest news on the demise of the mayor?'

Thierry seems to revel in the uncloaking of these *petit* local corruptions, as do I, particularly when they are not so *petit*.

The latest is that a senior official in the Cannes town hall has followed our Riviera mayor into custody on suspicion of trying to extort money from a gambling firm in London. He has been placed under investigation for alleged corruption.

'Some chappie working for him was caught redhanded by a British special investigations squad. At the Ritz Hotel. He was receiving a payment of three million francs in cash.'

'In London?'

'Yes, the sum was being handed over by a British firm in return for permission to install one-armed bandits at a casino in one of the beachfront hotels. It was the British company who tipped off the police.

The mayor's son, Gilles Mouillot, has also been placed under investigation, but has been released under supervision. Father, Michel, is in prison and on hunger strike, which is delaying matters. A lawyer acting for the mayor has denounced the arrests and investigations, calling them politically motivated. He claims that they are connected with wrangling and factiousness between members of the centre-right coalition.

Everywhere here there are echoes of Graham Greene's excellent book, *J'accuse*, which exposed the nefarious dealings of Jacques Médecin, the infamous mayor of Nice, who swindled his city out of millions and then did a bunk to Uruguay, where the said millions had been stashed away for what he hoped was going to be a very sunny retirement. Our chap, Mouillot, hasn't been so nifty.

Thierry promises to keep me up to speed when I return from my trip.

Barbara's birthday is an ebullient yet easygoing affair. She blows out the four candles I have placed on her cake. Much wine is drunk, we sing and talk and play sixties rock music and old Van Morrison records rather too loudly and dance till late on the terrace by the pool. Her only disappointment is that her camera jams and neither she nor Jacob is able to unlock it. They cannot photograph the occasion. It suddenly occurs to me that Michel may not have taken his camera with him for his trip to Sydney. I run up to our bedroom and find it beneath my shoebags on the floor of the wardrobe, which is where he usually hides it.

I have no idea how to operate such a complicated apparatus but I return to the garden with it and suggest a few snaps. I set the zoom and the lens and the flash and everyone gathers round the table, arms linked, glasses raised, and shouts '*Fromage!*'

From the summer kitchen comes the unmistakable voice of Buddy Holly: 'Maybe Baby'. The quartet burst into laughter and raucous song, jigging as they hold their poses.

'Hang on! Wait!' I cry. 'I don't seem to be able to—'

'*Fromage! FROMAGE! FORMAGGIO!*' they shout and call like merry parrots, hammering out a recurrent squawk, clapping their hands. I fiddle clumsily, all fingers and thumbs, until, almost without my guidance, the camera clicks, slides, flashes and snaps, and I feel rather pleased with myself. Glasses are topped up, spilling over, and I promise to send copies on to Rome when the negatives are developed. And then I say my goodnights, exchanging *bisous* with everyone, and leave them all to plunge into the underwater-lit pool, uncork more bottles of bubbly and vino, smoke, chatter loudly and generally behave like Romans at a party, while I disappear off to bed to cries of '*Ciao, bella!*' '*Grazie mille, mille grazie!*' They promise to let themselves out and to lock the gate behind them. Lord knows if, by whatever hour that might be, they will remember, but aside from hanging out all night with them, what can I do?

My last image of the party, as I close the front door, is of Jacob: a lone figure sitting at some distance, a terrace above his loved one and their companions, fingers jammed in his ears to block out the noise, looking decidedly fed up.

I wake about five, climb out of bed and wander out on to the terrace, thinking that I should walk down the drive and check the gate. The pre-dawn is sharply lit by an almost full moon which is reflecting circular pools of luminous, citric light right across the Mediterranean; it is a breathtaking sight. I sit for a while in pensive mood, gazing upon it, considering the lot of Barbara and Jacob.

I am not one for matchmaking and never have been, but I find myself wondering whether I shouldn't introduce her to Lord Harry. Surely they would have more in common. Same background, both lonely . . .

Lost in these fruitless, not to say busybody, musings, it is some time before I realise that I am not alone. The clinking of a glass is what draws my attention to the terrace beneath me. There I see Barbara, perched barefoot on one of the cream-painted walls by the dining table, wearing nothing but a sarong. Her hair is wet and hangs like lengths of damp seaweed down her back; she must have been swimming. She has a lighted cigarette between her fingers and a three-quarters-empty bottle of wine at her side. The dogs, all three of them, are dozing in a semi-circle around her.

I go down to join her. As I approach she holds out her hand. It turns out that the others left several hours ago but she has lingered, preferring to walk back when she is ready to go. We barely talk; there seems little need. She thanks me for the evening and tells me that I won't ever know how special it has been and how appreciated she has felt. To me, these words only emphasise the appalling loneliness I feel this woman is trapped in.

As the sun comes up, she helps me clear the debris from the table and stack the myriad empty bottles ready for the local bottle bank, stays for breakfast and then I drive her to Cannes.

She is off to sunbathe on the beach. 'I'm only really happy when I'm by the sea,' she says. 'It calms me, brings me peace.'

'Me too,' I laugh.

'You are lucky to be having a baby,' she mutters, almost inaudibly, before leaving the car.

We kiss goodbye and agree to stay in touch.

'And don't forget to send the photos,' she calls as our old car chugs away. After dropping Barbara off, I decide to take a stroll along the Croisette. The beaches are humming with activity and the *restos* and cafés *au bord de la mer* are buzzing with a new breed of holidaying visitor, many of whom have bleached, backcombed hairdos. They are ordering drinks, fixing extravagantly painted faces and reading Russian newspapers and magazines.

Once I begin to take notice, I see that every beachside bookstall has Russian journals for sale. The newsagent has *Vogue* on display in Russian for the mafia molls who might enjoy a little light beach reading. Russian restaurants are springing up everywhere, both in and out of town, and the fashions in the women's stores are being slanted towards the new market. This is not the usual seasonal changes or a pitch at the wealthy Arab consumers, who still exist, though since that 'blasted Gulf War' the Arab trade has not been what it was. No, the outfits on sale now have a retro look, but not as in the fashion corridors of Paris. This is fetchingly out of date, late fifties, early sixties, meretricious colour combinations; the dressed-to-kill rocker look that every young Russian might have aspired to during those sealed-off years of communism. Thierry is spot-on: a new Mafia is moving in, but no doubt the town of Cannes is grateful for them.

Three days later, I fly to London. René and his water diviner never made contact, never appeared. On my way through the departure lounge at Nice airport, I notice two posters advertising Russian television stations. My flight is announced, and as I approach the boarding gate I pass a young man dressed in a loud suit. He is shouting into four mobile telephones all at once. The language he's talking is Russian, with a few English swearwords thrown in for spice.

A new page in Côte d'Azur history.

Before leaving for Birmingham, which is where the shooting of my television film is scheduled to take place, I visit my gynaecologist. I admit to my tirednesses and the occasional shooting pains. He recommends that I undergo an amniocentesis. I am wary but agree. The risks are minimal, he assures me, though marginally higher for a woman such as myself with a history of miscarriage.

On the day, it all goes off without a hitch. I learn that our baby is perfectly normal, followed by the even more joyous news that the child I am carrying is no longer an 'it': the life taking form is a she. I leave the Harley Street clinic feeling both nervous and totally exhilarated and make directly for a phone box to telephone Michel in Paris.

'What will we christen her?'

We decide to both choose a name and, just for fun, to keep them to ourselves; a secret from one another until the next time we are together which will be after my filming. Suppose we choose the same name?

'*Peut-être, qui sait?*' Michel laughs happily.

Think how remarkable that would be.

The reality of the approaching birth of our baby, our tiny little girl, is taking hold. Her arrival is months away yet, but now she has a name, no, two names. Spiritually christened, she exists in my day-to-day life. She has moved in, is already a participating member of the family. I pass my days visiting my hairdresser, lunching with my agent, meeting for drinks with my editor; I am city-busy and oscillating between states of excitement and nervousness, which leave me both effervescent and drained. I feel as though my whole being is smiling, glowing from inside.

'You look great,' people repeatedly tell me.

Yes. I am past all the enervating bouts of morning sickness and no longer a prisoner to my tomato obsession; I am a woman in her stride.

Some days my mood is vital, powerfully alive and sharp. I and my baby are omnipotent; a single invincible force. I talk to her, ask her advice, offer her mine. She shares my secrets, knows my shortcomings, forgives me because she is too tiny to know otherwise and, for the present, I am all there is. She is my invisible ally, as I am hers. She is my passport to another earth, another stratosphere of happiness, of bondedness. Together our love, this union of mother and daughter, this sorority, girls together, will make my world go round.

And then, at other moments, friends remark that I look tired, or rather pale. It's true. I feel inadequate. I have sleepless nights worrying that I have left this birth too late, that I am too selfish, too set in my ways, that I won't be able to meet the challenge, that something will go wrong, that our little girl will not be whole. Fortunately, the negative responses are less frequent and are strongly overridden by my more upbeat moods. The designer calls. 'Costume fittings, darling,' she purrs. 'We must meet and discuss your cozzies.'

I have been postponing this important rendezvous knowing that there will be a drawn-out session involving measurements, sizes and styles of clothes and that I may be obliged to give away my secret. I suggest that she and her assistant come over to my flat, where we can discuss the script over a bottle of wine.

When she arrives that evening, accompanied by the assistant, she compliments me on how well I am looking, 'radiant', she says, tactfully observing that I am perhaps a tad on the plump side. I shrug this off with a comment about my French lifestyle: 'The wine and good living, you know.' We settle down to discuss the costumes required for the various scenes when a ring at the doorbell interrupts us. I am not expecting anyone. Excusing myself, I go out into the hall to press the intercom.

'Yes?'

'Flowers for Miss Drinkwater,' a voice announces.

This flat is not in the most salubrious district of north London and though we are well concealed on two floors at the very top of the building I am usually cautious before pressing the lock-release.

'I am not expecting flowers. Who are they are from?' I interrogate, but the crackly male voice does not say. Yet because I am not alone I feel less wary, so I press the button that opens the street door, calling out an apology to the two women in the living room, suggesting they help themselves to more wine and explaining that I will be with them shortly. I open my front door to await the delivery boy who is climbing the winding stairs. I see the bouquet of eighteen red roses before I see him.

It is Michel!

I cry out and both designer and assistant look up anxiously from the living room. The designer hurries to the door. 'Is everything all right?'

I nod. 'It's my husband,' and I run down a few steps to greet him and to throw my arms around him. 'What are you doing here? I thought you were on your way to Sydney.'

'Changing planes in London. I wanted to surprise you. I can't stay, I'll miss my flight. I have a taxi outside,' and he hands me the flowers, kisses me softly on the mouth, whispers

'*Je t'aime*,' and disappears out of sight with a final blown kiss. 'Take care of her,' he calls up softly.

I return to the two women, who look at me curiously. 'My husband,' I repeat. 'He's just flown in from Paris.'

'Isn't he coming in?' asks the designer 'I hope that we . . .'

'No, no, he's on his way to Australia and wanted to . . .' I consider divulging our news and then decide not to. 'He just came to give me these.'

'Shit, that's too romantic!' says one of them.

'He must be French,' declares the other.

Buried within the bouquet – I find it later – is a gold chain as slender as a strand of hair with one tiny emerald worked into it. It matches my engagement-cum-wedding ring.

It is the Irish in me, my superstitious nature, that has decided against broadcasting news of the baby, as well as the fact that I shall be filming for only three weeks. Had I been contracted for a longer period, out of courtesy to the designer, who would have needed to be prepared for the inevitable costume alterations, I would have discreetly included her. As it is, the entire shoot will be over in no time, so there will be few, if any, physical changes and, as much as I hate to, I have promised myself I will diet rigor-ously. So I guard our cherished secret, and the following afternoon I set off by train for Birmingham.

A Darker Climate

Surfacing from an uncharacteristically deep sleep, I open my
eyes into a twilight zone, into the shadowland between
drowsing and waking. Though my lids and limbs feel slug-
gish and my responses dull, I am instantly assaulted by two
very different sensations, both of which send shockwaves
through my system. Encompassing me is a heaviness, as
though life itself has been becalmed, and the other, a raw
ache rapping at the pit of my stomach.

I lie motionless, stiff as a board, on my back, staring at the
ceiling, attempting to deny this pain which has the nagging
quality of a pre-menstrual cramp. I want to close it out, to be
attentive only to the bursts of middle-of-the-night London
traffic. I lift my hand and brush it gingerly against my stomach. Although heartened by my belly's crescent fullness, I am
unable to rid myself of the fear that all is not well. Should I
rise, make hot tea, take an aspirin? Or should I relax,

breathe deeply and try to sleep again? I close my eyes, hankering for Michel, pining for him to be here alongside me, relieved that I am not filming in the morning and that I can sleep late if I choose to. I roll over on my hip to ease the discomfort but this does not alleviate it. On the contrary, the sensations are worsened; or perhaps they are exaggerated by my focus on them. I grow scared, worrying for the wellbeing of the minuscule female foetus growing with faith inside me.

Supine again, I keep my eyes firmly shut and move my hand from side to side across the rounded flesh, massaging it, intent on creating a pain-free zone down there, to transmit waves of serenity, of security to the tiny girl agitating within me. It seems to work; the pain eases and I drift off, swimming in and out of wakefulness, until, some time later, something alerts me to the fact that my thighs are damp; damp with a sticky warmth that freaks me, sending distress signals up and down the length of my body. I turn fast and put on the bedside light, pressing my other hand tight against the source of this wetness.

Drawing my arm out from beneath the bedding, I stare in horror at my palm, my fingers and my wrist. Sickened, I throw off the cover as though it were on fire and gaze down upon my lower regions, all of which are blotched in haemorrhaging blood. The sight of it, claret-dark and viscous, scares and nauseates me just as violence scares and revolts me. I kick the duvet away and lift myself, breathlessly, to a sitting position, noticing the clock, which shows something after 3am. I don't know what to do. I feel panicked and uncertain and alone and unwilling to face up to what this must mean.

I have to call someone, do something, take action, but who, what? Michel is in Australia. Even if I telephoned him – it is mid-afternoon in Sydney – what could he do? Why alarm him? I lift myself unsteadily to my feet and stagger down the stairs to the lavatory. I feel the blood escaping, slipping down my inner thighs. I am heaving in dry gulps as though I were choking although I know that I am not. It is fear, shock, confusion, as well as a passionate, a desperate need for this not to be happening. Clots as well as steady trickles of blood are slipping out of me. The ease with which they fall belies the gravity of my situation. I am losing my baby. Am I? Am I really losing our precious little girl?

The pains are shooting up my back and pressing vice-like against my stomach. I am dizzy and weak, seated on the loo, chest slumped against my knees, head hanging towards my feet like a vomiting drunk; I have no ability to move, no strength; the pain has me in its grip. But I know that I must take some action.

Eventually I crawl to the telephone and dial the number of Chris, a fellow actor and a loyal friend.

'What time is it?' he slurs sleepily.

'Come over,' I whisper. 'Please. Come now.' He lives nearby; he has keys. Thank God he has keys.

'What? Are you all right?' He doesn't wait for a coherent reply but accepts my stuttering negatives and assures me that he is on his way.

I drag a towelling robe from a hook on the back of the bathroom door, wrap it like a sarong around my lower torso and slump to the carpet in the living room, curled up like the foetus which is tearing itself out of me, because I have no strength to climb the stairs again. I am trembling and cold and frightened and the blood is still raining out of me. The pain clenches in fits and starts. Perhaps it's not too late. Perhaps this is not as serious as . . . but I know that it is. I have miscarried before; nothing quite as dramatic as this, but I recognise the signs. Above all, that dull ache throbbing round the base of my spine, digging into the lower half of me.

Chris finds me there on the floor. He fights back his distress at the sight of me. 'I'm taking you to hospital,' he says manfully.

I manage to convey my wish to be seen by my own gynaecologist. Chris goes in search of my address book, finds the number and telephones the specialist's home. Richard listens, instructs him on where to take me, details of how to get there and what to do in the meantime. Then Chris rings for a cab because he wants to be with me, to be able to hold me instead of having to drive; to care for me, and I am so grateful.

Dawn is rising bruised mauve and tangerine-sharp beyond the city's granite-grey high-rises. This part of London seems unfamiliar to me. I cannot recall ever having been here before. Curled, blanketed figures are dead to the world on the pavement, overturned bottles at their sides, as the cab swings in through the open iron gates of the hospital, and stops.

'We're here,' my friend whispers, leaning across me to open the door.

The damp, chilly weather bites into my senses. I hear the echo of my shuffling feet. I am weak, close to fainting and still bleeding. The morning light lours. It is close to 5am as Chris guides me through into Emergency. I see only two ambulance-drivers, deep in conversation, smoking, drinking coffee out of brown plastic cups and then, waiting by the reception desk, I spy Richard, still in his overcoat. The expression on my specialist's face prepares me for what is to come. With the help of my friend, who then discreetly disappears, he leads me through to a scrubbed, sulphurous-smelling cubicle, slips off his coat and switches on a monitor while I am disrobing myself of whatever ill-assorted clothes I have managed to cover myself in. Once I am horizontal on the trolley-bed, he begins to trace the ultrasonic scanner across my stomach. I shiver as it contacts my skin, recalling that curiously smooth, ice-cream cold sensation. The last time one of these instruments touched my flesh and X-rayed the inner contours of my body, reading me as nothing else has ever read me, it reported life within. That was barely two weeks ago. The gynaecologist at my side now is the same man who performed that earlier sketching of the inner me. On that occasion he was pointing out the silhouette of the tiny girl growing inside me. 'See here?' Richard had said then. 'Those white lines are the arms, and there is the head. And here, see, it's a girl.'

This morning, it is a different scenario. He does not turn his clean-cut face towards me but frowns, concentrating hard on the screen, which I cannot see. 'There's nothing there,' he says eventually.

Stupidly, and because I choose to, I take his words to mean that the machine is not functioning, or that there is no problem, until he turns his grave blue eyes upon me. 'There's no heartbeat, Carol, no life left. Nothing to save.'

I screw up my face and close my lids so tight I see lemony shapes dancing in the blackness of my mind. I feel dampness burning the contours of my eyes and my throat is constricting as though swelling from within. I want to beg him to look again. 'Nothing at all?' I plead.

'I'm sorry. You have miscarried.'

I cannot utter another sound. Seventeen weeks of joy, of anticipation, ejected. *Why?*

'Stress, overwork or nature's natural selection process.' He does not seem to know. 'A great many more women than you would think suffer similar losses. I doubt there was anything you could have done to save it,' he tells me. Kind though his words are, they do nothing to alleviate the pain of the loss.

'I'm going to ask a nurse to get you ready. I'm taking you up to the operating theatre to clean you out. I want to make sure there's no residue to become infected. And then, Carol, you will need to rest.'

'I'm filming tomorrow,' I mutter defiantly, angrily.

'No, you won't be strong enough for that. They will need to change the schedule.'

He rises, places a hand against my shoulder. 'Try not to worry or upset yourself now. I'll call the anaesthetist. Would you like to see your companion before we sedate you?'

I nod.

I wake into a world in which my head is throbbing in a thick and muzzy way, where the base of my spine is as rigid as an iron rod and my innards feel raw, as though my interior flesh and organs have been scraped with a paint-scraper. I moan involuntarily, blinking out the glaring light of consciousness, toss my head from side to side to rid myself of the pain and then close my eyes again, sinking back into the secure cave of darkness, drawn back down into a deep, drugged sleep.

I open heavy eyes. Figures are leaning over me; white masked faces leaning over me. Slender, chirpy young women and men in midsummer leaf-green uniforms. I think I hear white leather clogs echoing along corridors. I must be on a trolley being wheeled. No, I am static and in a bed. Sheets and covers and pillows are being tucked in around me. People are fussing over me. My head is spinning; my mind is turning corners. And I have a desperate thirst.

'Thirsty.'

'Here, drink this.' A glass of water is pressed against my parched lips. A cold hand slips behind the base of my skull, raising me up. I suck and draw and dribble clumsily, lacking control, and then, head resting once more against the newly plumped pillows, I disappear, plunging yet again down the rabbit warren corridors of my damaged self.

When I eventually regain consciousness, Richard is standing over me. 'Hello, there.' He takes my wrist, feeling for my pulse. 'It all went smoothly,' he says. His smile is kind, and professional.

'Was there . . . ?'

'It's all gone. We've cleaned you up. Nothing to worry about.'

A wave of grief presses hard against me, rolling titanically through my guts. In that split second, I have no desire to live.

'There were no signs of infection. How are you feeling?'

I cannot begin to explain, which is what I reply.

Someone, a woman in white, enters the room and takes my temperature. Richard watches on, lingering at my bedside.

'I want you to rest. You are going to need plenty of rest.'

'What time is it?' I drawl, as if it matters.

He glances at his watch. Half past three.

'In the afternoon or the morning?'

'The afternoon.'

I try to recall how I arrived here and where exactly I am, grappling with images of recent events. 'I'm filming tomorrow. I have to be in Birmingham tonight.'

'That's out of the question. You have lost a fair amount of blood and your system is in shock. I will only agree to discharge you if there is someone at home to take care of you. Otherwise, I really would prefer you to stay here tonight.'

I telephone. Chris returns. He drives me back to the flat. He makes hot tea while I lie on the sofa refusing to climb the stairs to the bedroom. I don't want to be alone up there, don't want to return to that threatening space. Not yet.

'Have you said anything to Michel?' he asks, when he appears with a cup of Earl Grey sweetened with two spoonfuls of the Provençal honey I brought with me from France. I think of the beekeepers back home, life back home, our precious, funny little olive farm, and I smile. A tear threatens. I feel emotional and unsteady but determine not to give in to it.

'Are there any messages?'

He plays the machine. A young man, Peter, from the Birmingham location has left me my call. According to his garbled news, they have lost a day due to bad weather. My new call is on set at 6am the day after tomorrow. This requires me to be in Birmingham late tomorrow afternoon. Their loss has gained me one day for myself.

'You'll have to tell them,' Chris says. His tone is unintentionally nagging, almost bullying. It is his manner, I have found, when he is faced with unfamiliar problems and he is concerned. Here he is, my pal and a gay man, attempting to cope with a situation which is well outside the realm of his own experience. 'When did you last talk to him?'

'Who?' I close my eyes, brushing a hand across my forehead, trying to recall. Time and the whole sequence of events are in a warp.

Yesterday – or was it the day before? – I was in Birmingham, standing alongside a fellow actor, my co-lead, posing for a photographer who was on set to shoot location stills for the BBC publicity department.

'Big smile, Carol. That's it. And, Den, eyes this way, please. That's it, and again. Great! Thanks, guys.' And I was beaming, laughing in a carefree way, savouring the knowledge that there were three of us in the photographs, not two, and no one knew it but me. Considering the health risks, I was tempted to ask Den to put out his cigarette, but I decided to remain silent. He would have been amenable but I preferred not to give the game away. Den is one of a breed of working-class theatre actors who has found success in television; he is short, stocky, intense and talented but ego-driven and a heavy drinker. One of the lads, and not an obvious confidant for me. Still, he is a father and a warm-hearted guy, and I may need to confide in him now. Was it really only yesterday evening that I arrived back in London?

'Carol, are you listening to me?' Chris insists. 'Have you spoken to Michel?'

Did Michel and I talk before I went to sleep yesterday? Was it yesterday? Yes, I think we did.

'I shan't call him now,' I answer. Chris brings over the telephone and, instead, I dial Birmingham, asking to speak to Laurence, the first assistant. He is responsible for drawing up the schedules; he keeps the show on course and is the right hand of the director during the weeks of principal photography. Denise, the production assistant, informs me that he is not at the base right now but is travelling somewhere between the location and the studios. She promises to have him ring me back. I thank her and emphasise the fact that it is rather urgent. Laurence returns my call almost before I have replaced the phone.

'Carol? Laurence here. Is there a problem?' I can hear the tension in his voice. The logistics, the smooth running of the shoot, rest on his shoulders. In the background his radio mike is crackling, transmitting the cries and orders from the shooting base.

'Cut!' 'Check the gate!'

'I've been taken ill.'

'*What?*'

'I mean I can film, if I have to, but I was wondering if there is any chance that . . .'

Chris heads back into the room from the kitchen, teatowel over his shoulder, waving wildly at me, signalling that I must not offer to go.

'Carol, there's no way I can change the schedule. Not unless it's a case of life and death. We're already over a day behind and the forecast for the rest of the week is rain, rain and more bloody rain.'

'*Hair in the gate!*'

'Oh, shit, I don't believe it! Hang on, Carol.' I hear him fiddling with the radio. 'Tim, Tim, can you hear me? What's going on over there with the stock? That's the third fucking hair in the gate this afternoon! Tim, Tim, can you . . . Carol, I'm going to have to call you back. Stay where you are, OK?'

'Laurence, I'd like to speak to Paddy. Please could you ask him to call me when he has a break?'

'He's . . . Yeah, OK, I'll give him your message. I have to go. Tim, *Tim?*' And the line goes dead.

Chris is hovering at my side. I don't look up. 'I've asked the director, Paddy, to call me, but it does sound rather tense up there, and I feel sure that I'll have to go,' I explain. 'I won't need to leave till lunchtime tomorrow, so . . . I'll be fine by then.'

'No!' he all but yells at me.

'Please, don't shout.'

'Well, tell them the truth! It's only a telly film, Carol. They can change the shooting schedule if they have to.' But he doesn't believe his own words. An actor himself, he knows that when the cameras roll, for those involved during those few intense weeks the film takes on a paramountcy, an aggrandised significance, that outstrips life or, in this case, death.

When Paddy returns my call, which, surprisingly, he does rapidly, he sounds frazzled and as though the very last thing he needs is a problem with the leading actress. 'What is it, darling?' he demands wearily.

'I've . . . lost . . . a baby, Paddy.' I am met with silence, and so I hurry on. 'I had a miscarriage in the early hours of this morning and . . . and I was wondering if . . .'

I hear him drag on his cigarette, the deep tiredness in the exhalation of his breath and the unspoken accusation: why didn't you tell me when I cast you that you were pregnant?

'All right, I'll speak to Laurence. But the weather forecast is lousy. We'll have to shoot interiors for the rest of the week, and that means you, I'm afraid, darling. In any case John, who's arriving tomorrow, is only contracted to us for the second half of this week. He has another shoot to go on to and I've got to release him on time. It was always going to be tight fitting in his dates, and now, with this bloody weather and the damaged film stock . . . I'll ask Laurence. I am sure that he will say the same, but we'll see what we can do. He'll call you later.' And again the line goes dead. By now I am regretting that I ever mentioned anything.

Chris persuades me to sleep, and it is while I am sleeping that the message comes through: I must return to work. The alternative seems to be that the shoot stops and it – me – becomes an insurance claim. I persuade both Chris and myself that I am fine, that by tomorrow I will have rested and will be raring to go. Now my friend tries to talk me into telephoning Richard, which I adamantly refuse to do.

'And you still haven't spoken to Michel. He has to know, Carol.'

This does it, this breaks me. It takes me out of the realm of the functional, dealing with my professional life, into the fragile, more vulnerable world of what has been taken away, what is no longer the future, our future, and the fact that Michel does not know yet. He is going about his Australian day – possibly getting out of bed as I think these thoughts, which makes it the ideal moment to speak to him – cherishing the knowledge that he is soon going to be father to his third daughter, and our first child. Outside, in the grimy city, evening is beginning to fall. I hear the horns of frayed drivers attempting to motor home, to make it beyond the grill and fumes, the roars and disappointments of the city. And I am suddenly exhausted. How I long to return to Appassionata, to hide myself away, to lick my wounds, lose myself in that landscape, shelter beneath olive trees. I assure my friend that he has done everything and more and that now I shall sleep.

'I can kip down here on the sofa if you like,' he offers.

I shake my head and stand up to see him out. The room spins but I manage to keep steady as I wrap my arms around him. 'You're a real pal,' I whisper. 'Thank you.'

'Call Michel,' he states. I nod into his woollen-sweatered shoulder. 'And if you need me, you know where I am. I wish you wouldn't go . . .'

'Sssh,' I say. 'Thank you for being here.' And he leaves me with a tender kiss on my forehead.

Before falling into bed I telephone Michel. His frame of mind is upbeat and energetic; things are going very well. He has negotiated a couple of very good sales, and one of the networks has watched the promo reel he sent on ahead of the animation film he has been working on with Serge and they have expressed a commitment as co-production partners. 'They love it,' he says. 'I've been running to and fro from their studios over on the north shore to their bank in the city and back to Elizabeth Bay. The weather is wonderful. A real balmy Sydney morning. Hard to believe it's early winter here. The only thing missing is you.' I listen to his positive mood and decide against mentioning anything of what has happened. There is nothing he can do. The knowledge will only cause him pain; he will begin to worry about me instead of paying attention to his work and, though I hate to deceive him, I cannot bear to trouble or frustrate him. We say 'Goodnight,' and 'Have a great day,' and I set the alarm so that I will be up in time to pack my travelling bag.

When I arrive in Birmingham it is evening; a howling wet evening. The chill wind burns blisteringly sharp against my skin as I hurry from taxi to hotel, where a teenage receptionist hands me my key.

'Is there a call sheet waiting?' I ask her.

She checks the message-box and shakes her head.

'Do you know if they've wrapped?'

'Wrapped?' she repeats, having not comprehended the question.

'Are the others back from the set yet?'

'I haven't seen anyone.'

'Has Mr Dunmore checked in yet?'

She fingers through a guest list and confirms that there is a reservation for a Mr Dunmore but that, as far as she knows, he has not checked in and that, in any case, he is not due in today.

Puzzled, I nod my thanks and take the lift to my room, where I set down my luggage, draw the curtains to darkness and curl up on the spacious bed. When I wake it is after nine. I rise and go to the door feeling certain that the third assistant will have slipped my call sheet under it. There is nothing. Concerned, I call reception. No call sheet has been left for me. Laurence is not staying at this hotel so I ring his mobile. He is in the production office somewhere across town. They wrapped late and he is still working.

'I haven't received my call yet for the morning,' I tell him.

'Oh, hi, Carol. There's no call sheet for you because you're not working tomorrow. We've had a hell of day and lost another four hours. We've been landed with faulty stock. I don't know how many duff gates we've had since yesterday. Paddy is blowing his top.'

'Am I on standby, or . . .'

'No, you're free. We definitely won't get to you.'

'May I go back to London?'

'No, I'd rather you stayed. The schedule's all up in the air. You just never know.'

But John's not here, I am thinking, and the greater proportion of my remaining scenes are with him. Still, I decide not to argue the point.

And so the following day I rest in my room. And the next day, and the day after that. It is now the end of the week and I haven't seen a soul in days. If I had returned to London, even to Appassionata, no one would have noticed. Time drags and there is nothing to do but go back over my script time and time again, take the lift to reception, poke my head into the bar and scan the dimly lit interior for other bored actors, or walk the drizzling streets of Birmingham. I promise myself matinée visits to the local cinema to cheer myself up but find myself sleeping the afternoons away, waking after harrowing dreams. I grow depressed. Very depressed. My mood is bleak and empty and my life feels directionless, pointless even. I call Richard, who says that mood swings are to be expected; they are nothing to be concerned about. Even so, he insists that I make an appointment to see him before I fly back to France and I agree to call him when I return to London. I still haven't broken the news to Michel and now I feel unable to do so. I decide that it must wait until we are together again. But the withholding is weighing heavily on me, exacerbating my negative frame of mind.

Finally, I am called to the set, where I learn that during my absence there appears to have been a 'minor' change of the artistic interpretation of the nature of my role.

The character I am playing is an adulteress. She is a glamorous and enigmatic figure as well as being a capricious wife who is betraying her husband (played by Den) with one of their neighbours. This morning we are scheduled to shoot the love scene between the neighbour (played by John) and myself in the 'kitchen set, John's house'. I doubt that any woman who has recently miscarried a much-longed for baby feels good about herself or her body – there are many insecurities, both physical and psychological – and I have not even begun to address these issues rising within me. To act out the motions of lovemaking in front of a camera not five feet away at a moment when you are as vulnerable as this calls for technique, skills, tricks. Actors are schooled at revealing their secret hearts, albeit wrapped in the flimsy mask of character, but there are times when you ask yourself whether you are capable of getting out there and performing.

This morning I need to create the illusion of wellbeing, or as the French so succinctly describe it, *être bien dans la peau*, and an actor's trick I frequently use when a situation requires it is to pick a song and sing or hum it to myself over and over, to try to call up a particular frame of mind, a mood, to replicate an emotional state. So here I am, alone in my dressing room, staring blindly at my well-thumbed script, bottling up a swell of negative emotions, humming 'These Foolish Things', attempting to recreate from memory Oscar Peterson's mellow rendition of this melody. It is a tune that never fails to make me feel feminine, sentimental and in the mood for love or, at least, a little cheek-to-cheek affection. Alas, not this morning. This morning my libido has gone underground.

A knock on the door is followed instantly by the bustling entrance of Tina, my dresser, with an armful of costumes: freshly washed tights and a black nylon negligée and matching housecoat, complete with bows and frills, pressed and ready on coathangers. 'The black nightwear is not mine,' I say casually to this young girl, whose job it is to look after me and see to my costumes and requirements.

'Yes it is,' Tina states emphatically. Confused, I request a brief word with the costume designer.

It appears a new twist has been thought up during my days away. So explains the designer to me when she appears in my dressing room.

'Which is?'

'Are neighbour and wife really at it? Or does the affair exist only in the distorted mind of the husband?' Much of the plot hangs around this question, it now seems, and, in order to underline the torment of the character of the leading actor (Den), the director has decided that he wants to overplay the love scene between myself and the neighbour to 'draw out the eroticism, not to say bestiality', to play up the torturous pictures in the head of the husband. 'Paddy came up with the idea a couple of days ago, didn't he mention it?'

Speechless, I shake my head.

'This black number's a bit in-your-face, I know, darling. Not quite the character we've been drawing with the other outfits, but you mustn't be concerned. It *is* sexy, in its way. You'll look fabulous in it. I've been watching the rushes; you're glowing. You're pregnant, aren't you?'

My heart feels as though it has just been knifed.

'Is that why your husband turned up with those roses? I've been telling everyone. How romantic can you get? No one's ever done such a thing for me.'

I am choking back the tears which threaten to send rivulets of black mascara streaming down my face.

'Don't be upset about the cozzie. You look a bit tired, darling, are you OK? It's all that hanging about in that bloody awful hotel. What a dump that place is. Have you eaten there? Don't, and don't worry. Sue in make-up'll soon put you right. Do you want me to fetch Paddy?'

I consider this, and then before I can give a decision, or

even gather words from out of my choked emotions, there is another knock on my dressing-room door.

'Who is it?' It's the designer asking. She can clearly see that I am utterly devastated, and though amazed that a costume should reduce anyone to such misery, she decides to speak up for me.

'It's John.'

The actor playing my supposed lover, the neighbour in the piece, is a pal, though we haven't seen one another for donkey's years. We were at drama school together, along with Chris, and then, eighteen months or so later, we were both offered a year's contract at the same provincial repertory theatre. Far from London, in a distant unknown northern city, we shared a flat together. It was a rambling, Victorian space which neither of us could afford, but we had great fun together. So, although we have not actually set eyes on one another for the best part of fifteen years, there is a bond between us that goes back to those special days of studentship and actor internship when we were soft at the edges, when one is so open to new friendships, when life promises dreams for the taking, and we were intent on stardom.

'Come in,' I manage.

The door opens and in walks a successful, well-fleshed-out forty-something man, equally handsome, equally prepossessing, with those honey-warm eyes, but long ago gone is that shy, soft-voiced juvenile with his floppy scarves, shoulder-length hair and well-worn sneakers. We fall into one another's arms, hugging tightly, shouting exuberantly. As actors do.

The designer exits discreetly, saying she'll catch up with me before we shoot.

'Has he told you what he wants?' John asks when we finally disengage. I shrug, dreading what's to come. 'He wants, and I quote, "raw lust, bestiality, darling".' John begins to giggle.

I try not to expose the insecurities welling within me. I know that I am not called upon to actually desire John, which I don't, nor have I ever, though I adore him and find him gorgeous, but it would spice up and authenticate the scene we are about to be expected to perform in front of the camera if I felt good about myself and capable of exuding a little passion.

John laughs at my downturned face.

I try to disguise the troubles flipping through my mind. 'He's chosen a costume. I wasn't even here . . .'

'Hey,' says John, wrapping a firm arm about my shoulder. 'I've never known something as trivial as a cozzie get you down. If it's "raw lust" he wants, honey, you and I can provide it. You're not to fret.' And with that he brushes a light kiss against my hair and disappears from my dressing room, leaving me alone in a very empty and unexpectedly alien environment.

When the third assistant's knock on the door comes, panic rises. I fear that I cannot step outside the hidden harbour of that space, let alone reveal this outfit before approximately forty predominantly male crew members. Beneath a floor-length dressing gown of my own is the horrendous and deeply unflattering negligée. But the job demands it. I take a deep, deep breath, and out I go.

Once on the set, there is a tense wait while some technical problem is addressed. Sue, my make-up artist, is tinkering with my hair and chattering away while I stew silently, desperate to fall upon a solution which will not cause a fuss. I catch sight of Paddy pacing up and down, glowering at his watch and casting malevolent glances in the general direction of the electrics lads, who appear to be responsible for whatever has caused this latest delay. Alone on a chair, in an unlit corner, behind our fulminating director, sits John, browsing through a newspaper.

In an instant I decide to take the bull by the horns. I leave my seat and hurry across to him. Blurting out to him the bare bones, a potted version of my history over these last few days, I plead for his support and then, to emphasise my case, I untie my dressing gown and reveal the deeply vulgar outfit. John lifts both hands to his face to mask a grimace of theatrical horror.

'Leave it to me,' he whispers conspiratorially.

The upshot is that I am led away to shed the scantily clad look and change into a frock and high heels. The scene is then rehearsed in a closed set. With the lights and cameras ready to shoot, the enactment of our illicit passion for one another is played out on the kitchen table. I hate every second of it. Limbs entangled, we huff and puff like creatures in the zoo as we are obliged to exaggerate our carnal cries and heavy breathing. Still, only a moderate amount of flesh is exposed, far less than had been threatened, and John gallantly shields my vulnerability. After the scene has been completed from all of its various angles we are both wrapped, given the all-clear, and we leave the location together to be driven back to the hotel, where we order a bottle of good wine and settle down to catch up on long-lost friends and gossip. I can relax now, knowing that I have few scenes left to shoot and the worst is over.

Back in London, two things are uppermost in my mind: my appointment with Richard and then, once I have been assured that all is well, my safe and speedy return to Appassionata to await the homecoming of Michel and the breaking of news I have postponed too long. Richard agrees to see me at his clinic in Harley Street on the day I telephone. The examination is brief and straightforward.

Afterwards, he leads me through to his capacious consulting room.

'Well, the good news is that no infection has set in and you are healing nicely.' He smiles, pausing to rest his hands on his desk; he glances at my file in front of him though I can see that he is not reading it but merely fiddling with it and shifting it a centimetre or two. His manner alarms me.

'What caused the miscarriage?' I ask 'Was it the amnio-centesis?'

He shakes his head. 'No, I am quite certain that the amniocentesis was not responsible, or you would have aborted sooner. A foetal cardiac arrest is my belief. There are signs of intraventricular haemorrhage.' He pauses again. A frown creases his forehead and I can see that he is weighing his words with care.

'Is there something else?'

'As I said, you are healing, but . . .'

This hangs in the air between us as he slowly shifts his gaze from the table to fix it on me.

'But?' I inhale, mouth dry, heart beating fast.

'I suspect another pregnancy might be out of the ques-tion.'

'We will wait,' I butt in. 'I know that Michel . . .'

His eyes, those blue-grey eyes set in a handsome, youthful, public-school face, remain concentrated on me. 'It's not a question of waiting. Yes, I would have advised a physical rest of, say, three to six months, but the case is slightly different here. You have a history of miscarrying. Still, until now, I have always held firmly to the belief that with rest and no pressure you would be able to carry a child through its term. I fear that may no longer be the situation. My belief is that it is not possible for you to carry a child the full term. You can conceive, that is not the difficulty, but any conceived foetus will sooner or later abort itself.'

I am stunned. The blow all but paralyses me, arresting my breath as though my life were hanging in the balance. In one clean swoop, dreams have been demolished. My head flops backwards and I exhale slowly, as though expelling from my mind, body, respiratory system the seed of such a prognosis. Eyes staring ceilingwards, determined against tears, against the rising hot anger, I resolutely examine the white cornicework, the central rose, and then I try to speak. I want to ask him if there is anything to be done, but my voice breaks mid-sentence; I bite back the swelling emotion, unable to continue. I am staring at a pair of clasped hands, mine, resting in my lap. A tear falls and wets my finger.

'Before you leave – when are you going? – before you do, I'd like you to see two of my colleagues . . . Or you might want to consider adoption?' He waits, and then, 'I could put you in touch with a therapist who . . .'

I shake my head.

'Well, I'll organise the two appointments, and let's wait to hear their diagnoses. Who knows, my colleagues may disagree. There is always the possibility that I am wrong.'

The Silence of the Sea

Throughout my life, whenever I have been in pain or have felt lost or confused, I have set myself on course for the sea. The sea heals me; its rhythms calm me; its boundless horizons revitalise and free me, easing out those cages I feel closing in around me. Today is no exception. The sea is the healing source I crave now. And tireless physical work. I want to bury myself and my misery in furious activity. No resting, no grieving, no taking stock.

For this I need to be back at the farm. I need the uncomplicated happiness of playing with the dogs, of preparing the house for the invasion of summer guests and the return of my husband, whose intense kindness I can no longer do without. And when I am worn out from work, I want to idle away time on the terraces and stare out at the distant skyline. At the end of each complete and fading day, I want to slip in a CD and drown myself in the blues, drink gallons of wine, take refuge in that Provençal light, those rays of bruised and coppery colours falling across the limpid stillness of the Mediterranean, until it is time to creep indoors and light the candles. And when the night draws in, I want to fall into bed exhausted and curl up like a damaged squirrel, ready to wake early with a list as long as my arm of tasks to be achieved.

Equally, I long to walk the beaches listening to the waves, to sit on the sand, breathe deeply and inhale the intense perfumes of pines and eucalyptus gums, to feed greedily off nature's munificence and, in isolation, unfold the disappointment and the sense of failure raging in my heart.

But I cannot face the airports, the queues, the nightmares of security and luggage, the gaggles of travellers and tourists I am bound to encounter during these early days of the height of the summer season. Even the journey from city to airport threatens to overwhelm me and my jumbled self, which gibbers and trembles as though shot.

My delayed response to my specialist's news is a defensive one, and not entirely logical. It leads me to embark on a series of decisions which threaten my safety because my reason is blinded by pain and is running haywire.

There are six more days until Michel is scheduled to arrive home from Sydney, which means that I have the time to choose *not* to fly, and so I decide to buy a car. The possibility of taking a train simply does not cross my mind. I will buy a car in London and drive it home, travelling south through France, moving at my own speed towards the land of olive groves and Judas trees, keeping pace with my thoughts and my solitude.

We have talked of buying another car since the Quatrelle drowned, I argue to myself. This is a fact, but the replacement vehicle of my choice is not the solution. I shell out every penny I have just earned, and a chunk more, on a second-hand Mercedes sports car. Into the boot I pile my chaotically packed bags and off I head for the ferry. I have not telephoned for a reservation; I barely know the registration number of my new acquisition; I have informed no one of my whereabouts or what I am embarking upon except my mother who, the moment she claps eyes on me when I make a stop at her home, en route for Dover, understands that I have lost the baby. She begs me not to act irrationally, to stay a while and rest or take the plane, but I won't hear of it. I must be on the move, must leave now, hell-bent on a course of my own fashioning: to begin again, pick myself up, dust myself down, be where I believe I am needed and where I have created a world; a world in which life and growth thrive. No self-pity. I must get on with the business of living.

She waves me off with that concerned expression of hers, which I know so well but barely register today.

I cross the Channel without difficulty, striding the ship's blustery deck relentlessly, back and forth like a soul lost in the swell, heaving in great gulps of salted wind, relishing the strength of its whip against my flushed face.

A certain calm descends when we draw in sight of the coast of France, but it does not last, does not stay my manic resolve. The ship drops anchor into a drizzling late morning, and I am on my way, choosing not to pause for lunch or refreshment of any sort. A full tank of *essence* and I hit the road again at rally-driving speed.

By the middle of the afternoon, having shot through the Champagne region with barely a glimpse at my surroundings, I become aware of an intermittent fluctuation in the car's performance. The rev-counter begins to flutter like a nervous butterfly. Peugeots, Renaults, Range Rovers, Porsches and other fast-moving machines gaining ground behind me begin to flash their lights, warning me to get over and out of their flight path. I have no knowledge of mechanics, and what this loss of speed or power means is unclear to me, but I swing to the right and out of the fast lane. I hear a clattering as though some vital part of the whole is trailing me. I mentally close my eyes, determined to believe that nothing is amiss and that this car is bloody well going to get me home in one piece. More or less as soon as I have completed this thought – slap-bang in the middle of the merciless jungle of a French motorway – my new acquisition grinds to a standstill. The engine is still turning, but the accelerator does not respond to the pressure of my foot and the erstwhile fluttering instrument has settled at zero. Now what?

Blind to the risks involved, I fling open the car door and step out, waving for help. Juggernauts are thundering by and horns begin to blast all around me, like rapid rounds of gunshots. The drivers, through open windows, are shouting at me in various European languages, threatening me with clenched fists as though I were doing this on purpose, or cursing me with degrees of blasphemy which amount to 'get off the fucking road', while I, stunned, am swept to and fro, weaving my way in and out of cars, until I eventually stagger back towards my stationary vehicle. I continue flailing my arms in the vain hope that one of these truckers will understand, stop and take pity. I have no mobile phone so I have no means, without assistance, of contacting anyone. After several dozen monsters have roared angrily by, one slows, his wheels or brakes emitting high-pitched squeals, and draws to a halt a hundred metres or so ahead.

The driver, a barrel of a man with blond, crewcut hair, clambers from the cab of his pantechnicon, waves and advances towards me. His gait is stiff, paddling, creating the impression that his joints are held together with screws. He is wearing a billowing scarlet T-shirt, khaki shorts, has hairy, muscular legs, solid boots and elongated cotton-wool pods sticking out of each ear. It is a means of protecting his hearing, no doubt, from the vehicle's constant rattling and the boom and roar of the motorways, but this, added to his overall appearance, inspires me to believe that I am about to be saved by a cuddly toy from outer space.

He is Belgian. He does not speak French, he explains – he must be one of the only remaining Belgians on God's earth who exclusively speaks Flemish and it's just my luck to fall upon him – but he manages to make himself understood with a spattering of English and jolly-sounding German.

After several exchanges achieved predominantly through hand signals, minutes spent staring beneath the bonnet of my wretched car, head-shakings, tuts and grave sighs, he offers to drive me to the next SOS telephone, which is a half a kilometre or so further along, or that is the gist of what I understand from the statement, 'Hare nix gut. Must you SOS calling frome ze point. Nix longe. Dry hoondred metres.'

While I, in the middle of this scorchingly hot, noisy and traffic-clogged afternoon, want to scream – not at him; he's a sweetheart – or just walk away, yes, that's it, walk off the road into the adjacent brushland, the wilderness, curl up beneath a leaf and disappear. Lose myself in the landscape, leaving everything behind me, particularly this useless sports car.

But this vat of a Belgian is a kindhearted soul who ruffles my hair and tells me not to cry, 'Not zo krying, pliss.' Then hands me his mobile phone 'Vife, you, telefon, want you?' he asks.

I shake my head, uncertain what he is offering. He shoves the phone at me again, more forcefully this time. 'Vife, Herr, Madame und Monsieur, wanting you, telefon?'

Eventually, I understand that he is lending me his mobile to call my husband.

'Thank you, but no.'

'*Pourquoi?*'

'Sydney.' He doesn't understand. 'He's in Sydney. Australia,' I reply with emphasis.

He nods uncertainly but quickly withdraws the phone.

I haul myself aboard his impossibly difficult-to-get-into cab while he rips off a length of ham baguette sandwich and offers it to me. I refuse, he shrugs and we rattle up the road to the SOS point, where he deposits me. He must be 'runnig', on his way, he explains, while writing on a sheet an excuse for his stop. 'Ist verboten de liffts,' or to help anyone out at all, it seems. Still, I am mightily grateful to him for his monumental kindness. He ruffles my hair once more, and I muster a smile for him as he waves like an old friend, calling, 'Bye bye Frau Sydney!', and zooms away in his articulated machine.

At the yellow distress box, I am informed, when I get through, that the wait will be an hour and I am firmly instructed to remain by the car. I decide that I have time to visit the next service station, which I see just a short walk ahead of me.

There, I buy a much-needed coffee, hand over 100 francs for the highest-unit phonecard on offer and put through a call to Michel in Australia. He is sleeping but instantly picks up the anguish in my voice.

'Carol? *Chérie*, what is it? What's happened?'

'We may be cut off. I'm on the motorway going back to the farm; my car has broken down.'

'Car? Which car?'

The sound of Michel's voice over such an immense distance and his concern flood my emotions and I am unable to contain my feelings. The tears pour helplessly out of me. Crouched on the floor in the cabin of the callbox, I am hiccuping and blubbering misery.

'Carol, Carol what is it? What's happened?'

'I lost her. I lost our little girl.'

There is a pause, a parenthesis, a heartstopping silence. Twelve thousand kilometres away, in another hemisphere, another time zone, my husband is taking this in.

'I'm sorry, Michel.'

'*Chérie*, where are you? Are you all right? Well, no, obviously you're not. What are you doing on a motorway? Where . . . ?'

And so I pour out my tale, or incomplete, disjointed parts of it, of the loss of our child. 'We're going to be cut off.'

'Leave the car, get to Paris. I'm coming back. Wait for me in Paris.'

'I didn't go through Paris. I'm somewhere near Beaune, I'm not sure where exactly.'

'Leave the car, then, wherever you can. Does the insurance include a relay? No, don't think about it; I'll deal with it when I get there. Go home. Promise me, you'll go home.'

I promise with a silent nod, but the line has gone dead.

Our home is our shelter from the world. Not only because it sits alone on its hill, set back from the lane and is protected by dozens of venerable, arcane olive trees and modest acres of terraced land. It is a place where Michel and I can be together, where the interface that exists between us can continue to evolve and take on its own shapes, where we can continue to create *us* and ourselves as individuals and where we can heal ourselves, lick our wounds and each other's, from the blows, the calamities and the uncertainties of life. A house is so much more than a house. It is a great deal more than its physical representation. Or it is to me, at least. For this home, this farm, is a place of healing for me in another sense, too. Perhaps in a way that it is does not need to be for Michel.

Certain eminent psychoanalysts claim that we spend our

adult lives attempting to heal the traumas of our childhood. I had never taken that idea fully on board until we moved here. For more than a decade I trawled the coasts of the world, alone, looking for 'my house by the sea', but it was not until I met Michel, until we found our abandoned olive farm, Appassionata, and set about the arduous and satisfying task of singing the place back into existence, of giving it back its elegance and its vibrancy after years of neglect, that I began to understand what I had been searching for and what I am now doing.

I am trying to heal the scars of domestic violence. To release the weight of that entrapment. To redraw the canvas, to paint over with rich, sensuous colours a childhood that was tormented by fear and burdened by guilt. To create beauty where before there was sorrow. The colours that dominate my memories are the red of my mother's painted fingernails and lips, and red again for spilled blood, the result of brutalities, the black nights in my bedroom as I lay awake listening to the hammer-and-tong exchanges in the living room beneath me, and black again for the cavern of despair that engulfed me. My father was a hot-tempered passionate man; a musician of average talent but a superb bandleader, a toastmaster (in red frock coat), a master of ceremonies with a magnetic sense of humour; charming, handsome and an incorrigible Lothario.

Once my mother, who had the lips, curves and cleavage of a Gina Lollobrigida, had given birth to my sister, she and my father grew estranged in the bedroom. Twenty-six years old at the time, she shut down that expression of herself. She believed that she had good reason for her distance – perhaps she had – but whatever it was that happened between them gave him every excuse for his endless stream of infidelities and he began to stay away from home more and more frequently.

My mother is a staunch Irish Catholic, a principled woman with an indomitable and courageous spirit, innocent in the ways of the world yet well able to gauge the worth of the material universe as well as its appraisals of her. Whatever the circumstances, she believed that it was her moral duty and her right to cling to her marriage, to hold it together and, on occasion, I believe, she has mistaken prudishness and punishment for discipline and values.

Both of these people are heedful spirits and they certainly did not set out to traumatise anyone. In fact, at my father's deathbed, as he lay unconscious, slipping away from us, it was heartbreakingly clear how deeply and loyally my mother loved him, but they had spent their lives grappling with a post-war marriage governed by Catholic values which my father did not adhere to and my mother insisted upon, and they never found the common ground where those differences could be resolved. In spite of the emotional bond, the physical differences between them left no space for their individual personalities to come together and their frustrations grew dark and angry and eventually found their outlet in violence.

I was conceived in the early days, the heyday of their relationship, the courtship days soon after the wedding. I sometimes fancy that those months were my mother at her truest, a time in her life when she let herself go and gave flight to her passionate and beautiful self. She was in love, after all.

Although I was not the trigger for their marriage, I became the habitual object of their frustrations, the reason for their imprisonment. In short, I was blamed. Children in unfulfilled marriages frequently find themselves shoved into the role of hostage. My situation was perhaps more distressing: I was cast in the role of jailer. 'If it wasn't for you, we wouldn't be in this mess, this marriage.' These words were hurled out thoughtlessly at all too regular intervals; they

turned my blood cold and stripped my ribboned heart to
shreds.

   The world looked at and lived through my disturbed eyes
was an angry, violent place where folk who lived together
expressed themselves through physical and emotional bru-
tality; where furniture was slung from room's end to room's
end; where tables bearing hot food crashed to the ground
like shot beasts spewing clots of baked beans, soggy toast,
smashed plates; where I pressed my ear against closed doors
and eavesdropped on the tinkly sound of my mother's solitary weeping, hovering, not knocking, impotent to offer
succour. In fact, not only was I unable to help, as I understood it I was the cause of the tears. Where friendships made
at school disintegrated in an instant when the new attachment was, eventually, like all the rest, forbidden to come to
my home because I and my background were judged a 'bad
influence'. In among all this there were moments of tender-
ness for, as I say, my parents were not cruel people, merely
trapped in a marriage from which they felt unable to free
themselves, or perhaps, deep down, did not want to walk
away from.

My newly acquired possession is towed away to the nearest
Mercedes garage, who agree to organise its relay to Cannes
where, they assure me, the vehicle's British guarantee will be
sorted out. I learn from my insurers that I am entitled to a
hire car, but I decline it. At this moment in time, I am safer
off the roads. They offer me a first-class rail ticket instead. I
spend the night in a very indifferent hotel and then, with my
ill-assorted bags, cases and confusions, take a late-morning
express to Cannes. The TGV I am travelling on is not
equipped with bar or restaurant. This is most surprising for
a nation of meal-lovers, but my fellow passengers seem to be
au fait with the oversight and have come prepared. As *midi*

approaches – the hour for lunch – everyone in the carriage, bar me, begins unloading their lunchboxes, well-provisioned with sandwiches, *charcuterie*, a little *fromage*, coffee, mineral water, dried fruits, fresh grapes, oranges and Mentos mints. They lay out their generous portions of refreshment on their laps or on portable picnic tables, accompanying it with plastic glasses brimming with red wine.

Opposite me sits a huge woman with a Felliniesque bosom, kitted out in matching red cardigan and skirt and chunks of gold and ruby jewellery. Her feet planted firmly on the ground, skirt riding up to her thighs, legs wide apart, she has been nibbling since I boarded while at the same time amusing herself with a crossword magazine. Mouthing possible solutions to her puzzle, she is now chewing bovinely on a baguette sandwich of lettuce, tomato, ham and cheese.

Everyone is content with this lovely sunny day, a little light nourishment to keep inordinate hunger at bay and the impressive countryside flying past the window, when two new travellers arrive and a rumpus begins.

It appears to be a question of seat numbers.

It seems that we have all been allocated seats 21 and 23 in carriage 13. It was of no matter as far back as Chalon-sur-Saône. We all took a seat, any seat, and settled down. But now a heavily made-up Arab woman has climbed aboard at some inconsequential station with seven massive suitcases and a child and insists that two seats in our compartment, only one of which remains unoccupied, are hers. Much heated shouting breaks out and the matter threatens to grow disagreeable.

'I've been sitting here since Nancy and I'm not budging!' booms the woman who resembles an extra from *Amacord*, in between mouthfuls of food.

Eventually a guard appears on the scene and the entire carriage, to a man, save me, pounces on him, shouting hysterically, demanding facts, explanations and, above all else, apologies for potential damage to their digestive tracts. 'We were *eating*!' they yell.

'Sit where you can,' he announces. 'Carriage 14 has been forgotten; left in Metz.'

'*Eh, voilà!*'

'*Mais oui, on comprend maintenant.*'

The misunderstanding has been explained to the satisfaction of everyone. Unfortunately, the difficulty remains. The bevy of lunching women, and one rather timid husband who is nervously twisting his copy of *Le Monde*, are not willing to vacate their places, while the Arab woman mulishly refuses to seek out another carriage.

Eventually, when everyone is worn out, it is decided to turf the Arab child into the corridor and install her on suitcases, leaving her mother free to claim the remaining seat. Calm is restored and lunch is resumed. I watch the little Arab girl perching sulkily on one of her mother's numerous *valises*. She is hungrily eyeing the delicious offerings of the various passengers who are munching contentedly while gazing blithely out at the passing vineyards.

Nothing disturbs the ensuing peace now except our large companion in the red woolly outfit, who is travelling with a print-out of her itinerary. At each station she reaches for it and announces to us all the length of time the train is scheduled to stand in the station.

'Mâcon! *Deux minutes!*' At one minute forty seconds her stubby fingers with their burgundy-varnished nails and 'rubies as big as hen's eggs' (in Scott Fitzgerald's words), begin tapping the face of her gold watch. She peers at it and tuts crossly. This is followed by loud huffings and the rolling up of her crossword magazine so that it now resembles a short, thick cane. And then the train pulls out and she relaxes back into her lunch.

I believe I am the only one to notice a rather interesting

exchange taking place about now. The Arab child in the corridor signals to her mother from beyond the glass that she
wants food and the mother responds, also in discreet mime,
that she has none.

We roll along in silence for a short while until suddenly
the Arab woman wails loudly and dramatically: '*J'ai mal au
cœur!*' 'My heart! I'm sick! A pain in my heart!'

I am perfectly fascinated.

'*Ah, ma pauvre!* I have pills,' cries the fat woman, and
instantly begins rummaging in her handbag for her heart
pills and her mineral water – not still water but the *gazeuse*,
which, she assures us all, is better for the digestion. 'You
must have eaten something which disagreed with you,' she
continues.

'No, no, my heart feels tight. No, I haven't eaten. Nothing
at all. We haven't eaten since—'

'You haven't eaten? *Mon Dieu!*' The words are chorused
across the carriage. Folk jump to it. A *demi-baguette* is
found, a lump of Brie. The fizzy water is delivered. As are the
heart pills.

'Have you a glass?' the heart-of-gold fat lady enquires as
she passes over her bottle.

The Arab woman shakes her head faintheartedly.
'Nothing. No time to pack it.'

'Use mine. Yes, you must. I insist. I am eighty years old. If
I had any diseases I would know them by now.'

Eighty years old! This, too, is repeated like a Chinese
whisper by one passenger to the next. It is true that the
woman does not look such an age. The Arab mother keeps
up her play-acting admirably, determined not to let the age of
the other detract from the business in hand. She is now
drinking the water while fanning herself and moaning softly.
She resists the pill, but it is forced upon her and so, reluc-
tantly, she swallows it. We have reached Lyon. The timid

husband and his axe-faced wife are now leaving the train.
But not before the husband has been ordered by his wife to
place all seven pieces of the Arab woman's luggage up on the
rack and offer his seat to the ragamuffin girl, who takes it
without a second's hesitation. As they depart, they leave the
remains of their buffet for mother and child, who eat like
greedy street urchins.

I return to my private contemplations both amused and
surprised that this little scam has worked so successfully.

The last I hear, as they all descend the train together at
Marseille, the very best of friends, is our octogenarian
remarking: 'I ask you, what is more beautiful for any *maman*
than the gift of a little girl?'

A reminder, a stab of a pain, and I switch my gaze to
beyond the window, to the silver sadness of the sea.

From the station, a taxi delivers me up into the sun-scorched
hills, to Appassionata. When I arrive – cautious of the dogs,
the driver deposits me at the gate – I climb the olive-ter-
raced drive, pausing every few yards to touch and examine
the drupes, which are green and hard but fattening up nicely.
The trees glinting in the sunshine are, in the words of
Auguste Renoir, who lived his last years on the coast here at
Cagnes-sur-Mer, 'shining like diamonds'.

I pause to pick a purpling fig from our elephantine tree
and split it open with my thumbnails. A satin-white milk
bleeds out of the still unripe fruit and sticks to my fingers. I
lick them clean and then lift the fig to my lips and suck out
the pale rose, mildly crunchy seeds.

Le figuier. The fig tree. Its botanical origins are uncertain
but, most likely, it has been a native Mediterranean plant
from prehistoric times, growing wild with fruits which were
at first believed to be inedible. It is possible that this may be

the thinking behind its role in the Garden of Eden. Unlike the apple, it could not be consumed. It was a useless thing, good for nothing until its leaf was used as the earliest, most primitive form of underwear. Adam and Eve took it to cover their shame, their sex, their knowledge and nakedness. Or, if Titian's painting of Adam and Eve in the Prado in Madrid is to be believed, it was Adam, the man, who understood shame and covered himself. Woman was the sinner.

Puberty arrived early for me. I was ten. Around this time, men who came to the house, usually friends or associates of my father's, began to whisper obscene desires in my ear or touched me in places on my body which left me feeling ashamed of the fullnesses forming there. I grew to perceive myself as a she-devil who induced inexplicable behaviour in heavy-breathing, sour-breathed men. My parents knew nothing of what was happening and I did not have the courage, or faith, to say anything. I believed that, like their marriage, I was to blame for these male manners. I grew withdrawn and secretive. I spent hour after hour locked in the bathroom, washing myself, not clean but out of existence.

I chew on my fig and feast my eyes, inhaling the mid-year quietude. All around is stillness. The farm is at peace in the summer heat, except for the *cigales*, who are buzzing frenetically, living their final weeks to the hilt, making the most of it, searching for a partner while the going is good, for after their frenzied bouts of mating these little critters pass away. There are no signs of activity and then, in a trice, the dogs come bounding from a dozen different directions all at once, charging at me to greet me with welcoming barks and leapings and wildly overenthusiastic felicity. How pleased I am to have their affection. I bend and stroke and kiss them hard.

M. Halaz, our watering hero, is nowhere to be seen. He

must have finished his chores and trundled off for a siesta. His presence is everywhere, though, in the fabulous firework displays of growth.

Shrubs, flowers, climbers are explosions of breathtaking colour. Geraniums are tumbling eagerly from their terracotta pots in bouquets of scarlet and pink and striped reds and whites, hanging like swathes of uncombed hair over the tiled edge of the pool, where one or two stray blossoms have fallen and are spinning gently in the movement of the water. The bougainvillaea bushes straddling the four lower verandah pillars have shot up in a lusty tangle of leaves and flowers, reached the upper terrace and are snaking themselves around the balustrades. Our spring wistaria, which rarely flowers twice, is dripping with blossoming racemes, smaller, more fragile, but blooming, while the roses, which never fare well in our devilish midsummer heat, are bursting forth everywhere. Further to the left of the *terrain* are the vegetable patches. I see the aubergine plants are still fruiting tiny golden tomatoes. I cannot bear to look, and instantly swing my gaze a terrace lower, where the branches of our *quatre saisons* lemon tree are bowing beneath the weight of their offerings.

No one is entirely sure where the lemon tree originated. There are no references to it in any Latin sources. The first mention of *le citronnier* in literature appears to have been in south-east Asia, further east than the earliest-known olive-tree topography, but both the lemon and the orange tree have been growing on this south-eastern French coastline since the Middle Ages. Interestingly, that is much later than the Greek or Roman occupations here, so it is possible that it was neither of these cultures who contributed this member of the citrus family to the Provençal way of life.

*

In every direction, the garden is an intoxicating celebration of life, which is precisely what I have been craving, and the tiled terraces are as pristine as freshly scrubbed floors. I have every reason to delight in being back home, and how I do delight in it. This homecoming contributes heartily to my determination to move forward and not give in to the weight of sorrow that is gnawing at my gut. I have already wasted money and time on an ill-considered purchase and now I must re-establish my equilibrium and get back to work as soon as possible.

As I pass the stables, still struggling with my luggage, I see that Halaz has dug out every broom the farm owns as well as others I was not even aware we possessed and lined them all up. The count is nine, all of varying shapes and sizes; an assortment of textures and materials for a variety of purposes, standing sentinel like solemn soldiers against one of the outer walls, heads upwards, airing and drying in the sun.

The villa, which has been closed up during these away-from-home weeks, is heavy with trapped, summer inactivity. It reeks of dried herbs, forgotten flowers and, in the bathroom, lingering whiffs of my Chanel No. 5 perfume. I throw open the shutters to let the light flood in and find dust and cobwebs everywhere. Three bright-green stink bugs fall to the floor and lie on their backs, writhing. They are pests to our vegetable beds. Even so, I turn them over and leave them be. Geckos scuttle into shadows, climbing walls at a speed which amazes. On the dining table there lies a stack of curling mail, mostly bills, which can be dealt with later and, hanging like a tongue from the telephone in my den, is a faxed message from Michel. It welcomes me home, begs me to reassure him that I have arrived safely and acquaints me with great tidings: he has managed to change his flight and will be landing in London at dawn the day after tomorrow. Assuming there is no intercontinental delay, his 9.05 plane from Heathrow to Nice will transport him home well in time for lunch. Thirty-six hours to go till love returns on 'the wings of the morning'.

I decide that, after I have ripped off my clothes and dived into the pool – better to do it now before M. Halaz wanders back up and has another seizure – I will consecrate the remainder of the day to mundane, organisational matters so that tomorrow, tomorrow I can indulge my yearning by making an early-morning pilgrimage to the sea, though to which beach I am still undecided. I am considering Antibes.

Antipolis, the classical Greek name meaning 'the city opposite', was bestowed upon the port they founded west of Nice, directly across the Baie des Anges, in the late sixth century BC. Today it is better known as Antibes or, in the Provençal language, Antibou. There is debate even now among scholars as to whether the Greeks were intending its name to describe the harbour's relationship to Nice – Nikaia to the Greeks and Niço to the Provençal people – or to the island of Corsica or even to their most hostile of enemies, the Ligurians of Liguria, now part of northern Italy.

When the Romans conquered this province, threw out the Greeks and took possession of this northern Mediterranean coast of France, Antibes became as strategically important to them as Fréjus. They used it as a stopover for their coastal fleets travelling between Italy and Arles. So valued was the town that they honoured it as a *civita romana* instead of deeming it a mere colony.

Today, this seaside port and holiday resort is still famous for its harbour and many, if not most, of its inhabitants are foreigners or members of the itinerant yachting community. Soon after we found our farm, while we were embarking upon the lengthy process of moving down here, setting up home and actually acquiring the deeds, I used to

make regular Monday-morning coffee stops one lane back
from that port after kissing Michel goodbye at the airport,
where he was set to board the dawn flight to Paris. I would
sit at a table alone in the rising heat of the morning sunshine, drink several large cups of *café au lait* and watch,
with a child's admiring gaze, an elderly man frequently
seated at the table next to me, who was awaiting the
arrival of the London *Times*. He was, and remains, one of
my heroes, Graham Greene. Later, I was fortunate enough
to make his acquaintance and exchange precious words
with him, but in those early days, during that first warm
summer of discovery, I was too shy, too tongue-tied and
too in awe of him to strike up a conversation.

It was the owner of the café who told me that M. Greene
was a year-round regular at his establishment, and that the
acclaimed author lived nearby, not in Antibes itself but on its
verdant cape a short drive along the coast.

'If you haven't made a tour of the cape,' the patron told
me, 'you must. There are fine beaches all along its coastline.
And a wealth of artists and writers have passed through the
doors of its luxurious villas. The place is legendary.'

Of course, in the years since we first arrived here, we have
visited on many occasions the legendary *cap* that M. Greene
inhabited and I never tire of its rugged beauty.

Two childhood passions became my lifebelt and gave me the
wherewithal to battle on and to dream beyond those early
stages of life to a time when I would be grown up, when I
could escape and play roles other than that of the bane of
someone's life.

Both these pastimes were lived out in isolation, in the
make-believe worlds of a damaged child's creation.

The first was Tireless Scribblings. I bled Biros dry expressing heartfelt thoughts in a quest for meaning, for the key to

the puzzle, filling notepads with quotations squirreled from books, self-pitying poetry and, later, lovesick sonnets. I wrote plays such as *The Story of Robin Hood*, which I staged at school and at charity institutions. The Cheshire Home for the Retired was one such establishment. Looking back, I am convinced that none of those bemused pensioners had a clue what I and my classmates were about, nor what my almost certainly ill-constructed story was saying. I was twelve at the time. I walked home in the autumnal darkness feeling despondent and perplexed by their lukewarm responses. Twelve, and already staring Critical Acclaim in the back. Curiously, though, the experience cemented my desire to write.

My second survival mechanism was Dressing Up. At some stage my father had acquired an entire costume department from a local amateur theatre that had lost its funding and was closing down. Most of these he stored in a long glass conservatory in the garden, while the rest went into the spare bedroom, which consequently reeked of stale sweat, mothballs and the faint traces of the panstick stage make-up which still stained collars and cuffs. This was where I was exiled as a punishment, and punishment it could be. Late at night the costumes, particularly the dark frock coats, terrified me because I was convinced they were moving, inhabited by invisible spirits.

However, in the hours of daylight I loved this room, because it had a square wooden rostrum in one corner – something to do with the design of the stairs – which became my theatre. Here I painstakingly pieced together a monster circular jigsaw which I kept laid out for reference. It showed a bust of Shakespeare surrounded by a still life from each of his thirty-seven plays. I studied those drawn characters, trying to imagine how they sounded, moved and behaved. Decked out in impossibly large and fraying costumes from those metal racks, tripping over dragging hems, I attempted to breathe life into my interpretations, reciting with intense ardour and dramatic emphasis the master's lines, struggling to find meaning in words weird and unfamiliar to me, such as 'coxcomb', 'palfrey' and 'humours'.

In the course of any one, usually rainy, afternoon I could be transformed into Mistress Quickly, 'Proud' Titania, Hermione, Rosalind, Viola, Shakespeare himself, with his goatee beard, which I drew on my face with a crayon, as well as his wife Anne (my middle name) Whateley of Temple Grafton, whom I had vaguely read about. But the character I loved the best, the queen of them all, the glamorous mistress and goddess of love, was Will's Egyptian monarch, Cleopatra who, in my mind's eye, possessed the luxuriant black hair, the curves, cleavage, low-cut frocks, stiletto heels and red lips of my mother. She exuded passion, had inspired war and epic emotions. She would have no truck with the grubby, furtive fumblings of decrepit old men, which was how the visitors to my parents' house appeared to this pubescent girl.

To recite her lines, enact that embodiment of femininity, would inspire applause, bouquets of flowers and international acclaim. Thus it was here, in those nights of isolated agony as well as in the hours I spent in empty auditoriums watching my charismatic father rehearse with his musicians, that my actress's 'immortal longings' and deep-rooted ambition were born. My dreams grew grandiose. I pictured myself as a movie star – Katharine Hepburn in *Stage Door* – or as a grande dame of the theatre, and I longed for the days when I might stand on a stage, gaze beyond the footlights and be uproariously applauded and adored.

For many years acting and my devotion to its craft gave me a vocation. I channelled all my confused emotions into work and my creative universe, but I discovered early on that there were two areas of this life that were unsatisfactory. The first was that the parts on offer to women, particularly on television or for the cinema, were not as varied or as challenging as those I had allocated to myself in the spare bedroom. Usually the choices were delineated by men's ideas of the woman's role, the woman's look, and, in my twenties, I frequently did not have the right look, did not fit the picture. I was too plump, too voluptuous. Secondly, there always came the moment when it was time to go home: the end of the day or, worse, the end of the shoot.

Home was a rented top-floor flat in Kentish Town where I lived alone. Sometimes, in the early, struggling days, I would let out a room to one fellow actor or another to help pay the bills, and sometimes there were mates staying who were passing through town or who had been thrown out of their own base by an erstwhile partner. In other words, I had company. Frequently, we whiled away the midnight hours listening to rock and jazz music, drinking bottles of rather poor wine, Hirondelle or Bulgarian Bull's Blood. Sometimes, I went to bed with one male friend or another and, occasionally, I had an affair which, for a brief period of time, actually made me quite happy and reasonably excited about life. There was one longish-term on-off romance with a young actor I cared deeply for, but it did not last. He married someone else. So nothing, no one, assuaged the emptiness I carried around within me. It was profound, but it was also relatively unconscious.

I believe now that I shadow-boxed with love, cloaked everything in a romantic haze. Much of the loving part of my nature, the nurturing side, I had cordoned off somewhere during my tormented teens. Outwardly, I was feminine, flirtatious and romantic, but within I was defensive, brutalised and terrified to reveal more of myself than I could regulate. I feared that the *real* me, the angry, abused young person, would explode like a volcano and overwhelm anyone who came too close. I was incapable of entrusting another with my heart; it was way too scrambled an organ. The deepest of my female urges, the atavistic desires for partnership and childbearing, I poured into my ambition. I never disclosed my past. I rarely talked about my private life at all, even to very close companions. I spent my out-of-work days, or my off-set hours, if I was filming away from London, on my own, travelling, searching for what I described as 'my house by the sea', which I don't believe, back then, I thought would ever materialise.

The following morning I am out of bed and clear of the house by sunrise or, in Colette's words, *à la naissance du jour*, making not for the sixteenth-century fortressed town of Antibes, because the town's beach is small and not very interesting, but to that legendary peninsula the Cap d'Antibes. In this season there is no possibility of enjoying the coast or of hoping for a moment to oneself unless you arrive bright and early and are gone before the tourists have woken, for once they are up and about the beaches and the cafés are seething with activity.

Taking Michel's deafening old car because we have no other transport, I hit the coast on the Cannes side of Golfe Juan and from there drive alongside the gently lapping sea, hugging the pearly, calm waterfront. The sun is rising beyond the Alps into a cloudless, iris-blue sky. Chugging past Tetou and Nounou, the two well-known fish restaurants, both deeply fashionable and renowned for their delicious bouillabaisse and, in the case of Tetou, astounding prices, I am reminded of the time Michel and I dined at Nonou, where we were seated at a table next to Vera Lynn and her late husband, Harry. Afterwards, Michel asked me about the elegant woman we had been talking to and I told him that, during the Second World War, Vera had been dubbed the Forces'

Sweetheart. Her name meant nothing to him, which served to emphasise the years and the different lives we had inhabited before our worlds so sweetly collided. Our fathers, neither of whom were actually in combat, were nonetheless on opposite sides of the war in which Vera sang for the British troops.

I drive on, passing through the beach town of Juan-les-Pins which, thanks to the influx of rich, partygoing Americans, became the hot spot on this stretch of coast in the 1920s, the Jazz Age. I am making for the western side of the *cap*. Yards from the shore, perched in the sunshine on glistening wet rocks, I spy several black cormorants, and there are Mediterranean, black-headed and herring gulls flocking and swooping everywhere. This is hardly surprising, given that the early-bird fishermen with their baguette breakfasts, coffee flasks and woven fishing baskets inhabit this rocky coastline. I count eleven already.

I am right alongside the Musée Naval et Napoléonien. Stylish tracksuited joggers, sweatbands keeping expensively cut hair out of eyes, remind me that this museum neighbours the exclusive Hôtel du Cap Eden Roc, situated on the south-western tip of the cape. I peer in through its imposing black iron gates at the fabulous palm-lined alleys. This fashionable address was immortalised as the Hôtel des Etrangers in Scott Fitzgerald's novel *Tender is the Night*.

The Eden Roc was the first hotel on the Côte d'Azur to construct an open-air swimming pool. It was also the first to throw open its doors to summer guests. That was in 1923, the year Coco Chanel, in the company of the Duke of Westminster, broke with tradition and escaped Paris to enjoy this coast as a summer visitor. Until then the Riviera had always been a fashionable winter resort and dead to the chic world for the remaining months of the year.

I am travelling along John F. Kennedy Boulevard. Not far

from here, buried in a wooded *parc*, is the Jardin Thuret, created in 1856, where the British planted the very first eucalyptus trees, which they had imported from Australia. President Kennedy was also a visitor to this neck of the woods. Half a mile or so back, I passed the magnificent beachside art-deco villa where in times gone by he was a guest, as was Marilyn Monroe, along with numerous other luminaries.

In the early days, before I knew who had graced its terraces, every time we drove past that well-proportioned cube of white house, sitting *pieds dans l'eau*, from where you can climb straight out of bed, gaze beyond the rocky, shorelined garden across the sweeping, semi-circular bay known as Port de l'Olivette to Cannes and, still clad in your silk pyjamas if that's your fancy, dive directly into the Med, I used to say to Michel: 'I wouldn't mind owning that villa.'

I began to feel like Charles Dickens who, walking up a hill in the Medway town of Chatham in Kent and passing his favourite house, used to make a similar statement to his father every morning: 'One day I am going to own that house.' Later in his life, when he was a bestselling author, he bought the house of his dreams. When this villa went on the market recently and I heard about it, for no more justifiable reasons than avarice and curiosity, I telephoned the agents. Yes, they said, it is for sale. 'How much?' I asked. A snip, at £7 million.

Years ago when I first began looking for 'my house by the sea', I had no clear idea of where that Elysium would be, what it would look like or if it could ever exist, but what I knew for certain was that it would be an enchanted place, vibrant and ringing with joy and passion. My childhood had upped the stakes, as it were, for what was required of that house by the sea. Generations of families, visitors, artists and friends would pass through its doors and leave traces of themselves, their imprints, behind them. There would be animals, there would be music and laughter and a free-spiritedness fed by the nature and the climate and home-grown food and the chaotic, unlikely combinations of the people present. And, at the centre of it, the axis that made it all spin, would be love. A love which would offer me peace of mind and the freedom to creep away and write; a love that would encourage me, enable me to discover who I am. And a love that bore children, innocent infants running about naked, unselfconscious and safe.

I signal and turn right into a seemingly insignificant tree-shaded *chemin*, actually adorned with gracious villas, which leads me to the renowned Plage de la Garoupe.

Here I park and sit a moment to contemplate the awesome beauty of the natural arena laid out before me. In the distance beyond the Baie des Anges, the amphitheatre of Alps. In the olden days, before roads were cut through, they served as a natural protection for Nice against inclement weather and unwanted invaders. In winter, they are a deep purple and capped at the summits by snow. This morning, they are a blueish-mulberry in the early light.

I shan't swim in this bay today. It is full-blown summer and the sea is heaving with svelte ivory yachts. Many of the yachties ditch their detritus overboard, sullying the shallow waters. Before I was wise to their habits, I once swam into a used Tampax and, believe me, I, who will frolic in a turbid puddle, was out of those waves like greased lightning.

I change into sneakers, take my costume and towel and set off along the path, the *sentier pédestre*, which winds its way around the cape and which, at this hour, is almost deserted. As I approach the small easterly point known as Cap Gros I see two wetsuited divers wading into the water, hauling their oxygen masks and lungs. I wonder what they are going after. I have never dived these waters but I know that neither the visibility nor the marine life here is exceptional. Distant sail-boats at full mast flag the horizon. Startling white against milky blue.

Behind me, set back from the beach, hidden somewhere within the thickets of the lean-trunked *pins parasols*, is the renowned Château de la Garoupe, rented by Cole Porter in 1922, where Scott and Zelda Fitzgerald got regularly soused on whisky sours.

There are a handful of dog-owners at the water's edge, trailed by their fluffy boutique canines yapping and snapping and jumping up and down on their hind legs. How I would love to bring my rabble-rousers to splash in and out of the wash here but it would be impossible. They'd wreak havoc everywhere and terrorise all these chaps.

The sudden roar of an engine startles me and a young man on his white fibreglass water scooter comes skirring by, churning up the calm sea.

I spy another dawn bather. An elderly bowlegged gentle-man in a pale blue swimming cap – the French call them *bonnets*, so delightfully Edwardian – is clambering over the sharp, slippery rocks in his plastic reef shoes. I wriggle into my costume and follow suit. There are saltwater pools every-where, still as dark night, in among the dun-and-white rocks bleached by the dry heat. They sometimes give harbour to *les oursins*, sea urchins, whose five rose-coloured ovaries, dug out of the belly of the creature, make for one of the great seafood delicacies down here, particularly when used in omelettes or scrambled eggs. Today they are just another reason for the plastic shoes, because you don't want to acci-dentally step on a sea urchin and end up with one of its black spines through the sole of your foot.

Once at the water's edge, I wedge my buttocks securely

between two boulders, pause to inhale that haunting, sing-song wash of waves licking against a rough barnacled strand, dip my toes into the water, shiver at its delicious tingliness and then plunge myself, stomach first, into the sea.

My father was discharged from the Air Force into postwar Britain. When he met my mother, at a dance hall in south London, she was a trainee hospital ward sister. It was a whirlwind romance. Money was scarce. One Saturday morning, the young couple installed themselves in the top two rooms of my grandparents' rented four-storey house in Brixton, south London, and went off in Grandad's horse-drawn taxi cab to get married. No honeymoon was planned. But one Saturday not long afterwards my father checked his football pools coupon and discovered that he had won £180. 'It was a bloody fortune.' He was due to share this princely sum with his father, who had chipped in fifty per cent for the coupon, but his dad would take only £80, saying that Peter should keep the hundred as he was newly wed.

So my parents treated themselves. They purchased two train tickets and set off at the beginning of October in the observation car of the *Devon Belle* for a week's holiday at the Grand Hotel in Torquay. I was there, in a manner of speaking, accompanying them on that heady honeymoon. A silent, subaquatic witness seesawing about in the womb, my ear to the neck, listening to everything.

Later, they occasionally spoke of those days – how they strolled the beaches hand in hand, visited antique shops and country pubs and made a stopover in a farmhouse in Combe Martin – eulogising the holiday and my father's timely windfall. It was out of season, but 'the weather was gorgeous'. It was a benchmark for their lost happiness, I suppose. And I have often wondered if those seven harmonious days didn't sow the seeds of my addiction to the sea, my sense of it as a 'palmy state', a providential environment.

The water is deliciously cool and tangy. Once I have immersed my entire body, I flip over on to my back then kick out a distance so that I can float in peace and quiet without being washed back by the current towards the shore. Bobbing with the beat of the waves, arms and legs outstretched like a Da Vinci diagram, I surrender my traumatised body to the water's saline buoyancy, to its thalassic remedial powers, and ponder the ether. It seems that I will never know the pain of birth, the breaking of waters, the joy, relief and exhaustion of delivery. Ours was to have been a Christmas baby. I had been dreaming of long evenings by the log-filled fireplace, and now . . . the anguish of childlessness.

A gentle offshore breeze lifts dampened wisps of my long hair, which settle across my face. The sun, rising hot and fast to the left of me, penetrates my bare, scrubbed skin while illuminating the ghost of a muslin-white, gibbous moon. Overhead, in that same dense expanse of blueness, soaring over mountains and sea, a plane, no, two, en route for Nice airport, leave vapour trails. Two white zips, dividing up, peeling open, the inexorable azureness of this Côte d'Azur sky.

Why has this happened to me? That is the question to which I am seeking an answer. No, I am not seeking, I am demanding. I want to know *why*. Why *me?*

Perfect silence, save for waves and screeching herring gulls and distant cries from the shore.

Within the breaches of the division above me, no booming voice of God speaks back; no Old Testament explanation is forthcoming. Nothing is answered, nothing clarified. As far as the Man Above is concerned, I must sort it out for myself.

Or does the answer lie somewhere within the realisation that this is not simply another sticky situation? Throughout my life I have managed to engineer my way out of those. I pride myself on quick thinking, finding ways through, but I cannot negotiate or act my way out of this one. This is a given. One of those junctures from which there is no going back. Not dissimilar to the death of a parent or loss of a loved one, it has to be taken on board. I cannot cast this loss, this set of circumstances, aside. I cannot rejig or rewrite this script.

So now it is down to me. I must find a way through, *and I will*. I have everything to be grateful for. Not least the golden splendour of this morning.

And so, that's it, is it? The response to my cry? It is not for me to reason why. My role is to accept – or not – to get on with it, for there lies wisdom, or sanity, at least.

Tomorrow, Michel will be home and I am already grateful, eternally grateful, for his approaching presence, for the spell of his warm embraces and those fabulous blue eyes filled with care and compassion.

And the love that illumines my house by the sea.

Love Rediscovered

I see him approach, wheeling a trolley full of luggage, eyes cast to left and right, searching for me as the doors swing automatically apart.

'Michel!' I wave vigorously and, in among the early-morning coasties in shorts and well-polished suntans, he spies me and smiles broadly. I never grow blasé about this moment, this first sighting of him after a long absence. My stomach flips like a girl's as I hurry through the press of people. He looks zonked. That first embrace. He hugs me tight, so tightly I think I might faint. His lips brush my hair. I hear him exhale as though landing – here, where we belong – then, locked together, we make our way, bumping against one another, out of the arrivals hall.

Having someone there to care makes all the difference. It feeds the spirit. We tend one another. He has been travelling for twenty-eight hours non-stop, those long legs crammed into spaces they were not born for. He needs a shower, or a swim, but first a decent cup of French coffee, and then, afterwards, we breakfast on the terrace: yoghurt and strawberries and slices of honeydew melon and *six cereales* bread, spread with marmalade made from our own oranges.

'You are wearing the necklace.'

'I haven't taken it off, except to film. It's beautiful. Thank you.'

'No more travelling,' he says. 'We are neither of us going anywhere for at least a month.'

His hand on my hip, slipped around my waist, I feel reassured. There is time and there is reason to heal.

Days of intimacy. Talking, listening. I talk, Michel listens.

'I'm afraid,' I tell him. 'And I feel a failure.'

He hammers hooks into the trunks of a great oak and an ancient olive and hitches up the hammock in the leafy shade. We bury ourselves in it, wrap it about us, a vibrantly coloured cocoon, rocking together, cradled out of the heat.

'What name did you choose?' I whisper eventually.

'*Chérie*, please, try not to hurt yourself like this.'

'No, that's not what I'm doing. I'd like to humanise her. It will help me, if you don't mind. If it doesn't hurt you.'

He reflects upon this and then wraps himself tighter about me. I feel his breath against my cheek, the familiarity of his intimacy. One word, he whispers in my ear, and then, in the space of a single exhalation, it has disappeared, spirited away by the breeze in the overhead branches.

'Yes, I like that.' I smile, fastening on it. 'Can you guess what I chose? Well, I didn't choose, exactly. She did, I think. She *became* the name. Shall I tell you?' I insist.

'If you want to.'

'Carrot.'

He frowns, puzzled, I am sure, by the unlikely tag.

'Don't laugh.'

'I'm not.'

'Nothing else seemed to fit. I doubt that she would have been born with red hair or any of the characteristics we might associate with such a nickname. She would probably have been blessed with our olive skin and long unkempt curls. But the name persisted. I tried to shoo it away until, finally, I acknowledged it, welcomed her thus and we began to communicate with one another using it. Carrot.'

I turn towards him, his face in the dappled shadows. He seems to understand, or accepts my madness, at least.

Mornings, rediscovering one another. For ever touching. Growing reaccustomed to the silky or rough feel of one another. To the partnership of love. His medicine: 'strokings'. Hours, he spends, stroking me. Every part of me: cracks, crevices, curves, soothing away my pain. Evenings to ourselves. Sitting in rickety wooden chairs, silently, side by side, watching the sun go down. Waiting for night to fall. Nights in white linen. Pushing out the night boat, drowning in love. *Les nuits blanches.*

There are the occasions, though, when I wake towards dawn in a sweat, crazed, hair in a tangle, haunted by nightmares, and find him, like a Chinese puzzle, entwined about me. Limbs slipped into limbs. His breath on my shoulder. '*Calme-toi, chérie.* Come here, cuddle up close.' Tight against one another like spoons in a canteen of cutlery. Spooning, breathing in unison, I quieten.

And, later, after repose, eyes opening to discover another, baking new day. Glad to be alive. The morning sky the blue of tit's wings, *bleuté.* Yes, the days are as lovely as a story.

Into one of these baking days, these days of 'stroking', comes a letter from ONIOL. I stare at the envelope. ONIOL. Planting olive trees. It reminds me of spring, of our plans for the farm. Of our trip to Marseille. When I was pregnant. The letter lists the approved nurseries for the purchase of olive trees. Nearest to us is one deep in the heart of the Var, behind Hyères, in the *arrière-pays*, La Londe les Maures.

'Before the girls arrive,' Michel suggests, 'we should go and take a look.'

'I'd rather not,' I answer.

This baffles him. 'Why not? We can make a day of it, stop somewhere for lunch, find a *domaine* vineyard and stock up on rosé.'

'I don't want to plant the extra trees.'

He says nothing. Silenced by surprise, wary of where this is leading. And then, eventually, 'We need the extension, *chérie*, if we are to be offered our AOC. They won't accept us as serious *oléiculteurs* without the required minimum of trees.'

'We don't need an olive-oil award. We're happy this way.' I feel the catch in my throat. 'What I mean is, I don't want to get lost in . . . Let's just accept everything the way that it is.'

'Why?'

'I don't think I can . . . I can't cope.'

I gather up our breakfast plates, rise to move inside. He takes my arm. His blue eyes bore into me. Crinkled features burned by sun.

'Of course you can. There's no question about it. But I don't want to force this decision on you. Still, I see no reason why we shouldn't make the trip A leisurely olive-tree recce, and afterwards, we can find a hotel on the beach. We could stay overnight. The girls will be arriving soon, and I have spoken to Serge again about paying us a visit and I think the idea is beginning to appeal to him. So let's visit the nursery, see what we think and make our decisions later.'

'Do you think that old car will stand the journey?'

'It's doing better than yours.'

I smile. So does he.

'That's settled, then.'

We set off the next day at the crack of dawn, because that is what Michel likes to do. We take the inland road, avoiding the autoroute and the south-seeking tourists. Oleander blossoms, vivid colours everywhere and sweeping hillsides furnished in green by the herby brush of the familiar *maquis*. Passing through leafy lanes of chestnuts, with olive fields beyond, moving westwards until we reach the Var wine districts. To left and right climb the cambered hills, green with vines, their dark grapes ripening like pendulous udders awaiting milking.

As morning hails us, so too do the mountains of Maures, almost as if from nowhere; there, rising up in front of us. Lilac and rust in the early light. The wooded summits of the Massif des Maures.

'Oh, my God!' I exclaim, taken aback by the beauty, the stillness, the sheer mountainness rising up out of a burnished landscape. 'It reminds me of Ayers Rock. I don't know why.'

'High, empty sky. Hot, flat land, that's why.'

'The name Maures comes from the Provençal word *maouro*, meaning dark.'

We snake left, following the trace of the road, hugging the curve of the mountain base – no access blasted through its centre – and head for the coast.

'I think breakfast at the beach. What do you say?'

We hit the water west of the city of Hyères and negotiate our way to a very pretty fishing port. The world has woken up. Cars are zipping to and fro, hooting and screeching. Urban sounds. I smell coffee and bakery flavours. My stomach rumbles, and I grin.

'Hyères. A designated stopover for pilgrims on their way to Jerusalem. A favourite spa for the British upper classes in the eighteenth century. Tolstoy lived here, and then, later, towards the end of the nineteenth century, Robert Louis Stevenson. He said it was the only peace he ever knew. He wrote the opening chapters of *Kidnapped* here.'

At the quayside, we settle at a café-restaurant, order peasant-sized cups of frothy coffee and guzzle on them greedily while giving ourselves over to the cinema of the early-morning seaport, which is already in full swing, busy about its business.

From where we are seated, we are well placed to study the world of the fishermen. Several fishing vessels are in dock. Others are arriving, men disembarking. A handful are kneeling or bending over nets on a narrow jetty jutting from the quayside, occupied with the unloading of their overnight catch. I am curious to know what they are spilling out of those bulging nets.

'I could sit here all day,' I murmur, but no sooner have the words been uttered than a white van draws to a halt directly in front of us, blocking out both the early-morning warmth of the sun and our view.

From the driver's side, out steps a small, plump man, whistling, in dusty white overalls and wellingtons. He thumps the side of the vehicle, walks to the rear, opens up both doors and a gangling, spotted youth clutching armfuls of baguettes descends. This callow assistant has an old-fashioned baker's hat set askew on his head, lying flat like a raw mushroom. The baker waves to the bald-headed *patron* of our café, who is leaning against a sliding glass door enjoying a cigarette in the sunshine.

'Don't worry, they'll be gone in a second,' says Michel.

But no. Between them they deliver what must be at least a *hundred* baguettes. One load after another of warm loaves direct from the oven slung in sacks over their shoulders. How can one establishment possibly require so much bread? Finally they rev up and set off to make other deliveries elsewhere along the summer coastline.

The briny sea hits my senses, as does the unmistakable and overwhelming smell of freshly caught fish.

'What's their catch?' I ask.

'Mackerel, I should think,' suggests Michel. 'Or maybe it's sea bass.'

Ah, the delicious Mediterranean white-fleshed fish *loup de mer*. 'If it is, we're taking some back with us,' I smile. It is one of my favourite meals. A fleeting memory of our burned one catches me out; I choose not to mention it. 'In these waters they could have been lucky and found crab, *non?*' Soupe de Pélous, the Niçois name for a truly delicious broth made from locally caught crabs.

'I don't think so.'

Michel is right. I can make out the flapping tails of fish gasping for oxygen, expiring on the quay.

Now, the fishermen have emptied their nets and are attempting to sell their wares. They call loudly in deep-throated, resonant voices, a singsong language I cannot figure out. I hear French, but another, too. Sentences roll out that are incomprehensible to me.

'What are they speaking?'

The language they are talking is Provençal: a foreign tongue to us but, bizarrely, its rhythms are familiar, flirting with revelation until then the sense slips infuriatingly away.

While some of the fishermen start trading, others settle at the narrow wharfside and begin the business of gathering up the nets to dry them or stitch and mend them in the sunshine. Their deftness of hand, their dexterity thrills me. These are burly men with hairy, muscular arms and thick workaday fingers, kneeling on the quay in high rubber boots, wrists turning like dancers. They laugh broadly, with hearty gusto. Vigorously handsome, black-haired men. Lovers, husbands, fathers, hunters of the sea.

People approach to buy the fresh spoils. A few arrivals are tourists, Belgians or Dutch perhaps: broad-beamed, unhurried bodies, solid shoes, light complexions burned pink. They talk with the animated fishermen, choosing carefully, lifting one wriggling sea creature after another, dropping it back on to the slithery heap, digging for another. The hirsute seamen, who have not slept all night, watch on, advising patiently, laughing and joking with their clientele. It is all part of an ancient ritual here on the Côte d'Azur: choosing one's own produce; picking or rejecting each item with due consideration; discussing its quality at length. The serious business of food, of eating, of nurturing the body.

Replete from our several generous cups of *café au lait* and our fresh *tartines*, spread thickly with fig and peach *confitures* and a dark coppery-coloured marmalade that is so delicious it could only be equalled by ours, home-made by René, we want to linger a while longer watching the ruddy-faced fishermen, but we must be on our way. And so, eventually, we leave coins on the table and set off along the waterfront, which reeks of the recently landed fish and of diesel, past the wooden fishing boats bobbing in the deep-green water slicked with a rainbow coating of oil, and return to the road that takes us back inland.

Behind Hyères, bulldozed landscape. Industrial zones. Advertising hoardings. Signposts everywhere, all pointing to the airport. We get lost, snarled up in clutches of fuming traffic. Rush hour. Stressed faces, smokers, mobile-phone users driving like sharp card-dealers.

'Let's get out of here.' Michel swings the old Merc over to the left and, as soon as he can, does a U-turn. On we go for miles, trying to find our way, moving out of the city's breeze-blocked suburbia into the countryside. Hot dusty roads, straight Roman roads flanked by keenly pruned plane trees. Empty but for one rusting white Citroën rising up out of the distant heat shimmer, transporting a band of farm hands to the vineyards.

'*Le platane*. Plane tree. Its first mention in Greek literature was in the *Iliad* and then, a little later, in the *Odyssey*,' I murmur.

'What is happening with your book?'

I shrug, and turn my face to the window.

'Why don't you take another look at it?'

'Not now.'

Michel does not persist. We reach a roundabout. I lean from the window and catch sight of, nestling behind over-grown foliage, a handwritten sign directing us to the nursery. Two or three kilometres further along, we see it up ahead: a disappointing *hypermarché* of a place. Turning left off the road, we park on the gravelled courtyard and Michel hurries to enquire at one of the cash desks.

'The olive trees are not here. Follow the lane. You'll need to take your car.'

Rolling slowly along a pebbled path, past row upon row of fruiting trees – I have never seen so many trees – we come upon a wooden shed with a handful of cars outside. This is the office.

A young man steps forward to greet us; he has been expecting us. He smiles warmly, shaking our hands, the epit-ome of wholesomeness.

'I'll take you to the *oliviers*,' he says.

He reverses his four-wheel-drive out of the shade and we climb aboard and hit the road again. Down lanes, past entrances to vineyard *domaines* with signs offering *dégusta-tions*, where, hidden beyond winding, vegetal tracks, can be glimpsed gracious *bastides*. Michel asks the young man if he can recommend one or two modest labels. He suggests two local wineries and then moves right back to the business in hand: olive trees.

'Of course, you are fortunate. Where you are situated, you have the *cailletier*, the famous Nice olive. It makes excellent oil. Here, in this region, no particular variety is cultivated. Here is a bit of a hodgepodge, which is why the area is not eligible for AOC status. The conditions, the soil, where you are, are ideal.'

Moments later, we swing off the lane into what, once upon a time, must have been agricultural land but is today the property of the nursery. A vast acreage dedicated exclusively to the propagation of olive trees. In every direction, as far as the eye can see, olive trees.

I step from the car into a silver ocean of foliage. Beyond are mountains and lavender sky.

'We have thirty-six varieties on offer here. Three sizes: three-year-olds, six or nine.'

Michel and I look about us in wonder.

'How many trees?' asks Michel.

'We aim to produce one hundred and eighty thousand a year.'

It is a mighty concept.

'One of our goals is to create the future heritage of Provence. This tree, *l'olivier*, one might say, is the signature tune of Provence.'

I turn to him in surprise. Signature tune? Yes, I like that: to sing the ancient ways of Provence into the future.

'Well, our order would be a modest one. Two hundred of the *cailletiers*. I think the six-year-olds would suit us. But my wife and I will obviously discuss it and confirm it with you in writing. Will you be needing a deposit, or—?'

'Lord, no, there's no hurry. You can settle the bill next year when we deliver them. If you decide to go ahead, that is, which I sincerely hope you will. There's an old Provençal saying,' he continues proudly. '"A hundred-year-old olive tree is still a baby." Yes, its finest fruit seasons are still to come.'

'It's your day,' Michel says to me when we are back in our car, having purchased two dozen bottles of rosé at one of the *châteaux* recommended by our nursery gardener, whose name we didn't learn. 'What would you like to do now?'

'Swim. If we can find a quiet bay.'

'We'll find a spot.'

Wading deep into the yawning blue sea, our thighs are caressed by brown twiny leaves of seaweed which, I discover later, is not seaweed at all. It is an aquatic plant known as *Posidonia oceanica*. In Corsica it is a protected species because it is a vital source of oxygen and nutrition for Mediterranean marine fauna. Waves slap gently against our naked navels. Michel's body is as brown as tobacco, as smooth as velvet. He throws himself carelessly into the warm water and swims fast. I follow, shouting and splashing after him. The exercise relaxes our tired limbs, aching from hours in the car. We float on our backs, staring up at the cloudless sky. It feels like a stolen day. The warmth of the sun beating down on us. Golden-hued. Almost sinful.

The wavy sand is packed with heat. Our bodies are packed with heat. We flake out on a dark, triangular rock which looks out across the semi-deserted beach to the flat blue water and beyond, to the Iles d'Or. Lapping waves and bird cries are our companions while the sun pours down upon flesh glistening with driplets of the sea and runnels of salty perspiration. I am lying on my stomach, deep in thought. Michel rolls towards me.

'Quite a sight, those olive trees, eh?'

'Yes. As is their philosophy. Remarkable. Still, we have all we need.'

He asks no questions, but leans into me and licks my shoulder, tasting the salt. Socks of damp sand cling to our sea-wet feet. A mauvy speckled lizard scurries by, pauses, stock-still, on the rock as though sensing our presence, flicks out its tongue and then disappears.

My fingertips have wrinkled in the water and turned a marbled, death-like white. It reminds me of my loss and I feel a wave of gloom wash through me. 'Please, don't let's order more trees.'

Later, inland, travelling home beneath a dramatic evening sky, we spot hand-painted signs pinned to pine trees announcing a *Guignol* performance this very evening. I beg to go. Michel agrees, although he does not share my passion for Punch and Judy shows.

In a dusty plaza in a lonely rural village, it is a pitiable occasion. Half a dozen kids, a gang of local lads, are running to and fro, a couple of them in bare feet, shouting, mocking the show. The French word for brats is *les mouflets*, which aptly describes these kids. They are slinging pebbles at the puppets, jeering at the sad puppeteer.

I recount to Michel how, when I was a child of eight or nine, I worked as the puppeteer's assistant for my father while he performed his weekend Punch and Judy shows. I can still see the battered navy case that housed the clothed wooden figures, and in which they were transported from gig to gig. I could recite every word of the dialogue in those days, from beginning to end. Even today I can recall chunks of it. How I used to love to peer out from the rear of the tent and watch the sea of entranced grown-ups and children, all sitting cross-legged on the grass, shouting words of warning to the characters:

'Judy! Judy! Look behind you!'

'Where?'

'There!'

'Here?'

'No, there!'

'Crocodile!'

'Policeman!'

'Ghost!'

I grow silent when reminded of my father, of the confused child I was, and of my own girl so recently lost. Michel guides me back to the present by asking me why I don't begin to write again.

I have no enthusiasm for work; no confidence in it.

He lets the matter drop.

The story being enacted here is marginally different to the tale I remember from my childhood. It seems to have a more political bias to it, but it is hard to grasp precisely because *les mouflets* are still screaming and throwing sticks.

I turn my head this way and that, searching for someone to call them off. But all I see is a trio of old men with hand-carved canes, olivewood, perhaps, seated side by side at the square's perimeter beneath a dusty olive tree. They stare into the middle distance, motionless, as though made of stone.

'Well, I wouldn't want to be the proud mother of any of this bunch,' I whisper crossly.

Summer Eclipsed

Les filles arrive, Michel's twin daughters. Eighteen, and beautiful as unfolding flowers. Although still adoring of their Papa, they are growing up, setting out on their own lives. Their talk is of their individual futures. Vanessa, with her long, auburn hair, her cinnamon-tanned skin and full, pouting lips, is intending to read modern languages at the Sorbonne in Paris while Clarisse, slender, soft-curled and poised, who appears to view the world from a more passive stance, is preparing to settle herself in my flat in London in readiness for a foundation course at one of the major art schools.

They swim, they read, they sunbathe, they natter together, they help with the table. Vanessa makes salads picked from the garden and her own style of potatoes, which are coated in our oil, baked with strong, hard cheeses and served up creamy and delicious. They take the scooter to buy the *brioches*, almond *croissants* and the *sablés* for breakfast or disappear down country lanes on outings of exploration, returning, with wild flowers, for meals or for dips in the pool. In so many ways they are independent; they are no longer children. Their lives are ahead of them. They do not notice my sadness and I say not a word. They enquire after my work and sometimes we discuss my projects but their energies are centred on their own lives. They are two regular teenagers; it is as it should be.

'Are you at work on a novel?' asks Vanessa.

The fact is I have no work. The material I was researching all those months back – for my book about this region of France, its changing history, its flora – has been relegated to a drawer, forgotten, abandoned. 'Just an idea I had,' I tell myself now. I still make the ritualistic trek to my den, padding along there every morning, sitting at my table, staring at my computer, or out at the awakening day, but it is habit more than a fervent need to write. I find myself sifting through papers, relocating one pile from here to there or simply gazing out of the window. Lost.

'I am lost,' I tell Michel. 'Directionless.'

'What about the new trees, our AOC, have you thought any further?'

I shake my head and shrug. I cannot throw myself into farm activities. In any case, there is little I can do to further our plans because it is August and the world of the south of France has closed down. Only the amenities for tourists are sparking. For the rest, it is holiday time. I flick through my bee tome, turning the pages, staring at diagrams, but I have lost heart in this project as well. The images remind me of spring and I cannot bear to think back to spring. But I know that I must attack something.

To offset apathy, and because the plants in the flowerbeds are all but strangled by weeds that shot up during the watering reign of M. Halaz I spend the days weeding. Reminded of

water, I call René. We have heard nothing from him since
before my departure. I leave a message with his wife, but he
does not return the call. He is probably out fishing on his
boat, and who can blame him? The weather is stunning. The
sun shines hotly. The sky is cloudless. It is hyacinth blue and
clear as a bell. Lazy summer. Yet, this time, it disappoints me
that he lets us down.

I am engrossed in a tribe of wasps, trying to shoo them
away – they have congregated round a freshly halved water-
melon I left out in the summer kitchen because it won't fit in
the fridge – when we hear our unoiled gates creak open and
the dogs begin to jump and bark. 'Ah, this could be René,' I
call out, and hurry to greet him.

But no, it is Quashia. The return of Quashia!

His nonchalant stroll up the drive, a supermarket carrier
bag in one hand, bearing a gift of sorts, I am sure, as though
he were arriving back from lunch, is greeted by whoops of
joy and much embracing.

'Welcome! Welcome!'

The wedding ceremonies were a huge success. Over a glass
of mineral water in the shade of the *Magnolia grandiflora*, he
acquaints us with the details of the celebrations, which have
cost him every franc he had saved. He has brought us video
cassettes of the occasion. Eight hours' screen time.

'Eight hours!'

'Well, it lasted for weeks,' he laughs. The feasting of this
family, that clan, the neighbours; the relocating of the bride;
the preparation of the food. 'Here.' He hands over the plastic bag that contains the tapes. 'See for yourselves.'

Michel assures him that we look forward to it, and I smile
to myself, knowing that it will be me who sits through those
home-recorded festivities.

'I hope you negotiated a good price for the bride,' I tease.

'I made a fair deal, but now I'm stony, stony broke.' The glint in his eye tells me how pleased our Arab friend is to be back.

'Any news from René?'

I shake my head and Quashia grins. 'The invisible man!' He looks about, appraising the garden. 'I hear it hasn't rained here in months, but Halaz has done his bit, I see.'

'Yes. I dread the water bill but . . .'

'Got yourself a water diviner?' he joshes.

'René found someone, but . . .'

'. . . you haven't heard from René. What's happening about a new watering system then?' he asks.

'Nothing.' I don't share my doubts about planting the new trees.

'Well, let's get to it. We need to get that second basin up and running.'

He rises, rolling up his sleeves. He never wastes a second. And perhaps, now that he is here, we will get to work.

Michel and Quashia wait while I change into shoes that can negotiate the hill and then, together, we climb up to the basin.

'The front wall must be repaired first. No point in touching the container yet.'

Michel nods. 'Correct. But it's a drystone wall and carrying too much weight. Yes, it must be rebuilt, but also reinforced. It has to be securely shored up or the stones will come loose again and it will disintegrate as soon as any stress or weight is laid on it. Once the wall has been secured, the base of the basin needs to have new foundations.'

Quashia frowns. 'I can join every hose we own and create a water supply from one of the higher taps. We probably have just about enough metreage to reach this spot, but how can we transport sand and cement up here? There's no proper track. If the builders' merchants dump everything in

the *parking*, as they usually do, I'll have to transport it by
wheelbarrow and I'll be at it till Christmas!'

He has a point. We are practically at the furthest extreme
of our land. There is no road up the rear of the hill and
nothing except terraces in front. The tracks that cut through
the terrace walls would have been carved out for the ease of
beasts of burden, mules, nothing else.

We look around, reflecting on the problem.

'How about a chain?' suggests Michel eventually. I don't
think either of us understand immediately. 'Let's sit down
and work out the quantities of sand and cement we'll
require, and then decide how many men could deliver it up
here in, say, three days.'

Quashia gets the idea.

'Do you think you could muster some of your cronies to
work in this relentless weather?'

'Two of my wife's brothers are staying nearby. And there's
another fellow I know. He's a good worker. It's time those
buggers sent a few francs back to their families. When shall
we start?'

While Michel and Quashia clear the land surrounding the
disused basin, I am dispatched to the builders' merchants to
place our order. It is deserted. I find both manager and drivers lounging about in the air-conditioned Portakabin,
smoking, drinking coffee, bitching about life. As I enter they
fall silent, eyeing me as though I have just trucked in from
another planet. I smile, offering a breezy *bonjour*, and they
return my greeting with grunts, wondering, with barely
veiled amusement, what this foreign woman who busies herself with sacks of cement and always debates the price wants
this time.

'You can't charge me five hundred francs for a delivery of
sand! It's out of the question,' I argue.

Lucien, the site manager, who I occasionally run into at the gym, shrugs. 'It's two tons,' he says. But eventually he proposes 250 francs.

I am convinced they add on a few hundred from the start, knowing that I will insist upon the same advantageous terms given to the professionals. We settle on 250 and he agrees to find a driver who will be able to deliver before the end of the week. I nod gratefully, perfectly aware that there is a quartet of drivers standing right behind me who are engaged in little aside from staring at my rear view in shorts.

I have given up on hanging out in my den, accomplishing nothing. Instead, for want of something productive to throw my energies into, I make an inventory of the garden, scribbling notes on my findings, listing plants, flowers, wildlife. Today, I am following the voracious antics of a praying mantis. I came across her yesterday when I was checking the progress of the grapes. There she was, holed up on the underside of one of the vine leaves. Extraordinarily, she has been there ever since, but her camouflage colouring is very effective and I had to hunt hard to find her again. Has she been taking it easy, caring for her digestion, after dining on her partner? I read that few male mantids are actually devoured by their women. The males seem to know the score and, once coitus has been achieved, they zip off out of the way, sharpish. This morning, I watched her trap and devour a tiny, jewel-skinned lizard. Quite shocking.

Before lunch and his siesta, after he has seen to the watering, Quashia goes in search of his three assistants. Two are as ancient and wrinkled as he, but the third is tall, handsome, young. His heavy boots and sloppy clothes aside, his looks and bearing would cast him as an Arabian prince. They sit with Michel at the round table up behind one of Quashia's newly renovated walls and the negotiations begin. Men's business.

The girls show signs of growing restless. I think they are uncomfortable lying by the pool with such visitors about. They propose an outing, but we are all agreed that it would be too crowded, too stultifying to visit the coast. In any case, Serge is due to arrive any day now. At long last he has accepted Michel's invitation.

Later, when the business in hand has been settled – the materials are arriving tomorrow and the men will set to work the day after – Michel suggests an adventurous alternative. Tomorrow we will take a little trip inland, towards the mountainous region of the Haut-Pays Niçoise, to visit the Gorge du Loup, where we can swim and picnic in relative tranquillity. Serge is travelling alone by car from Paris and, to make his journey marginally shorter, Michel organises a sundown rendezvous in the town of Tourrette-sur-Loup, the gateway to the gorge.

Tourrette-sur-Loup, constructed out of the mountain face, is known locally as 'the town of violets' because those purple-blossomed flowers grow wild there and felt-carpet the olive groves in springtime.

The next morning we leave Quashia to organise the truckloads of materials and set off after breakfast, juddering along in the smoking Merc, which reminds me that I should phone the garage and enquire after mine. But then again, it is August, and I don't much care to think about that car.

En route we make a swift alpine detour to a farm nestling in several thousand hectares of herb-scented pastureland. Its nearest neighbour is a pretty mountain hamlet. The farm is owned and managed by a handsome young goat farmer and cheesemaker we met a little over a year ago, at a Provençal honey festival in Mouans Sartoux. Although that village is not a million miles from our home, on that particular late-spring Sunday we felt like aliens because the locals were conversing in Provençal. The fishermen we observed near Hyères jumped between the two languages, but at the honey fair, French was shunned altogether. There are many faces to Provence, and its history is rich, diverse and embedded in our daily lives, but until that Sunday I had not been aware that Provençal was a spoken language.

Marcel, the goat farmer, is an esteemed figure in these parts because he is a published poet who writes in Prouvençau, but we are not making this stopover to partake of his poetry. It is his goat's cheese, probably the most delicious we have ever tasted, that we are after. Among his specialities is Banon, a fresh, light *chèvre* sprinkled with nuts and then wrapped in a chestnut leaf. Banon is a region in the Haute-Alpes, and by rights the name belongs to cheeses that hail from those pastures, but even if his goats are not reared in Banon, his cheese is an epicurean delight and well worth making the journey for.

Marcel is the proud owner of eighty-five nannies and three dark-coated billies. The nannies produce the newborn kids in early spring, at the end of February or early March, and are milked daily from two weeks after giving birth right through to September, which explains why you cannot find fresher cheese than right here at this farm. From late September until early October, the goats are put to mate.

On one of my previous trips to this hilly hinterland creamery, Marcel explained to me, and I ask him to repeat it now for the girls, that Provençal was one of the languages of Occitan, the traditional language of southern France. It is a dialect of the *langue d'oc*, or Langedocien, which literally means the 'tongue of the Occitan'. Its roots are closer to Spanish, or Catalan, which is prized as a sister language by Provençal speakers, than to French, which has a Latin root.

Once upon a time, Prouvençau was widely accepted as the literary language of all France and northern Spain.

Mediaeval troubadours and poets wrote poems and songs in Prouvençau and sang or recited them to their fair ladies, the mistresses of the courts. 'Their sentiments were of an altruistic nature, which is to say that they sang or recited the idylls of pure love, homages to the women of their dreams, rather than clamoured to consummate the physical passions, the carnal aspects of their desires. They were not looking to conjoin with their loves; it was more to celebrate them in words and music and offer the works as gifts to the heavenly creature of their choosing,' expounds Marcel.

'Might it be from this tradition that we find the root of the verb "to court", to try to win the hand of, the favours of?' I ask him.

He shrugs in the way so common down here. '*Hélas*, in 1539,' he continues, 'a statute known as the Villers-Cotterêts approved French, rather than Provençal, as the official administrative language in Provence. After that, over the centuries, Provençal fell into disuse. It threatened to become a dead language, but we are campaigning . . . *Eh, bien.*' He falls silent, his expression hangdog, as though the loss were a personal affront to him and his heritage. And I can well believe that it is.

I cast a curious eye towards the girls, who are gazing at him, listening intently, with shining expressions. Perhaps they are smitten not only by young Marcel's romanticism and his swarthy good looks but by his dark velvet voice. If so, I can't say I blame them.

'I wonder if you would like to add your names to our collective?' He is addressing the girls, handing each of them a form which contains a bulletin for new adherents to fill in. I have already sent one off on behalf of Michel and myself.

'*Un mouvamen souciau en marcho!*' it announces in this ancient tongue. 'The rest,' he points out, 'is written in both languages. As you can see, the form states clearly that we are neither a political party nor a sect. We are an independent body fighting hard for the recognition of our mother tongue. We want it taught in schools and spoken in our day-to-day lives. It is a quintessential part of our culture.'

The girls read the forms while I decide upon several small circular cheeses encrusted with herbs or peppers and Marcel wraps them for us. Through the window I glimpse Michel waiting by the car. He wanders over towards a small herd of goats. I smile, divining his thoughts.

'Were you able to find a use for all your tomatoes?' Marcel asks me.

I turn back, confused.

'Was the recipe I gave you helpful?'

And then I remember that I have forgotten to thank him. He advised me to halve our harvested tomatoes, lay them out on our flat roof to dry in the sun, and then add them to his very delicious *chèvre à l'huile*. The last time I visited him must have been three months back, during our tomato surfeit, after René suggested the idea to me. I nod brusquely, shying away from the memory.

Elegantly parcelled cheeses in hand, we wave our *au revoirs* – Marcel invites us to return later, if we fancy, to lend a hand with *la traite*, the evening milking – and set off, but not before Michel has reminded us that to accompany our mouthwatering *fromages* we will need yards of fresh, soft bread. 'Eyes peeled for a good baker, please. You know, *chérie*, I still think we should buy a goat of our own,' he says. 'Look at them.'

'What if they eat our olives?' I counter, but I suspect that, in the fullness of time, my objection will be overcome.

A kilometre or so along the way, as we approach the outskirts of the mediaeval city of Tourrette-sur-Loup, we make another stop for the required baguettes. This *boulangerie*, like so many here, is also a local *pâtisserie*, and the fresh fruit tartlets on display look too tempting to ignore. We choose two: a lemon and almond and a pear and apricot, and I ask the woman to wrap a couple of their onion tarts while she's about it.

'Mmm, what's that smell?' I have been seduced by something flavourful that I can't quite identify, sweet yet nuttyish, wafting from the rear of the building. The homely baker's wife grins, picks up a tray and flourishes the house speciality. '*Pâte de guimauve, fait à la maison!*' she cackles.

Home-made marshmallows. I have never seen them on sale before. At least, not direct from the oven like these. We buy a greedy man's portion, white and pink and soft as downy pillows. Our good lady weighs them up and off we go, leaving the shop laden with goodies – I feel the seeping warmth from the bread and the bagfuls of sweetmeats clutched against my chest – and I am suddenly reminded of my late father visiting us here, and what delight he found in the artistry of Provençal bakers and cakemakers.

Before too long, we are parking the car in the village of Pont-du-Loup. We unpack our shopping, our home-made picnic and our swimming gear, and embark on our hike. Passing a small *maison de confiserie* bearing the name of a well-established French confectionery house, we resist the temptation to step inside. Here, in the foothills of the lower Alp region, a few modest farmhouses cling to the twin hill-sides that converge at the foot of this canyon. We move into single file and prepare to penetrate the uninhabited interior.

This cleft, riven into two gigantic faces of salmon-beige rock, which, even in this dry season, has a substantial river running right through it, is a majestic sight. Gone is the lush, subtropical beauty of the coast. This is an altogether more awesome landscape.

'Any idea why the river is named Loup?' I yell to Michel, who has taken the lead. He shakes his head.

Loup means wolf. No doubt in former days wolves travelling in hungry packs hunted these mountains; it could be the origin of the name.

The dust track at the river's edge, *la rive*, is narrow and winding. Mountain streams puddle the path. If there is underground water to be prospected from our rocky smallholding, it would be fed by one of a million of these mountain runlets. Which reminds me that I must, somehow, track down René. It only now occurs to me that I have no idea where he lives; all we have are telephone numbers.

In winter this track would be mulched in rust-coloured oak leaves, sodden with water and black sinking mud, but this is the rainless season. Today, the only hindrances to our procession are the broken branches we encounter, snapped off somewhere way on high, or monumental felled trunks which block the route like feudal drawbridges, but we scramble over or circumvent them without difficulty, passing our bags from one to the other.

I feel sure there are raptors nesting or hunting here, but, craning my neck, even squinting, I see only drifting smudges. Any bird soaring above is too remote for me to identify. The sky, a visible curvy mass between the two rims of the canyon, looks to me like an inflated blue mouth. Warholesque. Butterflies on either side of the steep banks flit from one perched plant to the next and I attempt to identify both flora and fauna, mostly unsuccessfully. But this territory is untampered with; whatever grows here is native. Species that have survived for millennia.

La garrigue Méditerranéenne. Numerous plants compose the garrigue. Dog rose, tamarisk, blackberry bramble, rock rose, holly, myrtle, rosemary, ivy . . . others I cannot recall now.

Our marching is hot going. It is a thirst-inducing, dusty activity. Even with the river pounding tantalisingly close and an abundance of verdant vegetation brushing against our sweating flesh, the enclosed space feels dense and airless. We climb up, we climb down, we swing left, we swing right, and each progression seems to take us further from the riverbed. Midges swarm like bolts of mesh netting and irritate.

'Look down there!' calls Clarisse.

Thirty metres beneath us is a sparkling rock pool. A perfect invitation to picnic and swim.

'But how can we reach it? The descent looks dicey.'

'Shall we try?'

The girls turn to Papa – *always to Papa* – who decides that it is more prudent to continue. 'There'll be a well-trodden access soon and from there we'll approach with safety. If not, we'll find another pool. There are several further along. Don't worry.'

No one doubts the wisdom of his words, and so on we step. The day is reaching its zenith and I am beginning to feel faint, woozy with heat and lack of oxygen, but I am keen not to create a fuss, particularly in the light of recent events, and so I fall back, discreetly taking up the rear position.

We travel on for half a kilometre, more or less, before reaching an iron bridge, painted green – almost the same brilliant hue as the praying mantis I have been observing. It transports us over to the far bank and to the left, which means that we have swung back on ourselves and, before long, we find a narrow conduit that delivers us to the very same splendid rock pool Clarisse spotted a while back. From this angle, the descent is perfectly accessible and without danger. Our footsteps crackle and crunch on dozens of tiny twigs.

'Wow!'

'How lovely!'

And it is: a lush and stony oasis. A lonely, hidden place.

Luckily for us, the pool is bordered by substantial balloon-shaped boulders where we throw our bags in the shade of half a dozen leaning holm-oaks – these native evergreens grow everywhere in this region – seeded tight up against one another.

We tear off our clothes and fall into the water. It gurgles and bubbles and takes our breath away as we scream loudly and immerse our sticky bodies, splashing to and fro. The water is fabulous. Vanessa skids her hands across the crystal surface of the pool and a white spume rises, soaking Michel's face.

'Hey!' he cries. And then both girls take up the game. I hear the call of *'Papa! Papa!'* echo round the gorge until Papa dives out of range like a seal hunting fish.

Afterwards, we rub ourselves and one another furiously and fast and then lay out the towels to dry on the boulders. The girls go off to explore the rocky clefts and two rather litter-ridden caves we passed back by a waterfall beyond the green bridge, leaving us alone with river and sun.

'Watch your step,' Papa calls after them, but they don't turn back. They are not listening. Arms linked, then hand in hand, long-legged beauties, hurrying away to share secrets, to lose themselves in rocks and thickets and be grown-up girls together. I watch them until they are out of sight, and then, a moment or two later, I unfold a rush mat in readiness for our picnic. Still thinking of the girls I lie back, supine and glistening wet, against the darkly freckled, porous rock. A tear threatens.

I feel the brush of Michel's damp hand against my haunch, not a sexual caress so much as a supportive one, reassuring and reminding me that here at my side is companionship and love.

And how would I manage without it?

The roaring river cools us with its spray while the vegetation growing out of the rock face is our organic, filigreed parasol. We bask and dry in the dappled heat like lizards on the voluptuous curves of the boulders until a couple of mosquitos appear from out of the undergrowth, approaching from dark, fetid everywheres to bother us. The location is deceptive. You don't expect to find them here but they zirr and dive-bomb, hoping to feed off our blood. I sit up and reach for a bottle of mineral water, flicking my wrist crossly at one of the intruders.

Michel breaks off an oak branch and fans it over me like a switch. 'Are you having a nice day?' he enquires, having surely picked up on my evolving mood.

I stare at the river, the thundersome rush of the river, roaring furiously by. We have to shout to be heard above the din of the fast-flowing crystalline water, but before I can answer, while I am formulating thoughts, we are disturbed by the unexpected ring of his mobile phone breaking into this intimacy.

'Why did you bring that thing with you?' I demand irritably.

'In case it's Serge.'

It is. He has had an accident. He is unharmed, but his car is a write-off. Michel shoots questions, establishes location details, then digs for our car keys and bends to give me a quick kiss. Before he sets off on this rescue mission, we arrange that I will wait for him here with the girls or, if it gets too late, at the café we spotted in Pont-du-Loup close by the mouth of the canyon.

When he has gone, to relax and keep troubling doubts at bay, I plunge myself back into the water. Returning to my rock, I begin to lay out our picnic. Plastic tumblers, even for wine – glasses here may cause accidents – and then the cheeses from Marcel's farm, our fresh bread, the marshmallows and various hams. I cover the whole with napkins to protect against creepy-crawlies and await the girls' ravenous return. Once this has been accomplished I settle with a book, only to be interrupted by something wet pelting the back of my neck. I think it must be a bird and lift my head. The next raindrop splats on my cheek. It is pursued in quick succession by several more, all as large as saucers. Drops are plopping heavily against the overhead trees – I love the sound – while the river in front of me begins to furrow and spin and groove with the force of the rain now sheeting down.

Glancing skywards again, I see chutes of rain descending out of louring black clouds. This is no quick summer shower. Hurriedly, I begin to pack away all that I have painstakingly spread out.

'Vanessa! Clarisse!' My cries echo back to me, but there is no other response. The mountain water cascades forth, thundering by like a high-speed train. Oblivious, on its sonorous journey to the coast, of the potential separation of a trio of women. The roaring, yowling wolf. We don't want to get trapped here. I pull on my shorts, gather up the bags, too numerous for me to carry alone, and look about for shelter. Could I make it to the caves? I doubt it. Not with this load. I am already soaked, sopping, streaming. I haul the bags back against the cliff face and shelter beneath the trees. It is surprisingly dry. The ground at my feet remains dusty, untouched by a single raindrop. Water gutters all around me but I am safe; huddled, shivering, but refuged.

Peering out into the rain, my thoughts turn to the book I had intended to write this year. Listening to René and his tales of days gone by had set me thinking of the wonders of the old order of Provence alongside the new Côte d'Azur. Crouched here on my hams, I could be a cavewoman. Time has slipped away. Nothing where I am has changed in a million years. I should get back to my book; find something. Or the sense of failure will bring me down.

A clap of thunder is followed by a rustling sound and then cries and, from out of a curtain of heavy, wet leaves and sheeting rain, the girls come bounding towards me. Young gazelles, unicorns to the rescue. T-shirts over their heads; helmets of sodden cotton. They are laughing, wide smiles, healthy teeth, exuberant with life and the thrill of this mini-adventure.

'We got lost!'

'*Où est Papa?*'

'Serge telephoned.' And I recount the events.

'We should get out of here!'

'Let's go!' yells Vanessa. They swoop up belongings and hare on ahead. I look back, squinting, checking our spot.

'The marshmallows! I forgot the marshmallows.'

There they are, stuck like rotting mushrooms on the streaming mottled boulder, waterlogged and drowning in the summer downpour.

'*Tant pis!*'

'*Trop tard!*'

By the time we belt into the smoky café – a squelching, giggling hysterical entry – we are drowned rats. '*Chocolat chaud! Chocolat chaud!*' we are screaming.

Large cups of hot chocolate and pizzas with *saucissons* and local free-range eggs are ordered and while we await these, we rub each other's hair with the dryish towels providently stuffed and zipped away inside one of the backpacks. Men, propped against the bar drinking and smoking, stare at us, eyeing the girls.

Surely they take me for their mother.

For hours we sit there, reading, watching the rain, which

eventually gives way to a street potted with shining puddles and a cloudy blue sky. Coachloads of tourists come and go, tramping the village's sole thoroughfare, chomping on sweets purchased at the *confiserie*. I observe it all – this unscheduled mountain day – through the window, including the girls' reflections, all the while asking myself, what if there were no Michel? What would remain between myself and these two vibrant creatures, reading and nattering at my side, guzzling Coke and ordering yet more hot chocolate?

I recall occasions during my troubled teenage years when I was dragged off to partake of disagreeable lunches with one or other of my father's mistresses. I measured them, those unctuous women, none of whom possessed the beauty of my own mother. I mistrusted those who went to great lengths to curry favour with me. And I disliked with an even greater fervour those who ignored me, purring and pouting at Daddy as though I didn't exist.

Who is the intruder in this threesome? I used to ponder.

Still, I am the wife of these girls' father, not his mistress. There is a difference, isn't there? Even so . . .

And finally, late in the afternoon, after we have positively gorged ourselves on cakes and pizzas and hot chocolate, Michel and Serge turn up and we make for home.

When we arrive, we find hillocks of soaked sand in the driveway. Fortunately, Quashia has had the foresight to store the dozens of bags of cement in one of the stables.

Life turns between repose and activity. All around us the Arabs are transporting building materials, shifting wheel-barrows, laying planks up and across the hill while the rest of us are centred round the pool. Michel and I flit between one and the other. I to supply gallons of drinking water, Michel to survey the work process, though Quashia has the chain under control.

Serge is staying on with us. Such a gentle, introspective man who sits alone for hours in a deckchair in the garden. He sketches, mostly.

Occasionally, I see Clarisse crouch at his side on the warm terracotta tiles engaging him in easy conversation about his work. Otherwise he says little, even at mealtimes. I find myself watching him, slyly monitoring him, with awe and curiosity. Like a dog on the scent I keep tabs on him. He seems so unsuited to the practical demands of everyday life that I fear for his future. How will he cope alone? What has he learned about grief, about how to accommodate it, that I can steal from him? I empathise with his desolation. It mirrors my own. He shelters his pain with such dignity, losing himself within the fabulous worlds of his animation storyboards.

He works.

Is the grief of a male different from that of a female? I would like to ask him, but I don't.

I observe him beneath our cream-white parasol, sketching a translucent-blue dragonfly hovering by the pool. And the next day he has created a character: an iridescent, queen-like nymph with a humanised face and the svelteness of the dragonfly. Out of this world.

I should be working too. When summer is over, I tell myself, when everyone has left, then I'll begin again. Dig out my notes. But the very idea of summer being over, of the emptiness it will bring, fills me with terror.

A letter arrives from London, from Richard, my specialist. It reaffirms our conversation in his office. The various tests and scans I have undergone confirm that, though there appears to be no precise physical damage, to carry a child the full term is not possible. I stare at the page, clutching on to it. There is good news, though. In every other sense, I am healthy. All the scans are clear. He rounds off the missive by suggesting that whenever I am ready I should telephone, make another appointment to see him, 'for a chat'. I fold up the letter and secrete it beneath my computer in my den. A lifeline deep within me, centuries old, millennia old, has been severed. Atavistic rights I took to be my God-given entitlement have been withdrawn, snatched away from me, leaving me, in a world bred to propagate, as what?

Standing out in the heat on the upper terrace, I watch the girls and Serge lazing round the pool, see their obvious contentment as they sketch, swim, dangle their toes into the cool water, do nothing more strenuous than basking in their day, and I creep back inside, close up the shutters to block out the tireless light, the singsong cries of the Arabs at work and the trance-inducing heat. I burrow deep beneath the duvet, burying myself in a cave of darkness, beating back despair. Lying in the bed alone, hot tears roll silently down my cheeks. And when Michel comes looking for me, I pretend to be asleep.

He is returning from a trip to the garden centre, where he has bought me *nénuphars*, waterlilies, for the pond. He 'wakes' me, takes me by the hand and together we settle them in the deep green water. Six white blossoms floating like miniature sails. The foot-long carp dart in and around them. They are exquisite. Several blue dragonflies arrive. Darners, I think these are – the females are less brightly coloured than the males. They congregate there, hovering, or anchored to the petals where their tails lift and fall like teeny silver pumps. An expression of their contentment?

In the evening he leads me back to the pond. 'Come and look.' There, clipped to the creamy rim of one of the *nénuphars*, we discover two slender, graceful insects.

'Narrow-winged damselflies,' smiles Michel, who has looked them up in one of my nature books.

I smile too, aware to what lengths he has gone, but his

attentions serve only to exacerbate my sense of inadequacy. I had not bargained on this inner turmoil, had not expected to be so poleaxed by mourning, to be thrown into such isolation by it.

In the not too distant future, we will be the proud owners of a second water basin, but from where will we fill it? We could reroute our exterior pipes, or create an extension branch from the piping fed by the Lyonnaise des Eaux's central reserve, which travels up from our pumphouse, but that will prove to be extremely expensive. I telephone M. Di Luzio, our plumber, from whom we haven't heard a word since the film festival. We need a quote for laying the extra lengths of pipe. But his message tells me yet again that he is away. Yes, it's holiday time. I attempt to find René once more to find out what news there is, if any, of his celebrated colleague, the water diviner.

'Well, I can't ask him to visit you now.'

'Why, because it's August?'

'No. He's driving north for the eclipse.'

Ah yes, I was forgetting that any day now the earth is to be totally eclipsed by the sun.

'I'll call you at the weekend,' he promises, 'when it's all over.' And we leave it like that.

Everyone, everywhere is being whipped into eclipse fever. Even our trio of Arabs and Quashia declare it a holiday. Each night on the news, each day in the newspapers, we hear of the route of the eclipse, which will sweep a diagonal swatch across our eastern hemisphere, namely – as far as the French are concerned – across northern France.

Provence does not figure in what is known as the 'totality zone'; we are too far south for 'maximum coverage'. But it is predicted that we should have between ninety-six and ninety-seven degrees coverage. This offers shops and local radio and television stations an opportunity to take full commercial advantage.

Michel sends me to the village to deposit a roll of film for developing and to fetch eye-protection masks, special eclipse glasses, so that we can stare at the sun without danger. I trudge from shop to shop but all the *commerçants* have sold out. '*Plus*,' they tell me, but assure me that another delivery is expected in the morning.

The following morning I duly return, a few hours before the predicted eclipse. I collect Michel's developed photographs, but have no luck with the dratted glasses. The shopkeepers shrug when I ask what alternatives they can suggest. 'Don't look,' is the best they propose.

Back at the farm everyone is disappointed. We have one pair between us – Vanessa bought a pair in Cannes – which we will share. We will station ourselves outside anyway and take it in turns to wear the special lenses. I suspect that the temptation to look heavenwards will be irresistible.

'Can the glare really blind us?' asks Clarisse.

'Better not risk it,' cautions her father.

Jessye Norman is due to give an eclipse concert at the magnificent gothic cathedral of Reims. Reims, the capital of the Champagne district in northern-eastern France is, today, the centre of the 'totality zone'. In 1429, the newly victorious French Dauphin entered that cathedral to be crowned Charles VII of France, thus becoming the first of a long line of French kings to celebrate their coronations there. At Charles's side was his companion in battle, the eighteen-year-old Joan of Arc. The Maid of Orléans was the same age then as Michel's daughters are today.

Michel switches on both televisions to full volume, opens the French windows in our bedroom on the east side of the house and dusts down our ancient transistor radio. We troop outside: Serge, the girls, Vanessa already sporting her glasses, tripping and giggling on the steps, Michel with cumbersome radio in hand and me at the rear, flanked by the dogs. The morning news has warned that all domestic animals should be kept inside but we have decided, because we are not in the totality zone, that there is no serious threat. Our furry faithfuls will be less perturbed in our company than locked up in the house.

We settle ourselves over near the washing line. Not having bothered to bring chairs, we perch on the drystone wall or squat on the sun-baked grass. Michel is kneeling, trying to stand the radio upright. He is fiddling with the tuning knobs, twisting and turning, searching for the station, while the ancient ghettoblaster hisses and whistles like a drowning kettle.

And then, miraculously, there is music: a blast of ebony notes. Jessye's opulent voice belts forth 'He's Got the Whole World in His Hands', but this is not the tinny reproduction we had expected from our radio. It is a sublime, surround-sound performance assailing us from every direction. Other homes across the hillsides must have come up with the same idea, for the soprano's supersonic voices are airborne; a fleet of aluminium ribbons soaring beyond the hilltops. We are, all of us, silenced and amazed.

'*J'ai commencé d'utiliser le noir pur comme une couleur de lumière et non comme une couleur d'obscurité,*' wrote Henri Matisse.

I have begun to use pure black as a colour of light and not as a colour of darkness.

Bathed in sound from the concert, I attempt to penetrate Matisse's vision. Am I not witnessing the living expression of it? I turn to share this but the others are now engaged in an astronomical debate. All except Serge, who is staring at his feet. He would be fascinated by Matisse's observations, I feel sure, but watching him, I defer, choosing to leave him with the privacy of thought. What memories are haunting him? I wonder. Is he floundering like me, rooting about, trying to reconstruct meaning?

'No, it was Copernicus, not Galileo! Galileo came later.' I hear Vanessa, charged by her young-blooded certainty. Such certainty. 'Copernicus was the first to understand that the earth orbited the sun and not the other way around.'

'That's right, of course,' confirms Papa.

I read that after England's last total eclipse, on 29 June 1927, Virginia Woolf wrote: 'We had fallen. It was extinct. There was no colour. The earth was dead.'

No colour. I try to picture that. The earth dead. Extinction. As I close my eyes to spear her image, I realise that the temperature is dropping. I feel chilly. And there is no birdsong. No songs of nature at all. The exquisite music, yes, and the conversation alongside me. I open my eyes. My skin has goosepimpled. The dogs at my feet are silent and uncharacteristically still. Lucky's ears are standing to attention; she is alert in the way she is when she sniffs intruders or trouble. The other two, Ella and Bassett, are prostrate at my feet, snouts buried beneath paws.

The universe is rotating, turning the clock to another setting. I see shadows lengthening across the earth, distorted elongations of the cherry and olive trees reaching across the groves, creeping towards us like spirits stealing forth. I behold shadows where there have never been shadows before. It is eerie, quite spooky. Souls of the departed tiptoeing out to play. I shiver, casting off this image quickly.

Although the day is growing dimmer it remains bizarrely clear, sharp. Neither dusk nor dawn, day nor night. Rather, a flash of lightning frozen in time. On the terrace beneath us the cacti resemble giant-eared cartoon figures. I hear voices rising from afar, the rattle of shouted conversations, nervous-edged cries in the valley as the world slides into darker mode;

a limboland of quasi-crepuscular noon. The heavens are retreating, as though the gods were switching off our universe, drawing the celestial curtains once and for all. For a moment I feel nauseous. I experience a profound sense of panic. I glance about me, taking in the family gathered here, the people I love. Each momentarily silent, lost in his or her own contemplations; awestruck, perhaps, or pondering similarly gloomy demises to this unnatural day.

Michel picks up his explanation of the death of megastars, describing white dwarfs and what causes them. How long does a star live? I ask myself. And then, bizarrely, I hear Vanessa raise the same question and Michel's response: 'The bigger the star, the quicker it dies.'

'Compared to the sun, how much bigger are these stars?' It is Vanessa once again.

'Varying sizes, but scientists are not able to measure precisely. Twenty times bigger, I don't know. But when they implode they form the most mysterious phenomenon in the whole cosmos. I'm sure you know it, Vanessa?'

She shakes her head.

'The black hole.'

The black hole. Yes, I know it. I've been there. I lift my eyes to stare at the sun, to challenge that black enemy. Throwing my head recklessly back, gazing impudently upwards, knowing I shouldn't, but what the hell; inexorably drawn to the phenomenon occurring billions of light years above. The glare is blinding; it shocks. A sheet flaps lightly on the washing line. It catches my attention and its snowy-white ordinariness drags me to my senses.

'What are you doing? *Chérie!*'

I close my eyes tight before the light brands my retina. I see silver and black rings, crescents, circles, cuticles, wafers of luminosity; my sight has been dazzled, momentarily zapped.

Michel reaches towards me, his hand grabs my wrist. '*Chérie*, please take care.'

Jessye is now singing Gershwin's 'Summertime' from *Porgy and Bess* as the darkening grows darker; a wink, centuries old, received as though in slow motion.

We are each marginally apart, in our space, transfixed, bewitched by music and the coupling of star and planet, this mysterious astral love song. Each of us, that is, except Clarisse, who suddenly rises and shifts places, settling herself at Serge's side. I study her as she draws her knees tightly up against her daisy-stalk frame, wrapping arms round calves to keep warm and then, so imperceptibly, tilts herself in his direction.

I am stunned. I hadn't read the special attachment between these two but now, in this ghost of a light, their future is chalked, pellucid-clear as though it had always been written.

Without ado, I spring up and hurry inside.

On the television, the news report from Reims is taking a dramatic tone: if the clouds don't clear the eclipse will be obscured. An anchorman is counting down the minutes, the seconds. I think I hear that it is raining up there, but I am not listening, not paying attention. I cross through the living room and enter the haven of my den, where I switch on my computer and begin to bang at the keys.

Do I have the right to be jealous of C's attentiveness to S? His loss is unquestionably worse than mine. I don't OWN grief. Am I jealous of their youth without being aware of it? Do I begrudge them their beauty, their shiny futures; the possibilities they hold in their hands, their almost certain fecundity?

'What are you doing?'
'Scribbling.'

'Yes, I see that. Won't you come back outside and join us?'

I don't answer. I can't speak. This day, this darkness, this family gathering is almost too much to bear.

'Please, talk to me,' begs Michel. 'What is the matter with you?'

'It's fine for you, you have children!' I snap, not meaning to, not even knowing what carelessly thought-through thoughts I was about to utter.

'It's easy for you to say you don't mind that we don't have children, that if I can't produce any . . .' I falter. 'That we are still a couple, no matter what. You have your family. Those girls are yours, *yours*, not ours. I am the one who . . .' my voice breaks. I cannot continue. Overwhelmed by the affliction which aches like a deep, black chasm, I drop my head forward over my desk. My forehead brushes against the keyboard which instantaneously produces an alphabet of confusion on the screen. 'I feel so many things. All of them negative. I feel inadequate, a failure,' I mutter.

Michel remains a moment by the doorway, where no door exists now because he took it away to open up the space and create a more luminous living area. He looks on helplessly in my direction.

'Shall we discuss this now, or . . . ?'

I don't respond because I don't know what to say. I had never intended to embark on this, but now that I have I pinch at the corner of the envelope hidden beneath my Apple Mac and slip it out. Richard's letter. Without a word, I hand it to Michel.

He takes it and reads it gravely. And then lifts his eyes to mine. 'Come here.'

I remain where I am.

'*Papa! Papa! Viens! Vite!*' It's Vanessa calling. He hesitates.

'Please go, they're waiting for you. They want to share this day with you.'

'*Viens, chérie*, please.' He holds out his arm. '*Chérie, s'il te plaît.*'

I flip a glance over to where he is waiting patiently for me and rise awkwardly, accepting his outstretched hand. He takes me in his arms and hugs me tight. 'I know it might feel like the end of the world, particularly today, but it isn't. We'll get through this together,' he whispers into my hair. 'I am here for you. *Je t'aime enormement.*'

We step out into a world that has been transformed.

Everything is lit as though by floodlight, everywhere cloaked in silence: an enchanted stage. The gloaming hour before the appearance of the Fairy Queen. Heads are tilted heavenwards – it is safe to look now – entranced faces pearly-skinned, lustrous in a world that is perfectly still.

Two images come to my mind: the parable in the Bible of Lot and his wife looking backwards and being frozen into pillars of salt, and, in the teachings of Zen, the notion of being so at one with oneself, so in union with the universe, that you can hear a blade of grass growing.

The universe shifts yet another notch, such a great lumbersome clock, and the sun's corona, that halo of oyster light made up of the superheated gases surrounding it, is glowing like a translucent wedding band. All five of us are transfixed by the aubergine heavens. We are in communion with the stars which, at the zenith of this supernatural, surreal day, are winking like expiring fireflies.

And all at once the spell is broken. It's over. Daylight returns. It comes like an explosion of shattering glass as a flock of herring gulls appear from out of nowhere and screech angrily, raucously at the silence. Tearing into the sable darkness, they fly low, beating their wings, swooping and turning. They are disoriented, not knowing if it's day or night.

'Surely it must be night, for we have been in darkness,' a

cacophony of creatures cry out in unison. The world is raging with confusion. Crickets, birds burst into song; I hear the crowing of a distant cock which, bemused, probably thinks it's daybreak, the braying of a far-off donkey, the cicadas zirring like there's no tomorrow – and, perhaps, cowering between stalks and leaves, they had feared there would not be one ever again. Noah has unbattened the hatches, lowered the gangplank; time to fly free. We are standing in the midst of a new dawning, a newly lit afternoon. I exhale deeply, sensing ineffable relief. I had never before measured how profoundly the flora and fauna depend on this time-honoured structure of day and night, the customary rhythms of the universe, at least as much as we do. And within these routine yet mysterious daily rounds, this ebbing and flowing, this waning and waxing, there exists both loss and gain, suffering and joy, death and birth. And rebirth?

At our feet, from the radio, Jessye's ivory-black voice belts forth, engendering faith. 'Somewhere', and then 'Praise God and Dance'.

René's Bêtise

The Arabs have said their farewells. Utensils and materials have been transported up the hill, their work achieved. Now it is down to Quashia to begin the construction repairs. M. Di Luzio finally returns my call. He is pleased to hear from me, enquires after my escalating success in films – have I been offered a role in Hollywood yet? – and then announces that he has retired.

Ah. I ask him if he can recommend another plumber.

'Well, I don't usually make a habit of suggesting anyone else, but it can't hurt me any longer so try Sordello. You'll find them in the Yellow Pages and they're in the village beneath you.'

'Thank you,' I tell him. '*Et bonne retraite.*'

'Retirement? Bah! I'd rather be working. My wife stalks me, watching every mouthful that passes my lips. No more beer. Oh, well, that's life. I might drop by to borrow some of your garden tools, if you have no objections; I've got myself an allotment. Well, it passes the time. Greetings to Michel.'

'Indeed,' I smile, replacing the phone.

Michel is not at home. He has driven the girls and Serge to Cannes. During their absence René drops by. As is his habit, he arrives with a gift. Today he comes bearing a bottle of eau de vie distilled from our plums. With a twinkle in his eye, he confides that it is illegal to brew home-made alcohol. Only one location in each village – 'and this is not the case in every village, mind you' – has the right to distil alcohol. Naturally, he has figured out a way to circumvent the system.

I thank him for the precious bottle and ask after news of the water dowser. 'We are cleaning up the *bassin*,' I explain, 'and we'll be needing to feed it some time soon, so if there's underground water here . . .'

'*Malheureusement*, he's not here. After the eclipse he decided to spend a few days in the Champagne district to buy some wines. He only drinks champagne, you see.'

I am beginning to doubt the existence of this fellow and am on the brink of saying so when a rattling screech breaks out above us in the parking area. We both lift our heads to see four magpies pecking brutally at one another, staking their territorial rights over a few figs shrivelling on the tree.

'Bloody magpies,' I curse.

'Did I ever tell you about the pet magpie we had when I was a kid? Margot was her name.'

'No.'

'Good Lord, Carol, those branches have grown!' cries our olive master, now pointing up at the cedars overhead. 'They're damned dangerous. You must cut them back. Otherwise you'll have the electricity board on your backs. It's illegal, you know, for your trees to brush the cables, and it could cause a fire. And I don't have to tell you about bush fires.'

'Yes, we've been intending to cut them back all summer, but what with one thing and another . . .'

'No excuse. I'll cut them back for you right now and, as I told you last time, I'll keep the wood. Where's Quashia?'

'He's working up at the second basin. Do you want me to fetch him?'

'No, I'll manage, but I'll need to use his chainsaw. I haven't got mine with me. I lent it to my son. Has Quashia taken the ladders with him? No, there they are. Good.'

And before I can say another word, René is setting about in a purposeful way. It is unusual for him to be in such a hurry. Usually, he prefers a glass of something and a natter first.

'I tell you what,' he calls out to me as I make my way back into the house. 'Why don't you pour us both *un petit verre* while I get the chainsaw warmed up? And then I'll go to work.'

I smile, and then call back to him. 'You don't think we should have the glass of wine later, after you've finished with the ladder?'

'Not at all. It's almost lunchtime.'

Seated on the terrace, a bottle of Beaujolais to hand, I ask him to recount the tale of Margot, the magpie he spoke of.

'*Ah, notre agace,*' he grins.

Agace actually means an irritation – *agacer* is to jar, grate, set one's teeth on edge, and it is used in Provence as a name for magpies because their wretched screeching can drive you to distraction. As does their habit of filching.

'Margot lived with us for eight years and she drove our neighbours and guests crazy. Us as well, sometimes. She was jealous, you see. She couldn't bear it if the cat got more attention than she did. You know, Carol, we were rather poor and my mother used to feed the cat with leftovers from our meals. Usually we ate pasta, *pâtes*, and the cat seemed perfectly content with her scraps of that, but Margot would go mad. She wanted the same, you see. So, when the cat was dozing or not paying attention, Margot would sneak to the cat's bowl, steal the squares of pasta and . . . you know that magpies hide things they have stolen, don't you?'

I nod.

'Do you know where she hid the pasta?'

I shake my head.

'We were poor, as I told you. We ran around in our bare feet and, while we were at dinner, the bird would sneak under the table and slip the pasta squares in between our toes.'

I stare at him incredulously and then burst out laughing. René is encouraged by my response. He nods, pours himself a second glass of wine and then continues.

'Our neighbour smoked a pipe. Margot stole the pipe and threw it in his pond. Eventually, a week or so later, he found it, dried it out, cleaned it up and put it back on the mantel-piece, and then, *diable*! it was gone again. Of course, at that stage, the neighbour hadn't realised that it was our blasted bird who was responsible, but we kids guessed. The neighbour searched in the pond, but it wasn't there because the bird was smart. She never hid anything in the same place twice. He couldn't find that pipe anywhere and gave it up for lost.'

René reaches for the bottle and proffers it. I shake my head. He serves himself a top-up.

'But I knew it must be Margot, so I went round to the neighbour, knocked on his door and said to him: "Monsieur Braccio, is there a reward for finding your pipe?" He laughed, ruffled my hair and promised me two francs if I found it. It was a fortune to me then. I told not a soul but I kept a watchful eye on our bird. And one morning, weeks later, bingo! I found it. The magpie was sitting in the neighbour's mimosa tree with the pipe in her beak. She liked to copy, you see. She had understood that the neighbour held the pipe in his mouth and sucked on it, so Margot mimicked him. There she was, happy as Larry, sitting in a fully blossoming golden mimosa smoking a pipe. *Diable.* I got my two francs.' He laughs triumphantly, downing his wine and refilling his glass. I am beginning to wonder if I should remind him about the tree-cutting, but before I can he has launched into another anecdote about the bird.

'She learned to whistle like my father, repeated our names like a parrot and called and whistled for the dog.' Here René imitates the magpie by whistling and calling in a high-pitched voice: '*Flora! Flora!* That was the dog's name,' he explains. The sound has alerted two of our own dogs, who come running in our direction.

'My father used to keep his work boots in the garage alongside a box of nails. Margot stole the nails and hid them in my father's boots, and he cut his feet when he put his boots on and stood on the nails. How we children giggled! Ah, yes, we loved her. She had fallen from a nest. My father found her and we raised her. Eight years she lived with us. She was so crafty. She taught me a few tricks.' He chuckles mischievously and downs the remainder of his Beaujolais – the bottle is almost empty – then sets to work on pruning back the cedar trees while I return to my den, both amused and amazed by our little Provençal olive guru. Just like Margot, he never misses a trick.

I am answering e-mail when I hear the cries, and because my computer is a laptop and works on both battery and electricity I do not immediately notice that our electricity has been cut off.

'*Mon Dieu! Diable! Putain! Qu'est-ce que . . .?*'

I run to the window and throw it open.

There I behold René, at the foot of the ladder, chainsaw hanging from his hand, pouring with sweat, red as a beetroot, covered in bits of cedar foliage, and sticks and twigs and branches everywhere on the ground. But what is most shocking is the firework display of flying sparks.

'Oh my God!' I cry. 'What's happened?'

But it is quite clear what has happened. The tree has been felled in the wrong direction (or 'it turned on its own in the wind', as René tries to convince me later) and has landed on the four electricity cables running via the pylon close by the swimming pool to the house. While stretching from the ladder to the tip of a branch, René has lost his footing and with it his control of the chainsaw, which has struck the central trunk of the tree, still zirring. The upper portion of the tree, partially sawn through, has cracked and barrelled earthwards, slapping against the overhead electricity cables as it spun. The weight has pushed the highest cable against the one beneath it, and so on, in a domino effect, soldering all four cables as one. Naturally, this has caused a short circuit in the system and our power has gone.

I stare down at the cables. They resemble giant lengths of liquorice, looping towards the ground sending massive streaks of sparks sissing skywards.

I am open-eyed, thunderstruck, by the pyrotechnics taking place before me. 'I'm calling the fire brigade!' I yell. 'Those sparks will set fire to the trees!'

They are indeed ominously close. And what of the summer-dry herbage everywhere on our land?

I hear a female neighbour's cry and then, from down the lane, the roar of another neighbour, Jean-Claude. René, in the *parking* below me stares up at me like a guilty child. 'I think the electricity may have been cut off at the entrance to your property,' he announces sheepishly.

If this predicament weren't so perilous I might be tempted to laugh, because I have never before seen René cowed by anything. The man who made a financial killing out of the Second World War and everything else that has come his way has now landed himself in a very sticky situation.

'I'm on my way down,' I tell him, closing up the window. I tear down the exterior steps to the ground-floor level, bellowing 'Monsieur Quashia!' as I charge alongside the pool, where the skimmers have gone dead. There is little hope that Quashia will have heard me, and, as he will be facing uphill as he works, I doubt that he will have seen the sparks flying, either.

I join René in the *parking*. He looks as though he is about to have a heart attack.

The fireworks are over and the cables have sunk to the tarmac in the *parking* like deflated balloons. I am hit full on by an appalling smell of burning rubber.

'Now what?' I am terrified, but the fact is I have not grasped the magnitude of the accident whereas René has. As I approach, he bursts into action.

'It's because they are *en alu* that they, the cables, are *fondu*. First thing,' he is shouting as he scurries into the garage with the chainsaw, burying it beneath some of Quashia's work clothes, while I follow trying to work out what he is up to, 'I wasn't working here, OK?'

'OK,' I mouth, because at this stage I don't know what else to do or say. 'But what should we do? Call the fire brigade or the EDF?'

'No! No!' He is turning in circles like a small trapped rodent, desperately trying to think his way out of this one. 'I've got it. We must play shocked.'

'I am shocked!' I retort.

There is a high-pitched voice calling my name. I peer out

of the garage. A woman is running up the drive. Who left the gate unlocked? How did she get in?

'Carol! Carol!' she is screaming hysterically.

It's one of our neighbours. 'Oh, God, not her,' I moan.

'*Diable*, I left your gate unlocked,' René confides to me under his breath. 'Quick, run down to meet her. Don't let her up here, whatever you do.'

I do as I am told. He puffs along behind me. 'On second thoughts, keep quiet. I'll handle it.'

'Handle *what*?'

'Er, *bonjour*, Suzanne,' I say to the woman, who I am not in the least fond of and try to avoid even on the best of days. 'What is it?'

'There's been a disaster!'

'Really?' I play-act.

'An accident somewhere. We have no electricity, nothing at all. Do you know anything about this?' Her voice rises and the tone grows shriller and meaner as she grills me.

I shake my head, waiting for René to chip in and 'handle it', but he says nothing.

She continues: 'The whole lane's cut off, as is the motorway – all the way to Antibes.'

'WHAT!!' I scream. 'All the way to . . .' Antibes is close to fifteen kilometres from us.

René steps briskly forward. 'Yes, I was in the garden sorting out a few plant problems, *quelques petits soucis*, for Carol and I thought I was going to be killed when the sparks started flying. Did you see them? I hope you weren't too afraid?'

'I was,' Suzanne admits to him in an altogether softer tone.

'You and Carol must sue the electricity board, as well as the local council, for negligence if the fault is found to be due to an oversight on one of their parts.' His placatory tone, his charming concern, his brazen *lies*, have Suzanne eating out of his hand, and I am left gawping at his audacity.

'Fret not, madame, I will telephone the EDF and get them over here right away.'

'I think Jean-Claude has already done that.'

'Oh, has he?' I hear the edge return to René's voice. 'Well, there's nothing for it but to wait, then. Would you like me to accompany you back to your villa? Although I am sure there will be no further risk.'

'*Mais merci beaucoup. Vous êtes très gentil, monsieur.* What about Carol?'

'Oh, she's fine.'

And René escorts Suzanne back down the drive, leaving me alone, listening to his sweet concern. 'Is there anything you need, *chère* madame?'

Moments later, he climbs back up the path to me and the broiled, perished chaos that is our parking area. He is using the oily rag in his hand to wipe the sweat off his brow, thus blackening his florid face.

'Well, that's dealt with her. Now, we'll have to play this one out,' he says sternly to me. 'According to her, your other neighbour—'

'Jean-Claude.'

'Yes, Jean-Claude, well, he has called the bloody electricity board and they are on their way as I speak. Let me do the talking.'

I nod. I would not dream of interfering. If there is a day to be won, it's René's.

I take a seat over by the pool, wondering whether I should fetch Quashia. I decide that the fewer the people involved at this stage, probably the safer we are. If Michel comes back now . . . At this very moment, a blue EDF van beetles up the drive and two burly technicians get out. They look like they mean business. I rise and move uncertainly in their direction.

Should I leave this to René, or should I come forward, mistress of the house, and say something or other? Offer help, plead ignorance?

René is pointing out the overhead trees, charcoaled by the sparks. They stare heavenwards with sullen expressions.

'*Bonjour, messieurs,*' I call as I approach.

'There's over forty thousand francs' worth of damage,' one of them states in a matter-of-fact manner which I read as a threat.

'All the signalling on the autoroute is out. We have one dead system, burned out back at base. It will take three days' work to repair this lot!' adds the other. 'I think forty grand is an understatement. Someone's going to have to pay.'

I feel my knees buckle. I am not sure if I want to be sick or lie down. What I am sure of is that I don't want Quashia to wander down the hill now and let the cat out of the bag by commenting on René's work. I glance across at our olive hero, who looks, at this moment, no bigger than a pea. 'Any idea what happened?' he asks manfully, but I hear the croak in his voice.

'Well, you are the last house to be affected, so my guess is the problem started here.'

René flashes a look my way. I think he is telling me to get lost.

'Would you gentlemen like a cold drink?' I offer.

'No thanks, ma'am.'

'No, thanks.'

'Well, when I first saw the sparks . . .' begins René, and I am obliged to walk away because I cannot listen to what I know will be a pack of lies. Forty thousand francs is £4,000. I, we, don't possess such a sum.

The next time I look up, from the other side of the pool, where I am seated, worrying, the three men are talking on a telephone. Then they are shaking hands and slapping one another on the back. René is smiling. He comes hurrying towards me while the electricians wait near the cars.

'Quick!' he cries.

'What?'

'Give me some freshly bottled olive oil. The last pressing you have. I'll repay you later.'

I hurry into the summer kitchen, where it is cool and dark and where we store the freshly pressed oil, and pull out two wine bottles filled with our rich, green produce. René grabs them from me, winks and scuttles back to the *parking*. He hands each man a bottle, each shakes his hand vigorously and then they drive off.

'What was all that about?'

'They'll be back later to begin the repairs but we – well, you, that is – are off the hook.'

'Us?' I squeak.

'You would have been responsible for the entire cost of the works,' he tells me proudly. 'But I saved the day.'

'How?'

'It turns out that I know their boss. He used to drive lorries with my son. Well, I know a thing or two about him, a bit of business that goes on here and there, and I told them to give him a call. We had a word. Well, you know how these things are . . .'

I don't, but I don't interrupt him.

'. . . and we agreed all round to register the fault at the motorway. The fact is, Carol, it shouldn't have had such an impact back at their base, so it wasn't really our fault anyway.'

'So that's the end of it?'

'Once they've been back to carry out the maintenance work, yes.'

'Right,' I mutter, not quite sure whether to congratulate him or berate him.

'I need a drink. Shall we finish off that bottle we began at lunch? It seems a long while ago.'

I nod and go off to fetch wine. Frankly, I need a drink too, but there's not much left in that bottle. I dig out another.

Sitting with René on the terrace, I am understandably pensive, anxious even, while he is in high spirits. His mood is triumphant.

'Once we get the dowser here and sort out your well,' he says, chewing on an olive, 'then we'll make that trip to my friend the beekeeper.'

I listen on silently as he promises yet again to introduce me to the 'best beekeeper in Provence', a friend of his since they were lads in the village. Now this gentleman is eighty-three years old but still a professional apiarist.

'When we were youngsters we were competitors for the girls.'

'Who won?' I tease, brightening a little to his mood.

'Oh,' he grins, 'we both did all right. Never touched the local girls, though. Only the foreign ones. Never get into trouble at home, is what I say.'

Well, you can't claim to have followed that dictum today, eh, René? I am thinking, but choose not to say this out loud.

Later, when Michel and the youngsters return, he asks me what on earth has happened. I suggest that we all settle down with a glass of wine in the candlelight.

'It will have to be red wine because the white is no longer chilled. We have no electricity.'

'What's happened?' he repeats.

'Fill your glass with warm wine, Michel, it's a long story.'

Alternatives

During these hot, languid days, while the sun punishes and where nothing but a jet trail disturbs the blueness of the sky, I have been observing Clarisse and how she tends Serge. Her attentions are discreet, unlike mine. Now I find myself studying them both. Pressed against windows, leaning from terraces, always observant of her, my step-daughter, of how she asks to see his work, talks to him at length about the characters he is sketching, the world he is creating. She is prising him out of himself; she listens attentively, chooses subjects that fire his imagination. She is the image of her father. She knows intuitively when to draw near, when to gently intrude and when to hold herself at a distance. Her approaches are graceful. *She* is graceful, never hasty. Tiny, geisha-like steps she takes, and never falters. Yet she has no experience in this – how could she have? – she is playing it by instinct. Still, what I see is her regard for this man so many – how many? Fourteen? – years her senior, and for who he is. I am amazed that one so young, a slip of a girl who has passed her previous summers here collecting wild flowers, a girl I judged as passive, can operate from such depths of compassion and human understanding.

Both Clarisse and Serge are fired by a passion for art and their ability to express themselves through colours and forms. They have that in common. It is their language, as it is a mother tongue to Michel, who lives his own life so richly through colours and forms. He, too, I watch, as he works with Serge at the long wooden table in the garden, pages and pages of artwork for their storyboards spread out before them, fluttering in a ghost of a breeze, pinned down with stones and pens and used cups. I cannot see their eyes, shielded by dark glasses, or hear their words from this distance, but I can read their enthusiasm for their film, their creation. And all the while Clarisse is there, fetching and carrying glasses of wine, bottles of water, or sitting a little apart, chin resting in her hands, elbows on the table, listening attentively, idly studying the sketches, drinking in the process of work.

She has been seduced by the business of filmmaking, that is evident. But there's more. She loves this bereaved man. No doubt about it. Her eyes, flowing over with the vernal joys and palpitations of first love, linger on him and tell their story. And what of him? What he does feel? A shy, physically gauche man at the best of times, he probably has no idea what he feels about any damn thing. I know I don't. Still, he responds to her. Fragile emotions. Unspoken words, tender glances, drawings exchanged – messages only they can read – long walks side by side or, more frequently, one trailing the other until they reach a resting place within the harbour of the fruiting trees. Sometimes they are gone for hours on end, lost among the butterflies and wasps and vintage heat. Love in the olive groves. It certainly is a love affair of sorts. With Clarisse at his side, his unthreatening companion, Serge is healing. I clock the changes taking place within him. He is picking up the pieces. And what do I feel? Bittersweet emotions engulf me. Those youngsters have time. Together, or individually, they have their futures. But what of me?

Vanessa, too, is absent most days. She takes the scooter and goes to the beach, returning late, flushed with sea wind (and kisses, I am sure of it), brown as chocolate licked shiny in the melting heat. She, too, has met someone, and she has flowered overnight. She has become radiant. I mention it to Michel. He frowns. 'I don't think so,' he says. 'Why would you think that?'

Because I am a woman.

Even if these girls are not my daughters, I am alert to them. To the treasures of their enchantments. And if they were my daughters I would enfold them in my arms and hug them with such force and josh with them, begging them to share their secrets with me. 'Recount your happinesses, your discoveries, whisper them to me.' But they aren't, and there's the rub.

The water bill arrives, and sends us reeling. Nine thousand francs for three months' supply. Even when we discovered a leak in the swimming pool a while ago, it was nowhere near as much as this. We have been charged for approximately 1,500 cubic metres of water. It cannot be possible! And then we remember M. Halaz and his remarkable results in the garden. Delighted as we were, they have come at a price. They have left us with a sum to pay three times higher than we have ever shelled out before.

'Think how much more expensive it would be if we were to plant the new trees,' I say to Michel.

'We haven't decided not to,' he returns.

I do not respond. I gather up our coffee cups from the terrace and carry them inside.

He follows with jams and yoghurts. 'What do you say?'

'I don't want to plant trees. I can't take on anything else.'

I may have given up on the olives but I am still struggling with the elusive beemasters, who have all retreated inland and refuse in this escalating heat to visit us here. One woman I have been talking to on the telephone scoffs at the idea of bringing her hives so close to the coast. 'Too many tourists, too much traffic and the area is overconstructed.'

'Not where we are.'

'*Desolée. Non.* It's far too polluted where you are,' she says. I sigh, because from her point of view, this is probably not unreasonable, and we may never find our hivemaster.

Quashia has completed the repair work to the *bassin*. Today, he and Michel will go to work on the interior, which resembles a jungle. We all traipse up the hill to take a look. When I stand on piled stones and peer inside the old stone chamber, I see it is a breeding ground for plants. There are tiger lilies shooting up and wild, willowy canes growing within and Lord knows what else has seeded. The cane of Provence, I tell them, is one of the earliest plants to have been found on this Mediterranean coast. Cannes takes its name from the canes that used to grow along its saline littoral. They are known to survive best in hot, humid environments.

'Here, look at this!' calls Michel. 'The wall bears a mason's name, inscribed into the stone. No date though, which is a pity.'

The terraces up here are bare, save for a few self-seeded baby pines, thin as pencils, swaying gently in the altitude heat. It is ideal land for planting olives, or for the hives. *L'emplacement des ruches.* Yes, I can picture a row of beehives up here, out of reach of the dogs. No one could claim this patch is polluted. I breathe in deeply and the resiny air sings through my lungs.

'What's that noise?' I ask the two men, who are deciding how best to approach the basin cleaning.

'Sounds like chainsaws,' replies Michel.

I look about, wondering where the distraction could be coming from, but the forest is too dense to gauge the direction.

'They are cutting trees over on the other side of the valley,' says Quashia without concern.

'But we're in a green belt. *Une zone verte*. Nobody has the right to cut down trees!' I cry. 'It's illegal!'

'No, it's fine, don't worry. They are only pruning them, tidying up the land.'

When I return to the house to make coffee I hear screams and shouts from the *bassin* and rush out to see what is happening. Quashia hares down the hill with the step of a teenager. A family of deep russet-red squirrels are inhabiting the basin and sticks are needed to encourage them out. 'We don't want to hurt them,' he shouts as he passes. 'Come back up and see.'

But halfway up the hill, I am interrupted by the arrival of the new plumber, M. Sordello. He seems a very excitable fellow, hooting incessantly and bawling from his van, door open, cigarette in hand.

'Anyone home? Hello, hello! Anyone home?'

'I'm coming,' I scream from the hill, puffing and panting back down the track.

'Jesus! How many dogs have you got? Call them off!'

'Three. I have already chained up the Alsatian. The other two are reasonably harmless.'

I outline our requirements and he takes one look up the hill and shouts – I learn later that he always shouts – 'I'm not climbing up there! Not in this bloody heat! It'll have to wait until autumn.'

'Couldn't we take a gentle stroll up so that you can give us an approximate costing?'

He huffs and sighs dramatically, scratching his balding head, twitching his beaked nose. 'Any chance of a cup of coffee first? I'm bloody exhausted. I hate this weather. Roll on winter.'

I go inside to pour the freshly made coffee. He follows me in, still smoking. 'How do you take it, Monsieur Sordello?'

'Black, five sugars.'

Five sugars? No wonder he is jumping like a jack-in-the-box. We go out on to the terrace, and I am pointing up the hill, explaining what we need, when I see Clarisse and Serge up ahead. Michel is waving to me. There is much excitement, but I cannot make out what is going on. Sordello seizes his chance to be on his way, promising to return another day, in the evening, when the sun is less fierce.

'I'll give you a bell later,' he shouts, zipping back out of our lives.

The squirrels have successfully escaped. They have levered themselves on to the olive stick Quashia has lowered into the basin, scurried up it and then leaped to freedom. All except one, a baby that lost its footing on the cane. When Quashia attempted to assist, the little creature freaked and drew blood from our gardener's wrist.

I spend the remainder of the morning treating his wound, which is worryingly deep. I want to drive him to the hospital or to our doctor for a tetanus jab, but he won't hear of it. The little squirrel is frightened but not harmed. We decide to let her go. How she leaps! She flies through the air, landing in a cedar tree, and from there scoots from tree to tree until she is lost in the verdant wild.

Serge left for Paris this morning, loaded down with work for his project with Michel. We said our farewells, with hugs and embraces, and then Michel drove him to the airport. All day long Clarisse has looked downhearted, tramping the hill in search of her father.

I have never felt jealous of Michel's family, never felt any desire to intrude upon or despoil that past life of his, the years he spent with the girls' mother and all that they built together. On the contrary, I have always heartily welcomed that past; it is a vital and significant fraction of the man I love, the man Michel is today, even though I know precious little about that time. Michel is inscrutable and he is discreet. That first marriage and those early years belong to him and those who shared it. Not to me. I have no rights there. The girls rarely speak to me about Maman, even though she and I have met on several occasions. I like her. She makes me laugh; she is neat, witty and pretty. Still, it is their world, their universe, and it does not include me. Only on rare occasions do I skirt its periphery. Michel and I, *we*, came later, when so much was already in place, but I have never perceived myself as an outsider. My relationship with him, his generous love for me, has given me a secure foundation, one I never knew before. It gathers me up, cocoons and protects me. But my misery is eating into it, breeding fears and doubt. Worries nag me. How will I heal? How can I move beyond this failure? What if Michel should leave me? What witness to our love would remain? He and his first wife have the girls; they are the witnesses to that young love. Without children of our own, there will be nothing. Our love will have been a fleeting instant in time; a memory.

The following morning, after a tormented night, I drag myself to my den, not even bothering to dress. I heave down files and riffle furiously through work notes, casting about for a structure that will gel the pages into some semblance of order, grappling for the logical progression I must have been building, because I *have to* get beyond this negativity. I must find purpose and the only way I know how is through work. From my window, I rest my tired eyes on the sprawling fig tree. I return to my table and I write:

> The perfume of the summer fig is a heavy fragrance. It is musky, milky and dominates the scents of everything growing around it. Gravid . . . mothers' milk . . .

I throw down my pen and, rising from my chair, return to the window. I look again. What do I see? I see lopped-off cedar branches and scarred trunks. Most of the figs have ripened, fallen to the ground and been squashed by the passage of cars. Their crunchy pulp and seeds, carried by tyres, have spread all over the tarmac drive and left a sticky jam. The magpies zap at it with their beaks, devouring it wolfishly. They ignore the fruit's dark purply skins. Those lie shrivelling like bits of dried leather leached by the heat to the colour of diluted ink.

I return to my table and take a deep breath. Somewhere beyond the room, the telephone is ringing. I barely notice. I am leafing through notes. I find the page.

The fig tree, *le figuier*. The fig tree appears in many paintings and there are, of course, frequent references to it in the Bible. According to Lawrence Durrell, the fig tree was 'owned' by the god Demeter, while Bacchus, the god of wine and good living, carved his sacred phallus from its wood.

Its logs give off an acrid aroma when burned in the grate. It is ill-advised to plant these trees up against stone walls. They require plenty of circulating air or else, in the heat, they smell like cat's pee.

'The garage in Cannes has just telephoned. Your car is ready.

Would you like me to ask them to deliver it, or shall we drive down together and fetch it?' I have not heard Michel's approach, lost as I was in my studies.

'Oh, hi there.' I sigh, placing pen on tabletop. 'No, I'll walk down myself and collect it later.'

'Don't you want me to come with you? To make sure they've done a good job?'

I shake my head. 'No, I'll be fine.'

He pauses. 'It's good that you're working,' he smiles encouragingly.

I bow my head. 'Not really . . .'

'Please don't be so closed off, *chérie*.'

'Am I? Sorry, I . . .'

'I feel as though you resent me.'

I shake my head again. 'No, I don't. There is resentment, but it is not against you.'

'Who, then?'

I cannot answer. Until we came here, until I found Michel and we took on the challenge of Appassionata, I never put my feet on the ground and felt the earth stay firm beneath me. There is not a corner of this place, this olive farm, that I do not love. Every cobweb shot through with light, glinting silvery as old badgers' hairs; every arboreal bird singing its song; the geckos, lizards, every creature (well, maybe not the snakes and rats); every storm, even those that crack and fizz, shut off the electricity, send the dogs into a yowling spin and terrify me; every sunbeam that warms Michel's smooth skin and mellows the shadows I have carried in my heart. I hear and see all of these wonders and more, but I will never hear our child's cry, see her laughter on a summer's day, suffer her fears as she enters the pool before learning to swim. I will never know if, when I took her hand in mine, she would have felt safe in the fundamental way I never did.

'Carol? Are you listening?'

'Mmm?'

'Let me come with you to the garage. We can take the car and go off for lunch . . .'

I shake my head.

Michel nods his acquiescence and turns to leave me. 'By the way, what happened to that roll of film I gave you?'

'What film? Oh, I took it to be developed.'

'And?'

'I collected the photos.' He waits expectantly. 'They must be in my bag or in the car somewhere. I'll find them. Sorry, I forgot.'

The photographs have been hidden beneath the passenger seat of the car in what is now a raggedy wallet. They must have slipped under there as I took a bend in the road and have lain undiscovered for more than a week. Michel finds them while I am at the garage. When I return they are on the table on the upper terrace, where he has prepared our lunch.

'Isn't this the journalist you introduced me to in Cannes?' he asks.

He holds up four photographs, each one taken by me. Of Jacob and the two Italian guests at Barbara's birthday bash. In each of the four pictures, where Barbara should have been, there is nothing, nothing but an illuminated smudge, a grey ghost of an outline. I pick them up and scrutinise them. I am no photographer, but even so.

'I don't understand,' I murmur. 'There were four people . . . Is this something to do with the flash?'

'It shouldn't be.'

'Must have been the glare from the candlelight, then, that bleached her out.' I take the pictures and, later, their negatives too, and slip them into a drawer in my den, disquieted by them.

Some mornings, like this morning, I wake and stretch and

feel if I could reach up and tap at the sky, tap, tap, tap with my fingernails, it would reverberate in gentle chimes. And I know that today will be a good day. Then, carrying our coffee out on to the terrace, we find trails of wet weeds everywhere and muddy pawprints. I am bewildered until I trace them and discover that one of the dogs has devoured the water lilies. Every one of them. Nothing is left but a trail of root systems to prove they ever existed. And the carp, too. All are gone. I am peering at the surface of the pond hoping to catch signs of life, just one living fish, when Thierry, the young man who cleans our pool, arrives on his weekly visit. His mood is buoyant. He has gossip to impart and waves exuberantly. Michel Mouillot, the ex-mayor, has been found guilty of corruption.

'But he is not actually serving his sentence in prison. He has been put under house arrest, *en résidence surveillée*, in a rather elegant villa in the Var. At our expense!' cries cropped-haired Thierry, dragging hard on his cigarette. 'We, who do an honest's day's work for a pittance. We, who pay our taxes and without complaint!'

I smile. I love it when the French get *très chaud* under their collars or, in this trance-inducing climate, their T-shirts, especially when it concerns matters of injustice or workers' rights and white-collar corruption. They rant and rave but our experience has shown us that, at any given opportunity, most would prefer to do business *en noir*, in cash, so that the money can remain undeclared. Thierry is not of that breed. His work is by contract and above board. He is intense and honest. He never accepts a beer because he has other pools and other clients to attend to, but he always stops for a natter, to pass on the latest news of local rackets, and then goes contentedly on his way, with a bottle of mineral water to which he has helped himself from the garage fridge. It does not surprise me to learn that he is originally from another, more northerly region of France.

The scandal of the mayor does seem to have run its course and matters are quietening down along our wave-lapped coast. A new mayor has been elected. Cannes is returning to the erstwhile lucrative business of promoting its perfect sun-kissed lifestyle, and most local enterprises appear to be regaining ground. Even the price of real estate is on the increase again. Although I did read recently that the villa of that old trickster – crook, actually – Jacques Médecin was bought by the state for what many considered was a vastly inflated price soon after he legged it to Uruguay, and has just been sold to a local firm of estate agents for less than a tenth of the sum paid for it. Mmm.

Clarisse flew off late this afternoon. She was headed for Paris, but only for a day or two. Soon she will be setting off for her new life in London. Summer is drawing to a close. Michel will be going away in a few days, too, to begin pre-production on his animation film. It will be almost as though I am alone. Vanessa wants to stay on a while longer, she says, though we rarely see her. She rises late, spends hours in the shower, dresses with meticulous care, endlessly brushing her lustrous mane, and then speeds off, a whirlwind of smiles and flying excitement. These days, she converses with me in English, relishing it as though it were the language of love. And for her it is. The object of her attentions is a young American, she confides. 'He iz verry tall and verry 'and-some.'

'Will we meet him?' I ask her.

'*Ça depend*,' she grins secretively.

'Depends on what?'

' 'e iz verry shay. And 'e is verry frightened to meet Papa.'

'Why?' I laugh.

'Because Papa is my 'ero. But I shall invite him to Paris. I want him to meet Maman.' And she kisses me on both cheeks and hurries away to town, waving as she goes.

She hasn't meant to hurt me.

When Michel returns from the market, he finds me curled up on the bed, red-faced, sobbing into one of our square linen pillows, blotched now with mascara. He kneels on the bed, caresses my tearstained cheeks, kisses my head and then presents me with a cluster of red chili peppers, still attached to their stalks and held together with a pale blue elastic band.

'For you,' he whispers, and lays them out alongside my face.

'What are these for?' I mumble, nonplussed, for we rarely cook with chilis.

'A bouquet for you.'

I sniff and attempt a laugh. 'Are you teasing me?' But no, he takes my hand and leads me through the *salon*, where a bouquet of equally red long-stemmed roses are displayed in a vase, and on to the kitchen, where he places the chilis in the woven basket piled high with raw vegetables.

'I don't understand.'

'I thought it was an interesting alternative to flowers,' he smiles, inching me towards him, hugging me tightly, while tenderly stroking my back.

'This sadness won't last for ever, *chérie*.'

And I see that it is yet more evidence of Michel's kindliness, his generosity and inventiveness. He will transform anything into a form, a shape, a display of colour, but what I don't yet see is how he is encouraging me to seek alternatives.

The Divinity of Nature

Everyone has left. I spend my days alone, endeavouring to write. The weather has grown hot, windy and turbulent. Scribbles of cloud fleet fast across the sky. Our swimming pool is turning green. This will resolve itself at some point, I have no doubt, but what is much more troubling is that the olive trees are growing jaundiced again. Many of the leaves are dull yellow and smudged with black, circular stains. As I finger a leaf, it falls effortlessly into my hand. This is the wretched *Cyclocodium oleaginum* or *œil de paon*, the malady that damages the leaves but not the fruit. It is a fungus, René reminds me again as we scout the terraces, that is difficult to treat. It was apparent last year, but not to such an extent. I thought we had handled the problem at the beginning of summer.

'We'll have to spray all the trees again once the drupes have been gathered. We can't do it now, of course – it would harm the olives.'

'What troubles me, René, is that I don't want to spray the trees again.'

'You have no alternative.'

'There is one organic product . . .'

'Please don't tell me there is another solution, because there isn't. All anyone will advise is to plant the trees a decent distance apart and prune them regularly. Well, we all know that.'

'It's copper-based . . .'

'It'd be preventive, not curative, Carol, and it's too late for that. There isn't a farmer in the area who'd give a sou for your alternatives. Spray the trees or lose the foliage.'

I sigh. This is a sticky issue between us. 'It's irresponsible. The more we spray, the more we unsettle the ecological balance,' I venture as we walk from one tree to the next, patrolling the extent of the deterioration. 'Have you noticed that there are fewer swallows? I read they are being killed off by insecticides.'

'Well, you may be right. I heard that too.'

I turn to scrutinise him. This remark is coming from a man who has always extolled the virtues of treating the trees by raining gallons of water-mixed chemicals on to them. His methods have always been in direct opposition to what he perceives as my whimsical desires to run this place as an organic farm.

'And the fact is, René, we *have* treated them, against my better judgement, and the fungus has returned. There has to be another way to beat it.'

'There isn't. We have failed because we left it too late. You dithered. If we had sprayed in February or March, before flowering, this would not have happened. And these blasted winds don't help anything. They're probably spreading it.'

We are in the throes of the third *mistral* in as many weeks. Out at sea, white horses are chomping the waves.

What has caused these turbulences? The greenhouse effect? The depletion of rainforests? The roads blasted through the Alps, which allow northerly weather patterns to penetrate southern regions when before there was no access? Or might it be the astronomical quantities of pesticides squirted all over the countryside? I have heard, read, been given so many diverse explanations and I have no idea which, if any, to believe. But I do know that the return of the fungus has made me determined to find an alternative solution. Not only is the product we have used possibly harmful, it is inefficient.

'I went to visit an apiarist in the Var yesterday, a gentleman who has been tending bees since he was fifteen,' I tell René. 'He has agreed to visit us in the spring with a view to placing fifty hives up in the pine forest.'

'Ah, well done.'

'He talked to me about an insecticide spray developed to protect sunflowers that has killed off millions of bees. Sunflowers are a rich source of pollen for bees. While the bees feed off the blossoms, this product attacks their central nervous system, stunning them, and the bees' innate sense of distance and location is befuddled, destroyed by the chemical. They die of exhaustion, searching for the flightpath back to their hives.'

René shrugs. He hates these conversations.

'After I left the bee farm, driving back through the countryside, I remembered an old codger who sat at a table next to me months ago in Nice. A man whose remarks I dismissed as eccentric. The dance of the bees; their language for communicating pollen sources and the whereabouts of their habitats. He said they danced till they were stunned.'

'You can't take on the world, Carol.'

We kiss goodbye and he promises to be back later in the afternoon with the long-awaited water diviner. This will not be M. Nick, but the other gentleman. M. Nick seems to have disappeared off the face of the earth since the beginning of the summer break, but we can do it without him, René is confident.

'If this monsieur finds water, then we'll call in M. Nick to confirm it. If he doesn't, then you can inform the necessary parties that a dowser has made a thorough search and has confirmed that there is no accessible water source.' He glances skywards. 'Let's hope this wind doesn't bring rain, or he won't be able to work.'

I smile. It is not something I would have given thought to, but it's logical, of course; a water diviner cannot search for water in wet weather.

The wind does not let up, but nor does it bring rain. I am in my den when the American four-wheel-drive purrs up our leafy approach. It is twenty minutes early and for a moment I am not sure who has arrived. The dogs are barking and I run to look out of the window. They quieten when they see René descending from the rear of the Ford. I bang on the window and signal that I am on my way down.

'Hang on to the dogs,' I call, hurrying to greet my guests.

Monsieur the water dowser is an impressive but unexpected sight. He is very elegantly dressed, in golfing cap, suede bomber jacket and exquisite leather shoes. In all my imaginings among the *dramatis personae* of life, this is not the character I would have created to play the role of Provençal local searching for water. The dogs jump all over him, sullying his clothes, and I am obliged to haul them away.

'Don't worry,' he laughs. 'I love animals.' He exudes warmth and good breeding. 'So does my wife, here.' He glances towards the front passenger seat, and out steps a tiny woman, thin as a twig and no taller than a robin. She has dyed blonde hair, a silk scarf which is blowing into her

face, and running shoes. I fear the dogs in their overexcite-
ment to greet the new arrivals might send this Piaf figure
flying, but she repeats that she loves them and declares that
I am not to tie them up. Her accent is thick and I cannot
place it.

René introduces us. As soon as the monsieur's name is
spoken I recognise it, and he registers that I do. He is indeed
a fabled figure, a person of repute throughout Provence and,
as it happens, also a native of our nearby village.

'Right, where shall we begin?' Monsieur looks about him,
appraising the width and breadth of the land. 'Is there a
track?'

'Yes, several,' say I.

'Are they suitable for trucks?' He is digging about in the
rear of his luxury vehicle for the tools of his trade.

I shake my head.

'No point in looking, then. I'm wasting my time.'

'Why not?'

'Well, if there is water, how will the drilling truck reach
the source and dig the well?'

I had never considered that problem. The truth is, I don't
think either Michel or I have ever seriously believed that
water might be found here. This house is constructed on
solid rock, the hill behind us is rock and, if appearances are
anything to go by, dry as a bone.

Monsieur has retrieved from his Ford a large square of
black material which puts me in mind of one of my late
father's Magic Circle conjuring props: the black scarf that
hid the magic wands. I smile at the memory. Carefully, the
cloth is unwrapped and I see two tendrils of metal, each
about eighteen inches in length and barely more substantial
than cuts of wire. This is the diviner. Wrapped up with it is
a chunk of coppery metal secured to a chain.

'The pendulum,' he declares and hands the cut of cloth,

along with the pendulum, to his wife, who is being all but blown away by the wind. He then asks René to fetch his notebook, calculation list and pen from the dashboard. Madame spins off to talk to the dogs while Monsieur exits the *parking* and crosses the lower terrace alongside the pool. He is staring at the tiles, as though his eyes were boring through them. His expression is one of serious concentration. 'There's water here, no doubt about it,' he is muttering.

'We are above the drainage system and alongside the pool,' I offer by way of explanation. He appears not to have heard me, or has chosen to ignore my flippancy. René hurries to keep up with us and whispers in my ear, 'If he says there is water here, there is. He has never been known to be wrong.'

Am I being made a fool of? I am wondering. Might this be yet another example of local *escroquerie*?

Once we clear the house and have arrived at the tiled terrace where our wooden table and outdoor chairs live, he places the elongated, V-shaped divining rod between his two little fingers and his thumbs. He levels the apparatus directly in front of him, like a pair of dividers, somewhere around waist-height, making sure that its narrow end, the joined tip, is pointing outwards. Now he begins pacing. Long, sure strides towards the hill and then left towards the farthest reach of our land in the direction of what we refer to as the 'second plot', because we purchased it later. I trail along with him, holding back a polite pace or so, but surveying him like a hawk. First, I train my attention on his face, and then on his hands. I am the daughter of an entertainer, a musician, a magician; I grew up on sleight of hand. If there's a trick in this, then I am determined to spot it.

Suddenly, and most unexpectedly, as we approach the

four cedar trees that stand sentry on the passage between the two plots, the rod shoots upwards and begins to quiver like an overexcited bird.

'*Eh, voilà!*' he says, and stops. The rod continues to quiver. It looks as though it has a life of its own.

René, bringing up the rear, repeats the maestro's words. '*Eh, voilà.*'

The wife is elsewhere, lost in her elsewhere world, shouting to the wind.

'Are you telling me that we have water right here underneath this terrace?' I ask. We are standing on a patio that we have laid using something in the region of two hundred square metres of antique hand-made *dalles*. If we drilled here, even if we did repair the damage later, we might never find such tiles again.

'Yes. And what is more, it intersects right here. There are two streams: one is coming from the hill and the other is flowing in this direction. If I can find the precise junction and you drill at that strategic point you can benefit from two rivulets, both drawing from the same well.'

'Well, we're not digging up the terrace!' I bark. 'I'd rather pay the water bills. Can't you find another stream further up the hill?'

Monsieur steps away from what he has claimed is the source and the rod wilts instantly. 'But you have no means of accessing it up there.' He wanders off, frowning, as though trying to solve a conundrum. I turn to René, who is occupied with Madame; she is bent double and looks as though she is going to be sick.

'Is she all right?' I ask.

Her husband strides past her and tells her to go and sit in the car.

'What's up?'

'She's freezing, not feeling well.'

'Would you like me to take her inside?' I enquire of her husband.

'Later. First we must find water.'

'Look, it's really not that important.'

'Wait, if it runs this way – the *parking*! Why didn't I—?' And with that he is off, marching purposefully back towards his stationary truck. 'Move those cars!' he commands.

Madame sinks on to one of the swimming-pool steps, head in hands, while I am instructed again to move the cars, which I obediently do, driving them virtually into the trees until Monsieur calls to me that I have shifted them a sufficient distance. His own monster machine he reverses halfway down the drive. And then we begin the divining proceedings again. A few paces here, turn to the left. Rather like square-bashing. I don't know whether to concentrate on him or worry about his wife, who is at my side now leaning against me, muttering. René is taking notes. The rod is up and quivering again.

'Look! Look!'

I am looking. In amazement. You would think it was battery-operated, the speed at which it is moving.

'*Où est la pendule?* The pendulum!'

Everyone is shouting, 'Fetch the pendulum!' No one, of course, can find it. Who had it? Madame. This creates a *petit* drama because she cannot remember where she has put it.

I am bemused by the panic and the rush. After all, the water, if there is any, is not going to dry up in the next five minutes.

While the trio search for the cloth-wrapped pendulum, I ask: 'Please may I have a go?' Monsieur, almost without thinking, hands me his rod. I weave it carefully through my fingers, resting it against my upturned palms, precisely as I have observed him doing, and begin to pace. No one is paying me any attention. I stride here and there and nothing happens, except that my fingers begin to ache, and then, while the others are engaged in trying to find the key to their Jeep because they insisted on locking it and Madame swears that she placed the pendulum carefully on her seat in the car, I retrace his steps. I can just about recall where he found the water and I approach gingerly, pause and wait. Nothing happens. I twiddle my fingers in an effort to manipulate the rod, to give it impetus, to thrust it upwards, to spring the stupid thing into life. Nothing happens. Back and forth I step over the spot. Still nothing happens. If there's a trick to this, a way to manoeuvre this appliance, I am hell-bent on finding it.

'You don't believe me, do you?'

I swing round guiltily. 'Yes of course. I just thought . . .'

'It's neither dupery nor illusion.' He smiles. 'Allow me to guide you, please.' Monsieur plants himself right behind me, lays the heel of each of his hands beneath the backs of mine and negotiates me gently towards the spot. As we step towards it, the *baguette* swings fast with inverted gravity, pointing skywards and twitching powerfully. I feel its strength and this man is barely touching me; certainly, he is not in a position to force my hands.

'I tell you what, let's finish the job. I'll use this pendulum' – he takes it from René – 'to measure the depth of the source and the force of the flow, the cubic metreage per hour, and then, if you are willing, we can go into the house, get my poor wife out of the wind, and discuss all this.'

The pendulum swings and whirls and the source is reckoned to be about forty metres deep which is extremely shallow, I am informed, and therefore should not be expensive to excavate. The flow is sufficient to fill our 200-cubic-metre swimming pool in two days. The only information we cannot glean at this stage is whether the water is *eau potable* or not. For that we will have to drill and then test but, even if it's not drinkable, it will certainly irrigate the garden. It would also irrigate the 200 young olive trees that Michel, in spite of my protestations, is still eager for us to plant.

If what has been demonstrated here today really does indicate the presence of underground running water, then we have fallen upon tremendous good fortune.

Once inside and out of the gale force wind, where they will not accept refreshment – Monsieur drinks only champagne, and we have none in (I should have remembered his preference, René did tell me) and Madame is not supposed to consume anything hot or anything too strong, but she will accept a small nip of port if we have it, though when I serve it she worries that it may contain a tad too much alcohol – we settle to a long discussion. Monsieur asks me if I recognise the name Michel Rocard.

'The former prime minister of France?' I ask. 'Of course.'

'The very same.'

He tells me that Rocard's father was an esteemed research scientist who did some studies in water divining.

'One of his discoveries was that certain people have magnetism sensitivity at designated pressure points in their joints, and this enables them to detect unmapped water sources. Perhaps there is truth in it, I don't know. Certainly it sounds logical, but we in Provence believe that it is not explained away quite so reasonably.'

'What is your explanation, then?'

'It is less tangible. One needs to have a feel for water. How can I put it? To be in tune with it. There are other similar gifts. A cousin of mine, for example – she's dead now – had another talent that is passed on only through women, mother to daughter, mother to daughter, and no matter how hard a man tries, he can never achieve this power.'

'And that is?'

'The relieving of sunstroke. Someone working in the vineyards, for example, who has been weakened, made ill by too much sun, would be sent to such a woman. How does she extract the sun from the victim? She takes a glass of water, any ordinary tumbler of water, places it on the head of the patient and rests her first finger lightly against his or her forehead. The glass remains in position as though glued to the crown. Within seconds, the water in the glass begins to boil. And it boils, believe me, I have witnessed this, like a kettle on a stove. When the glass has been removed, the sunstroke has gone. You won't read of any such talents in your guide books to Provence. These are secrets we keep close to our chest, and women who possess such gifts are regarded with a certain deference. It is not a *métier*, not a profession, you understand. These women have a touch, a feel. I cannot explain it any more clearly than that.'

We are all of us silent. Monsieur rises and removes his jacket, folding it neatly behind him on the chair.

'Water divining is not a *métier*, either,' he continues. 'Though insurance companies regularly approach my colleague, Nick. If there is a lawsuit which is related to underground damp, leaking foundations and the like, they call him in to locate the flow. This is a mysterious land, a puzzling culture to outsiders, and in our language we have rich expressions that cannot be translated but they aptly describe the way we see the world. We—'

'Your language?' I butt in.

'Provençal.'

'You speak it?'

'Of course, I was raised speaking it. As my wife here was raised speaking Corsican. Both languages were outlawed by the French government, who created statutes to enforce the use of French as the official language—'

'Ah, I know about this,' I rather rudely interrupt again. 'The Villers-Cotterêts statute of 1539!'

'How right you are. And it has taken centuries for both Provençal and Corsican – languages rooted in the psyches of their native peoples – to fight their way back. Interestingly, they are not such distant neighbours. I can understand a smattering of Corsican, just as my wife here can partially understand my mother tongue. Carol, you seem to have a passion for this area of France and for the olive tree in particular, isn't that so?'

I nod my assent.

'I will send you a copy of a Provençal poem, in French, of course, that recounts how we believe that the spirit of the ancient Greeks lives on in the olive tree. To a true Provençal all trees are sacred, but above all reigns the olive tree. One reads of many ancient cultures who enforced the death penalty against anyone who cut down an olive tree . . .'

His wife nods her agreement, as does René. I look from one to the other. There is a certain madness in Monsieur's wife but, by contrast, he has a businesslike manner. And yet . . .

'Spirits in trees,' he laughs. 'No doubt you are thinking that we are a little crazy, that all this is far-fetched?'

I shrug.

'I understand the reverence given to the olive tree. All my life I worked in the world of business. Well, I believe you know what my work has been.'

'Yes.'

'These days, I ask myself what all those years were about. Making money, of course. Building a reputation, yes, indeed, but it wasn't until I retired and decided to dedicate myself to my farm that I found fulfilment. I feel in tune with life now, with my olive trees. I have over three hundred and fifty and, like you, we have splendid oil and hope for an AOC.'

*

And so we talk on while, beyond the windows, I hear the wind whistling through the pines. As night falls and the moon begins to rise, I find myself still sitting cross-legged on a cushion on the floor, listening to these two men, friends for over seventy years. They speak of this land – 'this land', to them, is Provence, not France – and recount anecdotes of their childhood and adolescent days here.

Monsieur narrates us the story of a boy he knew as a child in his village, an unprosperous fellow, who took two of the spines from the skeleton of a discarded umbrella, soldered them together and found that he had the skill and all the tools needed to source water. I learn that there is a shop in Paris where you can buy pendulums and divining rods.

Monsieur asks me if I know anything about the Aboriginals of Australia, and I tell him I spent several years intermittently working in and travelling around that prodigious continent, that I have a passionate respect for what I understand of their ancient ways, and that I frequently cite examples of their thinking.

'Australian Aboriginals,' he says, 'can pinpoint an underground stream with no more than an outstretched finger. They also believe, by the way, that the earth, its trees, mountains, every natural thing, is inhabited by its spirit life.'

'Going walkabout! Singing land back into existence!' I cry. 'I have always fancied that we might be doing something similar here with this little farm, which was abandoned and dilapidated when we found it. Singing the place back into existence. Recreating its colours.'

He smiles. 'Something like that. Well, we must be on our way.'

I glance at my watch and see that they have been here for five hours. 'I am so sorry to have kept you. I ask so many questions.'

'Not at all.'

Outside, the passage of the wind has turned the inky darkness into a glittering diorama. Its force has let up now, as it frequently does at sundown. Monsieur and I pause alongside one another, lingering an instant to drink in the beauty of the evening, the frisson of movement that stirs the perfumed air like fluttering chiffon.

From a branch in the *Magnolia grandiflora* – a tree which was originally discovered in the southern states of North America by the French botanist Plumier, who shipped examples of it back to France to enhance a botanical garden created for the pleasure of Louis XIV – we hear the gentle clunking of the bamboo wind chimes I bought in the market at Nice and hung there. Quashia always remarks that they remind him of his boyhood days as a goatherd in the Algerian mountains.

'I can trace water with an accuracy of within inches, but I can't trap the wind,' Monsieur confides to me, or perhaps he is talking to himself. 'Imagine if it could be bottled and administered in tiny doses as an antidote to the madness it creates in some.'

We stroll on towards the *parking* and I wonder if he is referring to his wife.

'How much do we owe you?' I ask when we reach the vehicle where René is now helping Madame into her seat.

'Nothing at all. It has been a pleasure, and I sincerely hope that it will contribute to your enterprises here. Please come and visit my farm. I want to show you my olive trees. They are very fine. I will also show you where I found water on our land. Meanwhile, I'll draw you a plan of your underground systems. Do have it verified by another dowser, if you are in any doubt. And if I can assist you with anything else, please don't hesitate to call me.'

And then, as he steps into his car, he turns and, in impeccable English, quotes a line from Hamlet: '"There are more

things in heaven and earth . . . than are dreamt of . . ." eh,
Carol? *Bon nuit, et à bientôt.*'

Once I have waved them off, I pad slowly back upstairs.
Inside, I pour myself a glass of wine, put Mahler's Fifth on
the stereo and settle back on to the cushions, peering out
through the French windows at the stars. I am ruminating on
the afternoon's events, on all that has been said, when, from
nowhere, I recall an episode in my twenties that until this
evening I had completely forgotten.

I was a young actress following a vegetarian diet and a
rather trendy, semi-Zenlike existence, meditating on a twice-
daily basis, searching earnestly for Truth and Meaning in
Life. I was living in a rented flat in north London and in my
bedroom there was a magnificent orchid plant. I was no
expert with anything botanical; I lacked green fingers altogether, but I had been given the plant with its several
blossoming sprays as a present, a first-night gift, and I had
placed it in an antique porcelain pot in my attic room. I
watered it regularly and it seemed to thrive there, if the flowering of extra, waxy cream blossoms was evidence of health.
It was extremely beautiful, very graceful. Still, the plant
excited no particular interest in me until something utterly
fantastical happened. I was reading in bed the first time I
became aware of it: a faint but clear, high-pitched intonation,
like a barely audible single note of a chant. At first I took it
to be a problem with the flat's antiquated electricity circuit.
I switched off the power at the mains, but the sonar-like
sound continued. I was completely clueless as to what it was
or where it was coming from. It was more than a week
before I finally came to the conclusion that it was the plant,
laden with blossoms, that was emitting the sound. This
cannot be true, I said to myself. I am going mad.

The next time I had chums over to dinner I told them

about the plant. 'I think it's *singing*,' I said. They stared at me incredulously and so I trooped everyone up to my bedroom to listen. It was late in the evening, the hour of its 'song', and we all plumped ourselves down on the floor (I had no chairs: cushions spread out in hillocks was where I and my guests lolled about in those days). Everybody listened politely but with lighthearted scepticism. No one heard a dicky-bird, not even me. Frankly, I felt pretty stupid and wished that I had never mentioned the phenomenon, even to close friends such as these actor pals. Like myself, they were sometimes given to way-out beliefs or leanings, but not this one. They simply roared with laughter and accused me teasingly of hallucinating, of having consumed drugs or magic mushrooms. No amount of protestation on my part would convince them otherwise, and so I shut up about it.

Yet, when I was alone, I continued to 'hear' the plant. Occasionally, when another lay at my side, the orchid would begin its song, but I never remarked upon it, never mentioned it again. I chose to appreciate it silently, leaving my partner to fall asleep in peace and ignorance.

It was around this time, the early to mid-seventies, that I learned of a book that was causing a mild sensation. It was written by a South African anthropologist, ethologist and marine biologist called Dr Lyall Watson. He was a recluse, someone told me back then, living on some windy bluff in the west of Ireland, and a bit of a boundary-breaker as far as conventional scientific circles were concerned. The book, *Supernature*, became a bestseller and cult reading for millions. Naturally, I hurried off to buy it. The text was a revelation to me. Anyone who has read it will know that there are chapters in which Dr Watson recounts experiments carried out on plants to measure electrically their responses to human behaviour. I was astounded. Plants 'screaming' at the sight of a human being who had just cut a lawn? Plants responding favourably to beings who had a recent history of plant nurturing?

The point, for me, was that not only were plants living entities, but it seemed as though they might possess memories, be capable of recognising other living forces and reacting negatively or positively towards them.

I had no electric meter or graph by which to measure the responses of my orchid, but I began to silently propose the possibility that the plant was at peace in the space it inhabited, and recognised me as an ally. Was this going too far, being too subjective? Might the plant have simply been expanding to its environment, responding favourably to the lack of threat? Could it have been sufficiently unthreatened to emit contentment?

If you quizzed me tonight about whether I still believe the orchid was singing, I would answer in the negative. My interpretation was doubtless born of the world of hip romanticism I floated about in. Even so, I cannot dismiss the experience entirely. So, what did I hear? Dr Desmond Morris, when discussing the early stages of human sexual courtship in his book *The Naked Ape*, talks of the 'highly specialised and symbolised sound signals of speech' courting couples use with one another. 'A courting couple is often referred to as "murmuring sweet nothings" and this phrase sums up clearly the significance of the tone of voice as opposed to what is being spoken.' Might such a form of contact exist, on occasion, between man and plant? Might my plant have been emitting electrical impulses, electromagnetic signals? And if so, is it possible that I picked up those impulses, as one might be aware of another's heartbeat or a loved one's sweet murmurings? I was not plugged into *singing* exactly, but is it conceivable that I was 'in tune' with the only other living energy force in the flat? I do not have answers, and these are probably far-fetched notions, but listening to Monsieur praising his beloved olive trees, to his claim of being in tune with them, has recalled this unfathomed incident.

Beyond the valley, in front of our olive farm and to the right, there is a hill wooded with arcane and venerable pine trees. Each stands a good twenty metres high and has been growing on that hill for many decades. There are no buildings, no constructions of any sort over there, and from our upper terrace it is a green and bosky sight, a round shoulder of greenery. I have always understood the hill to be, as our land is, a designated *zone verte*, written into the council records. After all, it is an extension of the conservation area in which our farm is situated. So it comes as a shock to me when I am disturbed in my work by the sound of chainsaws. Not one, but several. I rise from my table and walk out on to the terrace to see who is creating the noise. To my horror I see one of those ancient pines being felled, then another and another; decades-old trees falling in quick succession. I run in search of Quashia, who is repairing one of the drystone walls brought down in the night by the wild boars.

'What's going on over there?' I ask him.

'They're cutting trees,' he replies. 'I told you a while ago.'

'You told me that they were pruning the trees, not cutting them.'

'The trees are dangerous.'

I am horrified. 'Dangerous? In what sense dangerous? To whom?'

'The council says they can be cut down.'

'Who has the council given this permission to, and why?'

'They could fall on the *foyer* and damage the roof if these strong winds continue. '

I cannot believe what I am hearing. This reasoning is preposterous. The trees are a perfectly reasonable distance from the building which was constructed in the sixties to house foreign labour on land compulsorily purchased by the local council from the previous proprietors of our farm.

I hurry back into the house and telephone the Mairie, the town hall. The young woman I speak to informs me that she knows nothing about the trees. I leap into the car and hurtle down the hill to the appropriate office, determined to find out what is going on before the entire hillside has been denuded. Eventually, after being sent from one office to the next, from pillar to post, I learn that the French *société* that owns the land on which the *foyer* is built have put forward plans to extend this housing estate. They have applied for planning permission once and were refused on the grounds that you cannot obtain planning permission to build on land that is classified as *boissé classé*, where the trees themselves are listed. On top of which, it is public land. They do not even own these plots. Their only hope, and a damned cunning ploy it is too, is to register the trees as dangerous, cut them down and then put in their request for planning permission on land now free of trees, worthless as parkland and which can be purchased for a sou.

I am incensed. Locked in my own loss, I have not been paying attention. I should have noticed what was going on weeks ago.

The felling continues. Not every day, and not at such a dramatic speed as on the day I first noticed it, but discreetly, so that the surrounding neighbourhoods are not alerted. Nevertheless, every few days one more tree disappears.

I telephone the council again. They inform me that we must put our complaints in writing. When Michel comes home on Friday, he sets to work. He writes not only to the council representative to whom I have spoken but to several different departments at their local offices, as well as their land registration people in Juan-les-Pins. These he copies to a frankly rather hopeless local organisation we subscribe to whose raison d'être is the protection of the local village and its surrounding green areas. He writes to the Department of Environment in Nice and to anyone else he can think of. All to get someone to take notice of the fact that these protected trees are being felled like sticks. I walk down the lane and glare miserably at the stacks of trunks. I behold lorries arriving to load and cart them away. I return to the council, visit some of the same individuals and then fall upon a tall, bearded man who agrees to pop by within the hour and find out what is going on.

This he does, and then he calls on us. He has warned the manager of the residence that the felling is an illegal act. He assures us that he intends to make immediate contact with the owners of the housing estate, a company operating out of Marseille, and will notify them by registered letter that they are liable to a hefty fine and that replacement trees must be planted immediately.

Le pin. Pine. Highly scented trees. Evergreen, coniferous. There are numerous species, and many grow around the Mediterranean basin. One of the most popular is the Aleppo pine. Originally from the ancient Syrian city of Aleppo? No, but it grows everywhere in the eastern Mediterranean.

Its tiered, oval cones are the pine's means of reproduction. The female cones are the larger of the two. The egg cells in the female are fertilised by the pollen from the males.

Pines are cultivated for the resin and wood.

I stand on the terrace and look out across at the hill, at the space where the pines used to grow. For the moment the felling has been halted, the damage contained. But who can say for how long? Bribes have the power to change laws down here and *escroquerie* usually wins the day. And I see no signs of replacement planting.

Arabs crouch there now, out of the heat, in the shade. Resting on their haunches, they smoke cigarettes and watch time passing, the way Bedouins do in the desert. I have no problem with those men sitting over there on their hams, idling away the hours. What I cannot get to grips with is the space itself.

I scrutinise that newly created emptiness, and it troubles me. Profoundly.

I read a while back that a scientific experiment set up by botanists in New Hampshire has found that certain trees give off pheromones, airborne hormones that are carried on the wind like alarm signals when dangers to the trees' health or survival are close at hand. Bodies of scientists are beginning to support the possibility of a level of environmental awareness being transmitted between living organisms. From tree to tree of a like kind, for example, in a forest.

I find myself, as I stand out here on our terrace, asking what if such ancient philosophies as the Provençal or Aboriginal philosophies are not entirely wacky? What if trees do possess a spirit life? If they do, what happens to that spirit when the tree dies or is chopped down? If the tree dies naturally is the spirit's departure different, more prepared perhaps, than if the end is more violent? If Dr Watson walked the hill I am staring at now and measured the responses of each of the remaining trees in the surrounding wood, what might he read on his electrical meter?

Would he be deafened by screaming? Screams of anger, outrage? Loss or pain? If we, living and going about our daily lives in the surrounding neighbourhoods, could but hear the reaction of the forest I am preoccupied by now, would we be forced to prick up our ears and listen? Would it make any difference?

The girls' school I attended was set in rolling grounds with many arcane trees and encircled by a small oak forest of its own. From the age of ten or eleven, that turbulent time, when I was caught up in the web of misery at home and had few allies I could confide in because I felt sure that all homes were normal except ours, I spent a great deal of time alone in that wooded park. Trees became my friends. I talked to them, or simply hugged them, pressed my cheeks hard against their grainy surfaces, ears glued to their trunks, musing with them as though they were people. And if I could not, for whatever reason, hide away outside, I would find wooden beams to hang on to: they were my life rafts. The material itself was reassuring. My dreams were of flying and of living in tree houses.

I remember an occasion when I had been witness to a scene at home. The words spoken, the information revealed were so distressing to me that I fled the house. I ran up the hill the mile or so to school, locked myself in the cloakroom and would not come out. No amount of rapping on the door or threats of punishment would budge me. When the afternoon classes resumed, I escaped into the grounds. I was shivering, weeping, clinging to an ancient oak. It took classmates to report me and several members of staff several hours to coax me away from – what? An object of stability, reassurance, intimacy? What did those trees offer me that I couldn't find in the human world? There must have been some communion taking place there, but I no longer know what. I have long since lost touch with whatever it might have been; 'reasons of the heart of which the reason knows nothing,' was the observation made by Pascal.

Now, sitting alone out here on the terrace, long past the gloaming light of an autumnal evening, in the stillness of the falling night, Schubert's *Quintet in C Major for Two Violins, Viola and Two Celli* playing on the stereo, I dig about for an inkling of reasoned comprehension. In the teachings of Zen, students are trained to work towards inner harmony, balance; to be so at one with themselves, so in tune with the universe, that they can *hear* a blade of grass growing. Might there have been a quintessence of life, a core energy in those trees, that I, the child, sought out and plugged into? The healing power of nature? Might those trees, along with my scribblings and play-acting, have fed me with the strength to survive?

The first side of the record has finished. I rise and walk slowly inside to flip it over, but instead make for the telephone. I am not clear what spurs me to call Rome, but I do. A desire to speak to Barbara? Not especially, but an urgent need to know how she is. I have been vaguely intending to do it for a few days but other matters have kept me occupied. It is Jacob I fall upon, blubbering and bemoaning the fractured future he is about to face.

Barbara was taken ill during the Venice Film Festival. Her jaw locked. She could not speak or swallow. When they returned to Rome, he took her to the hospital, where she was kept in for a series of tests and diagnosed with advanced leukaemia. Three weeks later, which is to say three days ago, she was dead.

I am speechless. Eventually I mutter some mindless and fairly meaningless condolences and hang up. In my thoughts, aside from the shock I am feeling, is the knowledge of those photographs. I make my way to the drawer in my den and dig them out with the intention of destroying them and then I hesitate, and don't. I sit in semi-darkness, staring hard at them. Staring *into* them. Four pictures taken by me and in every one Barbara is bleached out. For whatever reason, whatever technical cock-up or fault on my part, she is simply *not there*. I think back to those warm, early-summer gatherings, to the loneliness I picked up on, and I cannot dismiss the questions spinning in my head. Why is she not in these photographs? Is it utter madness, or even vaguely feasible, to wonder whether her spirit was already departing, moving on elsewhere? Going on ahead, to seek out her next spot? A kinder one, I pray.

Suddenly, her soft, tobacco-scratched voice replays in my mind. The Englishness of her, in spite of her bohemian manners, and the words: 'You are lucky to be having a baby.' And in our kitchen: 'I'd really love a kid.'

I wipe away a tear, slip the photos back into the drawer and wish her *bon voyage*.

I return to the telephone and call Michel. The rush in my voice must alert him. 'I have been a fool.'

'Is everything all right?' he asks.

'We must plant our trees. It is the way forward.'

'Splendid. I'd hoped you'd come to it,' he says, and kisses me, long-distance, goodnight.

Olive Finale

Days and days of deliciously golden autumn and then, from nowhere, we are pelted by a freak hailstorm. The stones are the size of golf balls and cause the loss of approximately a third of the olive crop – full and fleshy fruit ripening early after such a long dry summer; fruit that is piebald deep violet and green, falling and rolling, squashed beneath tyres, never having given of its produce.

1 November: *Toussaint*, All Saints' Day. Here, in France, it is a public holiday. In the past it was the day that marked the decanting of the new year's wines. It is also the day the Provençals regard as the beginning of winter, but this year there is not a hint of such a season. The weather is glorious, far more autumnal than wintery, and the olives that were not destroyed by the hailstones of two weeks ago have ripened way ahead of schedule. There are far fewer drupes on the

trees due to that recent shock of bad weather, but those that remain are filled out and are first class: great damson-black fruits, plump, luscious, oleaginous.

I stand in the dappled sunlight beneath the twisted, hanging branches of one of the older trees and gaze upwards in admiration.

'The birds are at a feast. If we don't begin harvesting soon, we'll have nothing left.' Quashia is at my side, head tilted in the same direction. It is a day off for him – nobody works on these public holidays, and he is taking a well-deserved rest – but still he strolls up to say *bonjour* and lend a hand with whatever essential chores need attending to, for they are endless; work here is never done.

'But if we collect the ripe ones and leave the green, we won't have sufficient to make our own pressing. We'll have to share with someone else,' I reply.

It is true. The mill requires a minimum of eighty-five kilos to press for a single estate. If we are lucky we may gather sixty kilos of perfectly seasoned fruit. We could pick another twenty-five of underripe olives to meet the quota, but then we lose out on the quantity of oil the drupes will produce: green fruit returns less oil than black. If we leave the mature fruits on the trees and wait for the rest, or a proportion of the rest, to ripen, we will lose an extensive percentage to the birds, who will steal the plumpest of the pickings before they have been harvested. This is one of the choices to be made, a part of the delicate balance to which I would never have given a second thought before we began to reclaim this little farm. Michel is not here, so the decision will be mine.

'I'll telephone René and I'll leave a message at the mill; I'd prefer to hear what they advise.'

Quashia says he'll wait. While I go indoors to make the calls he busies himself in his newly constructed woodshed, pulling out and dusting down our green and René's white nets ready to encircle the feet of the trees. That done, he embarks on an appraising tour of the garden to see which have branches burgeoning with ripening fruit and where the drupes have already begun to drop. We are short of netting, in spite of the thousand metres I bought. Some of it has been damaged, caught and torn during earlier harvests, other yards have been used to keep scavengers out of our vegetable gardens and the original roll was insufficient in the first place.

I am very surprised, because it is a holiday, when Christophe, the mill-owner, picks up the phone himself. He answers with a weary despondent '*Allo?*'

'How are you, Christophe?' I ask. Our paths haven't crossed since last year. His mill is located a fair distance inland of us, so we have no reason to visit that village outside the oil-pressing season.

'Ah, *bonjour*, Carol, not good, not good.' He doesn't wait for me to ask what's up but instantly embarks upon the problem every *oléiculteur* is facing this year: little if any fruit yield. 'It should have been a stupendous year with all those months of sun,' he moans. 'Yes, we began pressing this week, for those who have fruit. Come if you like, but we are only turning the mill on Wednesdays and Saturdays. Of course we'll press more frequently if there's a call for it, but I don't think there will be. It's a *catastrophe, une vrai catastrophe*.' I smile, not because I don't commiserate with the farmers' situation, but because I know Christophe sufficiently well now to understand that in his eyes life is either a *catastrophe* of monumental proportions or a veritable triumph. Today we have the downside.

I explain to him that our fruit is ripening earlier than expected, but not all of it.

'Same everywhere. It adds to the dilemma,' he interrupts.

'So I am not sure that we will have enough for a single-estate pressing.'

'I'll press for eighty kilos, as it's you, but I can't do it for less. There is the cost, you understand, of the machines, the fuel, the staff. Oh, Carol, what a *catastrophe*! How's Michel?'

'He's fine. Working hard, as usual.'

'Is he here?'

'No, he's in Paris in preproduction on an animation film.'

'He leaves you alone too frequently. You tell him that from me.'

How can this mill-owner be party to such information? René must have been gossiping. 'Come whenever you like. I'll accept eighty kilos, or why don't you find someone to share the pressing with you?'

'We'll look into it. Either way, we'll see you soon. *Merci*, Christophe. *Ciao*.'

I call René. He is sniffing and coughing. 'Only a *petit rhume*, nothing to fuss about. Too many olive trees to tend,' he explains. 'But how are you?' He does not wait to hear; he is already affirming that the olive season is a catastrophe. At Pégomas, where one of the farms he husbands is situated, there is not one single olive on any of the 120 trees. 'All lost in that hailstorm, every single drupe. Can you believe it?'

'I was about to suggest we share a pressing . . .'

He leaps at the idea. He has fifty-two kilos gathered from the lone tree in his own garden. A yield of fifty-two kilos from one tree in a year of paucity is exceptional, though still, of course, not enough for a pressing. He needs another thirty to make up his quota. He arranges to call by to collect this amount from us.

And so Quashia and I decide to begin the harvest, *la récolte*, or, in the case of olives, *la cueillette des olives*. 'We'll start tomorrow morning, then,' I tell him when I return outside.

'Why not right this very minute?' he asks, tugging off his shirt in his hurry to get to the garage to change into his work clothes. He looks happy.

'Because it's your day off,' I yell after him, but he is already out of sight.

While I have been on the phone he has started laying the nets. He prepared the ground, cutting back the grass, clearing errant stones, several days ago, anticipating my decision.

So here we are again at harvest time. *La olivaison*. The olive season.

I find a butterfly caught under one of the nets and while trying to release it I lose my entire afternoon's gathered load. With a sigh, I watch the drupes rolling down the steps and then I concentrate on the butterfly. It flaps and flutters until it is free and then flies away to alight on a terracotta pot, still, even in early November, blushed with flowering geraniums. I want to be able to identify the butterfly later so I pause to make a mental note of its markings: splashes of white with black spots, known as ocelli – they resemble dark, round eyes on its wings – and a tortoiseshell colouring which, in the sunlight, glows almost burned orange. Is this a Red Admiral? There were dozens of this species in the nectar-rich gardens of my childhood. Later, when I return to my den, I leaf through my guide and learn that I have lent a helping hand not to a Red Admiral but to another of its family: a *Vanessa cardui*, more commonly known as a Painted Lady. It is a resident of the Canary Islands and Madeira, but a migrant from North Africa – like Quashia! – where it establishes colonies along the coast. It can be found in the warmer parts of the Mediterranean until cold weather sets in.

While perusing my handbook I also discover that there is

a whole genus of butterflies, including the Red Admiral, whose Latin name includes the word *Vanessa*. Is Michel aware that one of his daughters shares her name with a species of butterfly? *Vanessid* is the adjective, I am informed by my *Oxford* dictionary. So might I say of my lovely step-daughter that her fretting about her weight, her perennial concerns about her appearance, are, in her case, *Vanessid* behaviour? I smile. I haven't heard from her in a while and I wonder how she is getting along with her American sweetheart.

The following afternoon, I leave Quashia with the rest of this early gathering and set off for a short stay in London. Before I depart, René telephones to confirm that he must have the olives.

'Call Quashia,' I tell him. 'He'll give you all you need.'

In London, I pass delightful evenings with Clarisse. When she is not at college or at the bistro where she works as a waitress to earn her keep, or off visiting galleries, going to the movies or lectures with newly made friends, of which there seems to be a manifold and motley collection, we lounge on cushions, drinking wine, gorging on steaming great bowls of spaghetti we have rustled up together, and she shows me her artwork, her impressive portfolios, and then we talk and talk until dawn. We are like students together. Or rather, she brings an air of lightness to my heart. In her company, I revisit those late-teenage joys and revelations. When the phone rings it is usually a young voice enquiring after my stepdaughter and I gladly take messages. It is a special time, a privileged interval; we are discovering one another.

Here, in London, I am not the wife of her father – of course, I remain that too, but what bonds us here is her passion for this capital city where she is launching herself for the first time and all that it contributes to this encounter with her developing feminine self. Here she insists we speak in English. *La France* and its language are skins she has temporarily shed. Here, her pleasure is the carving of her independence within a neutral environment – a pad of her own, a city she has claimed as hers – where she can express her newly gained liberties. She speaks of Papa in a way I have never heard before and which quite takes me aback. These days he has been transformed into someone other than her father: he is a man, and I see her begin in tiny ways to look at him in a more objective light. She does not mention Serge and neither do I. Perhaps she has forgotten him among so many new discoveries. Somehow, though, I suspect not.

On the plane home, replaying my stay in London, I am reminded of a comment Michel made to me back in the summer after the eclipse. 'You say the girls are mine. They are not, Carol. I don't own them, nor does their mother. They are their own people and, if you want it, you have a part to play in their lives, too.'

Reflecting upon my days with Clarisse, I see that perhaps there might be a role for me and if she will accept me, I will gladly take it on.

I return to grey skies and a world blasted by yet another fierce wind, but this is not the *mistral* that I have grown to know. This wind is called by some the *scirocco* and by others *vent d'est*, or wind from the east, because it travels up through Spain and blows across the southern coast of France. Actually it comes from the Sahara desert bringing with it pale red sand. The cars are covered in a thick film of it and the exterior world has taken on a salmon opaqueness. From inside the house, the wind rattling through the trees sounds like a train thundering through a tunnel. I stare out of the dust-smeared windows and spy a helicopter, like a determined dragonfly, ploughing through the dense clouds. Claps of dry thunder spook the dogs. Stepping outside, I am surprised by how warm it is; such a fierce wind suggests a biting chill, but not so. A desert wind that brings desert heat.

Many of the fruits are still too green to harvest but now the wind is driving them in shoals to the ground. Traditionally, olive-gathering begins on 25 November, the feast of Ste Catherine Labouré, but it looks as though we will be forced to continue to pick up what we can and press what we have before they wither and go dry, even if we must share the pressing.

Our load turns out to be 113 kilos, more than sufficient for a rendezvous at the mill, and Christophe's assistant is happy to book it in as a single-estate pressing.

'There are dozens in your predicament,' she explains, 'forced by nature to alter their pattern.'

Michel is still in Paris, so I decide to take the six crates to the *moulin* alone, my first trip this year.

The wind has polished up the weather, leaving it clear and sharp. The landscape is a melody of yellows and tiger oranges. Startlingly beautiful. Ahead of me, beyond the road, the mauve and umbrous, snow-capped Alps. Weekend joggers in the pine-forested parks, dogs following at their heels, running and scampering.

Upon arrival I am greeted by Christophe, who is dressed in bright green, a gnome in a black woollen Noddy hat that ascends to a rather comical point. He waddles to and fro with a face as red as Christmas but he wears the desolate expression of an abandoned woman. Although it is a Saturday the place is surprisingly empty – fewer olives this year, hence fewer farmers. As always, the conversations around me are of 'four kilos to this' and 'no, olives here'.

Gravely concerned but unflustered, except for Christophe with his Noddy hat, shiny cheeks, plimsolls stained with olive paste and his air of tragedy.

He is washing out with a water spray one of his mammoth machines that clunks and gutters – the Superdecanter 1000, purchased from Firenze; a fortune forked out to align himself with European health standards. It all needs to be paid for.

A small woman less than five feet tall in a black cardigan arrives, carrying an empty plastic container which, when full, will hold fifty litres of precious oil. She nods a greeting to Christophe and his son, sits down next to me and pulls out black rosary beads. Her feet in her unpolished black slingbacks don't reach the ground; still, she has a stalwart air about her. I watch her sneakily. Eyes front, head facing forwards, tiny pearl earrings, brittle, broken nails. I try to engage her in conversation but either she does not hear me or chooses not to – the noise in here is thunderous. Now her calloused labourer's hands clutching the beads are beating her breast. Perhaps she is lost in the world of her prayers? This little woman is a very familiar figure in a disappearing Mediterranean society: the widow, the aged mother, the matriarch and backbone of any family.

We wait. The air is cold and reeks of mashed olives. The few farmers present are pacing to and fro, as though in a hospital corridor, attending the outcome of their pressing. 'This year the oil-production industry is in crisis,' I hear.

I watch the miller's son, Gérard, who is a tad plumper this year, going about his work. He is using a small iron frying pan to catch the dribbles of pressed liquid so that not a solitary drop is lost or wasted as he changes containers, manoeuvring the trolley to position the next empty canister beneath the running nozzle.

One of the machines gets clogged. Christophe calls to

Gérard and together they push and pull at the appliance. Christophe grows impatient and begins to swear, beating it with a length of wood and then, when nothing seems to make any difference, they both shrug, Provençal style, and continue with what they were previously engaged in. Seconds later, when the machine rights itself, Christophe booms triumphantly while Gérard merely nods and goes about his business.

Everyone has left, carrying off their jars of oil and their receipts. Only the Latin mother and I remain. I smile at her but she remains implacable, her short legs swinging back and forth like those of a small child.

Attending the mill, delivering the olives, seems to be becoming one of my chores, except that it is not a chore. Who would ever have thought that sitting before seven great churning machines could afford me such satisfaction? Why? It is both the beginning and the end of a process. The conclusion for nature of this year's cycle of growth and giving and, for the farmer, the beginning of the journey to the kitchens, the tables, the stomachs – meals celebrated, eaten in ignorance of the labour this oil has required. Also, there are the medicinal properties of this ancient juice. It is indeed a revered offering from the earth, blessed and warmed by the sun and irrigated by the rains. Appassionata's bottles will go as gifts, for we are not running a business.

While I am musing upon who will enjoy the receipts of our bounty, my oil has begun to drizzle through. The matriarch at my side nudges me. I thank her, leap to my feet to run my finger through the spluttering oil, green as a gooseberry, and suck on it. It is lighter, less peppery, more citrony than last year, but fresh and delicious. Smooth and scrumptious. I am delighted and turn to share my delight. The venerable Latin mama gets up and marches towards me. She is from

Italy, she tells me now, but has lived in Provence for years. Then, when my produce is bottled and ready to go, she bends and, with one sweep of the arm, deftly lifts up all the containers and asks me where my car is.

'Please, don't!' I cry.

'*Non, non,*' she insists, 'let me. This is no work for you.' Before I can stop her, this insect-sized woman singlehandedly transports my entire twenty-seven litres to the car, where she deposits them, shakes my hand formally and disappears back inside to await her own goodies.

When I return home I find Quashia in a state of great anxiety. The news from Algeria is worrying. Villages have been destroyed in this spate of blusterous weather. And worse, all telephone communication has been brought down and he cannot contact his family.

'Do you want to leave? Shall I phone for a ticket?' I realise that he must go.

But the country has been closed off. Roads are blocked everywhere. He may not even get through to his district. 'No, I'll stay. Let's wait and see. How was the pressing?' he asks.

'Not bad. Twenty-seven litres. I've left five in the garage next to your clothes.'

'*Mais, non!* That's too much!'

'Don't be ludicrous, Mr Quashia. Without you we wouldn't have any oil at all.'

He bursts out laughing.

I send an e-mail to Michel: 'See you tomorrow. *L'huile nouvelle est arrivée!*'

I write this because it is also the week of the new Beaujolais, and the tidings '*Le Beaujolais Nouveau est arrivé*' are broadcast everywhere: in bars, restaurants, supermarkets. Michel is home for Sunday. We are neither of us fans of this wine, but I buy a bottle just the same, as always, to mark the season, I suppose. It is quite frequently sold in half-litre bottles of a simple and rather lovely shape, and the empties we fill with oil for the kitchen. This year, as every other, we pour two small glasses of the wine, make a toast to the new season's produce and then put the rest in the fridge for cooking.

Michel cannot stay on to help with the olive-gathering. Paris calls, work demands his undivided attention. These pre-production periods are as critical as the timing of a farm's harvest. It has been an all too brief visit. I drive him to the airport and we kiss our heartfelt goodbyes. 'I want to ease up on all this travelling,' he says. 'And spend more time at home with you.' His words serve only to make our parting more difficult.

As I return to the *parking*, in among the huggermugger of cars, the screeching traffic and impatient taxis, I spot a rusting Cortina, a boneshaker of a jalopy with English plates, left carelessly outside a bay. There is a sticker displayed on its rear window which stops me in my tracks. It makes me smile because, before returning to the farm, I have a small errand to perform. The sticker reads:

> Practise random acts of kindness
> Senseless acts of great beauty

The little matter ahead of me might well be judged as senseless but it has been on my mind for a while and I am keen to accomplish it. I take the coast road to Cannes and then pass on through, driving towards the Esterele, with its betelnut red soil. Here the coastline is more rugged, the beaches less busy, though in this early-winter season there are few about. I sight a deserted cove, park the car and clamber down to the water's edge. It is still windy. The waves are lapping at my feet. I dig into my shoulder bag and draw out four, finger-sized excisions from the photographs I took of Barbara and her friends. These are all that remain; the four impermeable shadows that were the Englishwoman. The rest I have torn up and discarded. I set down my bag on a rock, take off my shoes and wade into the water with the four blurred images clutched tightly in my hand. The wind is against me so my original idea of throwing them out to sea won't work; they will only blow back at me. I must wade out further, which is what I do, feeling my jeans grow heavy with salt water. When I think I have shoved out far enough, I bend down and plunge the photos beneath the surface, holding them under long enough to say a silent word or two and to soak them thoroughly so that they will not fly off. Or perhaps they will, who knows? Then I release them, bequeathing my souvenirs of Barbara to the ocean, turn and, without looking back, wade out of the water, rub my feet dry and carry bag and shoes up to the car.

I am trying to contact René but he is nowhere to be found. It is now the beginning of Ramadan. Quashia is working long days gathering olives on an empty stomach. He looks tired, worrying about his children back home. I am concerned for him. Does he want me to drive him to Marseille, help him find a boat passage? He shakes his head, also refusing all offers of so much as a cup of tea, reminding me that between sun-up and sundown nothing, not even a sip of water or a puff of a cigarette, may pass his lips. Still no news from René. Quashia and I are working alone and it is backbreaking. I fall into bed exhausted but cannot sleep because the dogs won't stop barking. Nothing quietens them. If I bring them into the house, they go crazy until I get up and let them out again. They bark and, in the case of Bassett, our little hunter, howl until dawn, until I am ragged and starved of sleep. The *sangliers* are about again. The wild boars are tearing up the land, foraging for food as the autumn fades and the darker season closes in. Quashia says that he spotted a family of six roaming the land the day before yesterday. They have created hummocks of mud and grass roots every-where in their search for fallen acorns from the oaks. They must be getting very hungry, but with their fossicking I am getting no sleep. Something needs to be done about them.

Eventually, out of the blue, René turns up.

'We haven't heard from you since you came by and took thirty kilos of olives to the mill. How did we do?' I tease, and I am both surprised and uplifted by his response.

'We are the champions,' he boasts. 'The quality is first rate and your olives, along with mine, of course, are producing excellent quantities of oil.'

'Any chance you could lend us a hand?' I ask, but he is occupied at one of his other farms.

'Everyone is gathering, fearing to lose what fruit there is. No time to waste. One of the earliest harvests I've ever expe-rienced. I'm afraid I need my crates. Can you spare them?'

Usually he lends us half a dozen; it is part of our arrange-ment with him. I cannot spare them, but what can I say?

'I'll be back with them to freight your fruit to the mill,' he promises, and off he goes.

So Quashia and I continue collecting the remainder of the crop ourselves, with nothing to store it in. The fruits on the trees are improving by the day: pudgy purple and jet drupes the size of small plums. I lay them out on a plastic sheet on the floor in the summer kitchen. The cool room reeks of them and, as I turn them, to keep them free of mould, I feel their sponginess; how oliferous they are and what a fine pressing they will make for us.

I confirm with the mill that they will still press for the allotted eighty kilos. Christophe agrees. The problem is I am not sure what quantity we have. I could gauge it easily when we were storing them in René's crates because each holds twenty-five kilos, but now, while every evening our mound gets higher, I have no means of weighing it.

Eventually, I head for the Co-opérative Agricole to buy crates. René claimed that his are only available in Italy, which is why I have never troubled before and why I am not altogether hopeful of finding any, but Frédéric produces half a dozen which he assures me are for olives. They are a different shape and size, but otherwise similar. I ask about the capacity.

'My guess would be around twenty kilos, perhaps twenty-five,' he tells me.

The same as René's, then; even though these are narrower and squarer, they are deeper.

I explain to Quashia later that it should work out the same. We agree to begin the transfer in the morning. After he has left for his cottage, I set about the job myself. I love listening to that gentle rumble as the olives roll and tumble. When the first crate is full, I try to lift it but it is too heavy. So it's a good load, I am thinking.

Suddenly, behind me, at the door, is René.

'I didn't hear your car,' I puff.

'New crates?'

'I had to,' I smile.

He has dropped by to see how we are getting on and to round off a hard day in the fields with a little *apéritif*, which he knows is perenially on offer here.

I dig out a bottle of rosé and we go inside. I am exhausted but not sorry to have company and settle back, ready to hear yet another tale of bygone days in Provence. Tonight his story is of Nina, who collected the groceries.

In the days after the war, René was appointed manager of a sheep farm in the Alp mountains. He arrived to take up his position with his young family in a truck. He was the very first to take a vehicle up into those steep inclines. The shepherds and farmers scoffed at him, claiming that such a contraption would break down, and serve no purpose on those serpentine uphill tracks. He begged to differ and, to show neighbourly spirit, drove from farm to farm offering to purchase and transport everybody's provisions the next time he was in town.

Each farmer shook his head and gave the same response, 'Nina shops for me.'

René was intrigued. 'Who is Nina?'

'The mule.'

And, sure enough, one of the locals owned a mule who set off once a week at dawn, visiting each farm, collecting from every household a shopping list and the cash to pay for the goods. They just placed their orders in one of Nina's two satchels. The mule then hoofed it all alone down the mountainside to the small town below. There she clopped from shop to shop, where the storeholders collected the lists and money and replaced them with the requested items. Nina was rewarded with a sack of hay and, when the shopping was done, she climbed slowly back up the mountainside, stopping to eat grass wherever she fancied, but making sure she was back by sunset. On one occasion, René's truck gave up, marooning him in the middle of nowhere. Night was drawing in, and he was hungry, cold and had no way of getting help – until he sighted the homebound mule. He scribbled a note and put it into Nina's packed satchel. The note read: 'Broken down. Need a tow.' The mule relayed the message back to the next farmstead and René and vehicle were retrieved, much to the merriment of the mountain locals.

Ah, he makes me giggle, does René. But tonight, as he is leaving, he also disturbs me with the comment: 'You know, Carol, you should weigh those crates; they won't hold half as much fruit as mine.'

'Surely they will, René?'

'*Mais, non.*'

The next morning Quashia and I agree that having waited ten days for an appointment at the mill – bookings are impossible to come by because everyone is harvesting at the same time – it would be a disaster if, when our load was delivered, it proved to be insufficient and I was obliged to throw in my lot with some unidentified farmer the quality of whose drupes I cannot hazard.

I run to the guest bathroom to fetch the weighing scales.

'Good idea,' laughs Quashia, and heaves the charged crate on to it. We are dismayed to discover that the entire crate-load weighs only ten kilos.

'That can't be right! The scales must be wrong.' We empty out the olives and put the empty crate on the balance. It weighs less than 200 grammes. The scales are accurate.

We have thirty-six hours left before I am due at the mill and it seems we have gathered only fifty kilos of fruit. Quashia encourages me. 'If we keep going, work until sundown, whatever the weather, we can make our mound.'

I see that he is tired, hours without a break, or food; I send him home to eat. The rules of his faith allow that during the season of Ramadan, of diurnal fasting, he can break his fast at sunset. I continue on alone in the garden. The trees seem as laden as they were when we began, days back. And many of the olives which have fallen to the ground and are lying in the nets have been eaten; all that remains of them are the stones. It's curious that the birds are so avaricious this year, a lean year for olives, when there is plenty of food for them elsewhere. Driving through the country lanes I have noticed bushes weighed down with bright orange berries, clusters and clusters of them. Our bay trees, too, are gravid with shiny, tar-black globules.

After the recent tempestuous winds and dramatic overnight storms, the evening has turned still. The sky is almost cloudless and there is – one of my favourite perfumes – nuttiness, woodsmoke in the air. It turns the light a mulberry-blue. I work alone, collecting errant drupes hidden beneath stones or plants, until it is too dark to see and I realise that I am gathering fallen acorns by mistake. An olive branch whips against my eye and it begins to smart and weep. Time to stop, time for a glass of wine, I tell myself, and climb back up to the summer kitchen with my laden pails. As I empty my freshly gathered fruit into the crate it dawns on me that I feel deep satisfaction; I am at peace. The pain, the loss and the sense of failure which have been tearing at me are easing.

For me the gathering of olives is a therapy. Some knit or embroider; I grow, gather and press olives. I enjoy the air on my cheeks, the earth beneath my destroyed fingernails, the rich aromas of the damp soil, the birdsong all around me; the simplicity and authenticity of life in the garden. It makes sense; adds up; doesn't demand comprehension, though it does demand commitment and can be physically backbreaking. But even that I enjoy: working until I am dead beat.

All the next day we toil. The blustering wind is up again, the sky slate-coloured. By lunchtime we have another ten kilos, which means we are still at least twenty short. I go upstairs to my office, using the interlude to catch up on my messages. Afterwards, I go back outside and find Quashia climbing among the silvery branches of one of the older trees.

'Did you eat?' he calls out to me as I descend the drive with my empty buckets.

'No time.' I am bending to gather the fallen fruit concealed within the windblown nets.

'You'll never get fat on the slithers of food you consume,' he shouts from his neighbouring tree.

'I don't think that's a problem I'll ever have to worry about,' I jape in return.

'How much do you think I weigh?'

'No idea.'

'Ten kilos!' And he roars with laughter. 'I just stepped on your scales. Ten kilos! Then I put one of the flowerpots on. Ten kilos. Everything weighs ten kilos!'

'No!'

We return to the summer kitchen and conduct several tests, weighing everything in sight. The scales are accurate up to ten kilos but above that the machine is blocked. We have been pushing ourselves needlessly; we have more than the quota stipulated by the mill.

We continue gathering but now the pressure is off. Our mood grows lighthearted and there are great cries when Quashia discovers a robin trapped beneath one of the nets. He brings it to show me, clutched between his work-scarred hands, and at first I think the little creature is dead or wounded. Bassett and Lucky lope along beside him, alert to possible prey.

'Please don't squash him!'

The tiny bird with its downy pumpkin-orange breast trembles, turning its minute head with terrified eyes this way and that, pinned in the warm, earthy clutch of this new and unfamiliar threat.

'He looks so fragile. Is he injured?' I ask.

'No, but he was panicking and flapping, tangled up in all that netting.'

'He's probably freaked. Release your grip a little and see what happens, but watch out for these two.' The dogs are panting at our heels. 'If the bird is injured we'll have to nurse him indoors or these hounds of ours will nab him,' I say, but the moment Quashia unclenches his grip, the tiny thing zips from the muddy cave of fingers and flees to its arboreal refuge in the sprucy pine forest up behind the house.

Later, having harvested all that there is time for, Quashia and I settle in the summer kitchen. Our crates are filled to bursting and on the floor, laid out on the plastic sheet, is our most recently gathered pile. Because we have worked under such constraint there has been no time to sort through, *trier*, these fruits; they are mixed with leaves, bits of twig, blades of grass and the remains of bird-eaten fruits. I am not allowed to deliver such unwinnowed pickings; we need to sift them, this hillock of what must be another forty kilos. Seated cross-legged on cushions on the tiled floor, either side of the laden sheet, we begin to work. Outside it is dark; in here it is cold and our breath rises like smoke because I have turned off the radiator to preserve the oil in the drupes. The heat would dry them out. Thelonius Monk plays on the old stereo system in the corner. We work in concentrated silence until I ask Quashia about his first wife, the mother of all those children I saw on the wedding video, who died so young.

He smiles and says nothing, staring into the speckled quilt of fruits at his fingertips.

'Sorry, I didn't mean to intrude.'

He shrugs. 'You ask many questions. What do you want to know?'

'How did you meet her? Who chose her for you?'

He shakes his head. 'My father died when I was twelve or thirteen. I've told you all that.'

'Yes.'

'I chose my wife. I was sixteen, she was fifteen. In those days, before the war with France, the system was less strict and we could marry younger, which is better. Look at me now: sixty-seven years old, all my children grown up and married and I have twenty-eight grandchildren with plenty more to come. That's how it should be. These days people wait too long, women don't have children. My present wife, she never had children. It's not good.' He pauses and I don't know if it has crossed his mind that I am one of those women. It certainly crosses mine.

'Tell me about your first wife, what was her name?'

'Nadia. Oh, she was beautiful! *Comme elle était belle!* There never was a woman as beautiful who walked this earth. Aside from you, of course, Carol.' He glances up shyly and we both grin. I clench my fists and press them to my lips to blow on them. My fingers are stiff with cold. I shift position on the cushions; one of my legs has cramp.

'We had nine children but two died, both at seventeen months. A boy and a girl, both walking and talking. We never knew why. In those days the hospitals and medical conditions in Algeria were very bad. It broke Nadia's heart. She never got over the loss of them, even though there were seven others to keep house for. She was living with my mother. I came here to France when I was seventeen to join my brother who, as you know, was run over and killed by an American Jeep. I went home whenever I could and I sent money every month. Fortunately, the bond she formed with my mother was very special. My mother looked on her as a daughter; she nursed Nadia at the end. The cancer was everywhere. She was forty-four and our youngest son, the one you saw on the video getting married, was only two.'

We continue for a while in silence. He is in his past with his beautiful Nadia.

'It took me ten years to find another wife. This woman is also kind and gentle, but she's very thin, fragile, like that robin I found. You'll see when you come to Algeria and meet her. Nadia was robust and strong, muscular and hefty, like you, Carol. Built like an ox.'

I hope I'm *not*, I am thinking.

'Yet she was the one to die. My mother survived till ninety. She returns, visits and talks to me regularly, as does my father, but never Nadia. Nadia's never been back to see me.'

I am surprised by this remark. This man who labours for our land, who is of the earth, always practical, is talking to me about spirits.

'Do you see your father, Carol?' he asks. 'Does he come to visit you?'

'I think so. Certainly, I am aware of his presence in my life and I light a candle to him every day. Well, most days.'

'My parents come to me in the village house where we lived, where one of my boys now lives. Never in my new house. Well, these matters are private, aren't they?'

'Might Nadia be sad that you remarried?'

'Oh, no! She would have wanted it. I don't know where she is or why she doesn't talk to me. We grew up together. I chose her, gave her my word that she would always be mine and she knows that I would never break that word. She will always be my sweetheart.'

The record has finished and I don't get up to change it. While Quashia dreams of Nadia, I consider our relationship and what a curious but special one it is. Who would have thought it? This creased-faced Arab, in his Persian wool hat and socks with the toes worn through, cross-legged on my floor, me opposite him. As he so often claims, we are family. I know and believe it now. And I thank whoever is out there, listening to us, watching over us, that he and we have been brought together. Quashia is the guardian angel of this farm.

I wake stiff as a board, back aching, to whiffs of last night's log fire still smouldering in the hearth. Outside, the day is warm and bright. I swim in the pool in the late November sunshine, splashing fast, to and fro, in the icy-cold water like a plump otter, and hurry to get dressed, ready for my second visit to the mill.

The hills are cloudy green and rusty oak. Low clouds hang around the mountains. An incongruous sight on the way through Grasse is a falcon perched atop a set of traffic lights. I weigh in our olive load at 124 kilos. Hurrah!

Once the forms have been dealt with, I am greeted below, at mill level, by a handful of men staring at a whacking great basin of olives and shaking their heads despondently. '*Trop vieilles, trop vertes*,' they are moaning. Moving alongside them, I glance at the harvest about to be pressed and must agree that the drupes do look rather sorry for themselves: skins peeling, flesh disintegrating, old yet still green.

I ask the worker who shovels and carts, always a cigarette glued to his lips: 'What variety of olive is this?'

'Fuck knows,' he answers, and slouches away.

My questions and constant interest bemuse these *oléiculteurs*. They are not fussed about the pressing process; they grow animated only when the oil begins to drip through. Passionate or despairing, they wear their emotions on their leathered faces. Arms folded, aimlessly pacing, they await the results, knowing the yield will be mean. They watch in silence, hoping for the best. Like the weather, this process carries with it a combination of unpredictable factors. I observe five men bent like storks staring silently at a pipe, and then the oil begins to arrive, to drip and now gush.

'*Pas mal, pas mal*,' they are saying. 'Considering the weather.'

'Bah, the weather,' one bleats, but their mood is softening. They chatter and begin to laugh, hands dancing, extrovert once more.

Gérard, the *fils* of Christophe, pays them no heed. He is cleaning, shunting bottles, stainless-steel containers, washing

with jet sprays. A gush here, another there. He is careful
never to mix one client's produce with another's. A sacro-
sanct affair.

Our turn next.

Christophe bustles in, a ladder rather too large for this
confined space on his shoulders. He is shouting and waving,
shaking hands with everyone. Due to the weight of his
paunch, he waddles like a duck.

'What news of your AOC?' he bawls at me.

I sigh. 'We are still waiting.'

'*Ah, oui*,' he shrugs, as though life is nothing but a business of waiting.

Our pressing begins. I pass the time talking to a retired
mason who has thirty trees. He bought his plot as a hobby
for his retirement. He moans about how hard it is to maintain the price of oil. 'I tried to sell for sixty francs a litre but
nobody would buy. Now I sell at fifty and they buy, but
they are not happy. They moan: "*Trop cher*."'

'Perhaps because they can drive across the border into
Italy and pick up oil at thirty francs a litre,' I suggest.

'*Mais oui*, but the Italians are like the Moroccans. They
mix their olive oil with cashew and pistachio oils to be more
competitive on the international market.'

I try to protest that this cannot possibly be so, but he will
not have it.

During a lull in the proceedings I jot down what the
mason has told me. He crosses over to me. 'Are you writing
about me?' he demands.

'No,' I lie.

'What, then? What are you writing?'

'Ideas,' I stammer, feeling embarrassed, wishing I had left
my notebook where it was in my bag. 'A thought here and
there, strung together.'

'Stories,' he continues. 'You're like the Italians. Mix a bit of this and that and call it extra virgin. There's no such thing as *extra* virgin. Either she's a virgin or she's not!' He roars with lascivious laughter.

And now the moment for our oil. I rush to the spout and watch those first drips plopping into the steel dish. Others gather around me. All is silent. I cast my gaze across the intent faces, peering from face to weatherworn face, and then I return to the deep sea-green liquid. I am apprehensive. Though I know the yield will be less than last year, I long for it to be excellent. Suddenly, I catch myself as these others might see me. My expression is sombre, concentrated, just like theirs. I am no different. This transformation from drupe to oil is as sacred and as important to me as it is to any of these farmers. I burst into a broad smile. Would I rather be learning lines or drinking champagne at the Ivy? No, not today. For this moment in time, this olive season, I feel content, I am complete. I have melded with the old order. I have become one of them.

Upstairs, as I approach the cash desk to pay for our pressing, I spy Christophe slumped on a trolley. 'How did you do?' he calls out to me as one gambler might ask of another.

'Catastrophic!' I cry, feigning despair.

He takes me seriously and clambers to his feet, huffing and puffing. '*Mon Dieu*. How many litres?'

'Sixteen.'

'That's better than most. Look at this morning's yields. And it's the quality. You have the quality. What would you do with thirty litres of dishwater? And wait till you've planted those two hundred young trees. You'll get your AOC, have no fear. It takes time. Life takes time.'

We all shake hands as Gérard, the *fils,* interrupts his work to hump my *bidons* of oil to the boot of my car.

'I wouldn't do this for anyone else,' he mutters shyly.

'Thank you,' I tell him, genuinely touched by his kindness.

Everyone shakes hands again and the frightful mason attempts to kiss me while the rest of us are merrily waving and calling, 'See you soon!'

'Four kilos to the litre next time!'

A curious band we make, I am thinking, as I trundle off down the hill in a happy frame of mind.

200 New Possibilities

Spring. The weather is delicious. Blossoms have spread like confetti across the garden. Blue-black hornets in the wistaria. Scurrying lizards everywhere, exposing nutmeg stomachs as they flip and slither into stone cracks. The air is dusty with yellow pollen from the fir trees and cedars. When the wind gets up, it carries the powder like a carpet of egg yolk.

Michel and I are out in the garden, occupied with stakes for the planting of the 200 olive saplings that were delivered two days ago.

This planting requires strategic planning: the aspects of the sun, the growth rates of the olive trees, avoidance of the shadows of the towering pines and, in accordance with Michel's perennial preoccupation, *überblick,* or the overview – the overall pattern of the groves. Michel rooted around in the garage for paint and found a pot of a lime-green colour which has barely been touched. It had been destined for the kitchen but, after one wall was painted, it was quickly rejected. He handed it, with brush and stirring stick, to me. In order that we do not forget where each tree is to be planted, he decided that we should make a tour of the entire land, place a small mound of stones or a stick at each planting spot and, in case the dogs or wild boars knock them about, mark them. Hence the paint. My job is to paint the stones.

We have been at this work for two days. Today is the last and we are dressed for guests and celebration but shod in wellies. As ever, the dogs are trailing at our heels. In the distance a backdrop of foxglove-mauve mountains, the spring Alps. There are birds everywhere. I spot one I have never seen before. He is large and lime green – the colour of my paint. His head is holly-berry red and he has sooty markings on his face. His beak is hammering powerfully at the grassed earth. I ditch my can and dig into my pockets in search of pen and thick, spiral notebook curled with use and crammed tight with ideas and daily sightings. I begin to scribble: 'Tree Planting, morning one: I see a hell of a big Green Woodpecker; he is whacking his beak at the ground, foraging for insects. They are known to plunder anthills.'

Michel is calling to me. '*Chérie*, we have a hundred and seventy positions marked, but thirty to go. It will soon be lunchtime. We have dozens of people arriving, and, I don't know about you, but I am looking forward to a glass of champagne in the sun on the terrace. *Depêche-toi!*'

I lift my head and laugh. 'You're right,' I call. 'Friends are coming. Let's finish our work and crack open that champagne.'

We walk back up to the house, hand in hand, passing on our way the 200 six-year-old trees standing in tight lines at the top of the garden. A lake of silver vitality raring to get going. Trees that, when they reach a hundred years old, will be smiled upon by Provençals and called toddlers. Trees that are the signature tune of Provence. Today we will begin the business of putting these saplings in the earth, where they will stay for centuries, long beyond our fleeting lifetimes, and to celebrate this occasion we have invited friends and colleagues to Come and Plant a Tree, drink champagne, stay for lunch, come for the weekend or just pop by.

Each tree will bear the name of its planter. René is coming; the water diviner and his Corsican wife; Lord Harry, whose wife has returned to him and we have yet to meet; Christophe and Gérard; our vet, who always arrives with flowers for his favourite actress. The gentle beemaster will drop by too to meet Michel and, I hope, finalise the arrangements for our hives; friends are convening from England, Germany and locally.

I want to mark these days of planting. To celebrate them joyously. And when these junior trees, this rip-roaring chorus of olive trees, are in the ground, growing splendidly, we can be classified as genuine farmers by the bodies who count. We are now affiliated to, have been contacted by, been sent information about, among others, the following organisations: ONIOL, La Chambre d'Agriculture, FDGEDA, FOPO, FSPAOC, FNPHP, FCO, SNM, FEDICO, AFIDOL, CEAO, ONIDOL, COPEXO – and the list will not end there. We have been registered as one of 20,000 olive-growers in France. Between us, we produce three and a half million tons of olives over 20,000 hectares. Our handsome young chief from the Chambre d'Agriculture, who will also call in tomorrow, has written a booklet, *A Practical Guide to Organic Olive Farming in the Alpes-Maritimes*, and has very generously sent us a copy, along with a promise to assist us make this step in earnest.

Our tables are groaning with food. The fridges are

crammed with chilled bottles. And the sun is shining. To any farmer, to Lord Harry with his apricots or a longstanding olive or fruit farmer, this step is a humble one, but to us, who started out with a newly discovered love and a crumbling house by the sea, who never in our wildest dreams saw ourselves in the role of farmers, this is an exciting, challenging decision. We are striking root – digging deeper, nurturing our discoveries, expanding and enriching our love affair with the Midi, with the ancient ways of this mythical land known since Roman times as Provincia: Provence.

There is an Arab proverb that Quashia – I hear him digging holes and preparing the soil for the trees up behind the villa – sometimes quotes. 'When the house is finished, death walks in the door.' This house, this smallholding, has a long way to go yet before its crumbling walls and unmade kitchens and unconstructed bedrooms and dusty stables are plastered, painted and furnished and, please God, death is and will remain occupied elsewhere.

Quashia spies us approaching and waves us up. Lucky bounds on ahead.

'Who's planting the first one?' he calls.

'You should,' returns Michel. 'Quashia's tree.'

'I'll get your camera.' I hurry on inside and hike up the hill with the Nikon.

Quashia has sent Michel off to fill two buckets with water. 'You go first,' he tells me.

'No, you.'

But he insists, and begins unpotting one of the half a dozen saplings standing in black plastic pots at his side. I take the baby from him and settle it gently into the earth, straightening it, welcoming it to the farm, as Quashia hands me a shovel. 'Pack the earth in tightly around it,' he orders.

I start shovelling. Michel returns with the water, picks up the camera from beside my feet and snaps. 'Carol's tree!'

And then another as I pour the water, and another with Quashia at my side, and then another and another. 'Who's next?'

Three six-year-old trees are planted and numerous photographs taken to record the occasion. Our new, extended grove is finally underway. I hear a car purring up the drive. The first of our visitors. It's party time.

The olive tree is a symbol of peace, of wisdom, eternity and continual rebirth. The births that I will know will not be my own children, children seeded by Michel and born of my loins. My children will not take form in the physical sense. They will be born of my passion, of my creativity, such as it is. There will be stories to hear, to narrate and pass on, there will be harvests to gather and the fruits of that labour to share, there will be friends to meet and make films with, there is the love of a man who is remarkable and who stands like an oak at my side, and there is the continuous but nonetheless inspiring discovery that pain and loss recoup life and regeneration.

I am learning, slowly, and not without heartache, to take what there is, to accept it gratefully, to *celebrate* it, treasure it, to seed it and work with it, before time passes. But as time passes there will always be new damage and renovation to address, the swings and roundabouts, the helterskelters of our lives and our damaged hearts. That's it, that is the moulding of my life. It's not a profound philosophy or a secret. It is quite simply the loudly joyous choice of paths at the crossroads. But it has taken me time to see it through the fogs of my own making. Still, as Christophe at the mill so succinctly remarked: 'Life takes time.'

And I would add to that, healing also takes time.

I never took the time to grieve the loss of my little girl, and to heal myself.

Carrot.

Only when I began to write about her did I unfold fragile memories; memories returning to be cried over and released. Perhaps the most extraordinary miracle has been that, as I wept for her and let her go, she returned. She bounced back smiling and full of life. These days her spirit is here with me everywhere. I see her now. She soars and laughs through the breeze or the still heat in the olive trees; she weeps with the rain at my shortsightedness and her smile radiates the day no less than the sun. She *is* this book. My child. My gift to Michel.

THE OLIVE FARM

Carol Drinkwater

The Olive Farm is a double love story. It is a lyrical tale of the real-life romance between actress Carol Drinkwater and Michel, a television producer, and of an abandoned Provençal olive farm – Appassionata – which they fall in love with and buy.

And as the olives turn from green to violet, luscious grape-purple to a deep succulent black, we are drawn seductively into Carol and Michel's vibrant Mediterranean world. We experience the highs and lows of Provençal life: the carnivals, customs and local cuisine; the threats of fire, the adoption of a menagerie of animals and a ready-made family; potential financial ruin as well as the thrill of harvesting your own olives by hand – especially when they are discovered to produce the finest extra-virgin olive oil.

Rich and resonant, *The Olive Farm* effortlessly captures the joys of living in a warmer clime, of eating fresh Mediterranean food, swimming in one's own pool, and sharing all this with the love of one's life.

BON APPÉTIT!

Peter Mayle

The early part of Peter Mayle's life was spent in the gastronomic wilderness of post-war England. But a business trip to Paris at the tender age of nineteen began an enduring fascination with the French and their love affair with food and wine. In *Bon Appétit!*, he brings to life all the charm and taste of France's culinary calendar: its fairs, festivals and traditions.

He visits Livarot, where his nose encounters its far from modest fromage, and revels in the spectacle of the annual competitive cheese-eating contest; in Martigny-les-Bains he learns the best way to eat snails; and he becomes the first English confrère of Vittel, haven of the frog-fancier.

What Peter Mayle discovers is the high level of enthusiasm for any event, however bizarre, that seeks to turn eating and drinking into a celebration. Warm, witty and mouthwatering in equal measure, *Bon Appétit!* is proof that the old saying 'Lovely country, France. Pity about the French', is only half correct.

'Affectionate and witty . . . [Mayle's] unerring eye for human eccentricity results in a highly flavoured evocation of a nation devoted to its stomach'
Daily Mail

Now you can order superb titles directly from Abacus

☐ The Olive Farm   Carol Drinkwater   £7.99
☐ Bon Appétit!   Peter Mayle   £6.99

———————————— ⬭ABACUS⬭ ————————————

Please allow for postage and packing: **Free UK delivery.**
Europe; add 25% of retail price; Rest of World; 45% of retail price.

To order any of the above or any other Abacus titles, please call our credit card orderline or fill in this coupon and send/fax it to:

Abacus, P.O. Box 121, Kettering, Northants NN14 4ZQ
Tel: 01832 737527   Fax: 01832 733076
Email: aspenhouse@FSBDial.co.uk

☐ I enclose a UK bank cheque made payable to Abacus for £ ....

☐ Please charge £.............. to my Access, Visa, Delta, Switch Card No.

☐☐☐☐☐☐☐☐☐☐☐☐☐☐☐☐☐☐☐

Expiry Date ☐☐☐☐   Switch Issue No. ☐☐

NAME (Block letters please) ....

ADDRESS ....

....

....

Postcode ....Telephone ....

Signature ....

Please allow 28 days for delivery within the UK. Offer subject to price and availability.

Please do not send any further mailings from companies carefully selected by Abacus ☐